Mahatma's Philosophy on Indian Caste, Religion and Education

Mahatma's Philosophy on Indian Caste, Religion and Education

R. Subramanian

CYBER TECH PUBLICATIONS
4264/3, Ansari Road, Daryaganj, New Delhi-110002 (India)
Ph.: 011-23244078. Fax: 011-23280028
E-Mail: cyberpublicationsdelhi@yahoo.com

MAHATMA'S PHILOSOPHY ON INDIAN CASTE, RELIGION AND EDUCATION

R. Subramanian

First Edition 2008

Published by :

G.S. Rawat for **Cyber Tech Publications**
4264/3, Ansari Road, Daryaganj, New Delhi-110002 (India)
Ph.: 011-23244078. Fax: 011-23280028
E-Mail: cyberpublicationsdelhi@yahoo.com

Printed at : **Amit Enterprises**, Maujpur, Delhi, (9810878184)

Preface

Gandhi's conceptualization of political life and redefinitions of such central concepts as liberty *(Swaraj)*, equality *(samata)*, citizenship *(nagarikata)*, rights *(adhikar)*, obligation *(dharma)* and tolerance *(sahisnuta)* also contain important insights and deserve close study. We shall take the first three by way of illustration.

Like many Hindu philosophers Gandhi took little interest in the concept of human nature, largely because he took a radically individualistic view of man. Each individual was unique, followed his own path of moral and spiritual evolution, and had a distinct *swabhava,* that is, a distinct and firm but relatively open and within limits malleable constitution or nature. It was true that all men shared certain *gunas* or qualities in common. However these were too general and indeterminate to account for the unique constitution of each individual. The qualities were also largely passive, capable of neither mechanical nor teleological casualty, and unable to explain human conduct. Since the concept of human nature had no explanatory power, it had neither theoretical nor practical significance for Gandhi.

—Author

Contents

1

MAHATMA'S EDUCATION

Introduction

The fundamental principles of social, political, and economic life were welded into a comprehensive theory which is called Religion in Hindu thought. The total configuration of ideals, practices, and conduct is called Dharma (Religion, Virtue or Duty) in this ancient tradition. From the very start, they came, under the influence of their religious ideas, to conceive of their country as less a geographical and material than a cultural or a spiritual possession, and to identify, broadly speaking, the country with their culture.

The Country was their Culture and the Culture their Country, the true Country of the Spirit, the 'invisible church of culture' not confined within physical bounds. India thus was the first country to rise to the conception of an extraterritorial nationality and naturally became the happy home of different races, each with its own ethno-psychic endowment, and each carrying its social reality for Hindus is not geographical, not ethnic, but a culture-pattern. Country and patriotism expand, as ideals and ways of life receive acquiescence. Thus, from the very dawn of its history has this Country of the Spirit ever expanded in extending circles, Brahmarshidesa, Brahmavarta, Aryavarta, Bharatvarsha, or Jambudvipa, Suvarnabhumi and even a Greater India beyond its geographical boundaries.

Learning in India through the ages had been prized and pursued not for its own sake, if we may so put it, but for the sake, and as a part, of religion. (It was sought as the means of self-realization, as the means to the highest end of life, *viz.*

Mukti or Emancipation. Ancient Indian education is also to be understood as being ultimately the outcome of the Indian theory of knowledge as part of the corresponding scheme of life and values. The scheme takes full account of the fact that Life includes Death and the two form the whole truth. This gives a particular angle of vision, a sense of perspective and proportion in which the material and the moral, the physical and spiritual, the perishable and permanent interests and values of life are clearly defined and strictly differentiated. Of all the people of the world the Hindu is the most impressed and affected by the fact of death as the central fact of life. The individual's supreme duty is thus to achieve his expansion into the Absolute, his self-fulfilment, for he is a potential God, a spark of the Divine. Education must aid in this self-fulfilment, and not in the acquisition of mere objective knowledge.

It may be said with quite a good degree of precision that India was the only country where knowledge was systematized and where provision was made for its imparting at the highest level in remote times. Whatever the discipline of learning, whether it was chemistry, medicine, surgery, the art of painting or sculpture, or dramatics or principles of literary criticism or mechanics or even dancing, everything was reduced to a systematic whole for passing it on to the future generations in a brief and yet detailed manner. University education on almost modern lines existed in India as early as 800 B.C. or even earlier. The learning or culture of ancient India was chiefly the product of her hermitages in the solitude of the forests. It was not of the cities. The learning of the forests was embodied in the books specially designated as Aranyakas "belonging to the forests." Indian civilization in its early stages had been mainly a rural, sylvan, and not an urban, civilization.

The ideal of education has been very grand, noble and high in ancient India. Its aim, according to Herbert Spencer is the 'training for completeness of life' and the moulding of character of men and women for the battle of life. The history of the educational institutions in ancient India shows how old is her cultural history. It points to a long history. In the early stage it is rural, not urban. British Sanskrit scholar Arthur Anthony Macdonell (1854-1930) author of A History of Sanskrit Literature

(Motilal Banarsidass Pub. ISBN: 8120800354) says "Some hundreds of years must have been needed for all that is found" in her culture. The aim of education was at the manifestation of the divinity in men, it touches the highest point of knowledge. In order to attain the goal the whole educational method is based on plain living and high thinking pursued through eternity.

As the individual is the chief concern and centre of this Education, education also is necessarily individual. It is an intimate relationship between the teacher and the pupil. The relationship is inaugurated by a religious ceremony called Upanayana. It is not like the admission of a pupil to the register of a school on his payment of the prescribed fee. The spiritual meaning of Upanayana, and its details inpsired by that meaning, are elaborated in many texts and explained below in the proper place. By Upanayana, the teacher, "holding the pupil within him as in a womb, impregnates him with his spirit, and delivers him in a new birth." The pupil is then known as Dvija, "born afresh" in a new existence, "twice born" (Satapatha Brahmana). The education that is thus begun is called by the significant term Brahmacharya, indicating that it is a mode of life, a system of practices.

Women as Rishis

The history of the most of the known civilizations show that the further back we go into antiquity, the more unsatisfactory is found to be the general position of women. Hindu civilization is unique in this respect, for here we find a surprising exception to the general rule. The further back we go, the more satisfactory is found to be the position of women in more spheres than one; and the field of education is most noteworthy among them. There is ample and convincing evidence to show that women were regarded as perfectly eligible for the privilege of studying the Vedic literature and performing the sacrifices enjoined in it down to about 200 B.C. This need not surprise us, for some of the hymns of the Rig Veda are the composition of twenty sage-poetesses.

Women were then admitted to fulfil religious rites and consequently to complete educational facilities. Women-sages were callee Rishikas and Brahmavadinis. The Rig Veda knows of the following Rishikas 1.Romasa 2.Lopamudra 3. Apala 4. Kadru 5.Visvavara 6. Ghosha 7. Juhu 8. Vagambhrini 9. Paulomi 10. Jarita 11. Sraddha-Kamayani 12. Urvasi 13. Sarnga 14. Yami 15. Indrani 18. Savitri 19. Devajami 20. Nodha 21. Akrishtabhasha 22. Sikatanivavari 23. Gaupayana.

The Brahmavadinis were the products of the educational discipline of brahmacharaya for which women also were eligible. Rig Veda refers to young maidens completing their education as brahmacharinis and then gaining husbands in whom they are merged like rivers in oceans. Yajurveda similarly states that a daughter, who has completed her Brahmacharya, should be married to one who is learned like her.

A most catholic passage occurs in Yajurveda (xxvi, 2) which enjoins the imparting of Vedic knowledge to all classes, Brahmins and Rajanyas, Sudras, Anaryas, and charanas (Vaisyas) and women. No one can recite Vedic prayers or offer Vedic sacrifices without having undergone the Vedic initiation (Upanayana). It is, therefore, but natural that in the early period the Upanayana of girls should have been as common as that of boys.

The Arthava Veda (xi. 5.8) expressly refers to maidens undergoing the Brahmacharya discipline and the Sutra works of the 5th century B.C. supply interesting details in its connection. Even Manu includes Upanayana among the sanskaras (rituals) obligatory for girls (II.66). Music and dancing was also taught to them. Brahmavadins used to marry after their education was over, some of them like Vedavati, a daughter of sage Kusadhvaja, would not marry at all.

Women in Education

Radha Kumud Mookerji (1884-1964) Indian historian, has noted: "An important feature of this educational system should not be missed. The part taken in intellectual life by women like Gargi who could address a Congress of philosophers on learned topics, or like Maitreyi, who had achieved the highest knowledge, that of Brahma. The Rigveda shows us some women as authors of hymns, such as Visvavara, Ghosha, and Apala."

The Vedic women received a fair share of masculine attention in physical culture and military training. The Rigveda tells us that many women joined the army in those days. A form of chariot race was one of the games most popular during the Vedic period.

People were fond of swinging. Ball games were in vogue in those days by both men and women. Apart from this, a number of courtyard games like" Hide and seek" and "Run and catch" were also played by the girls. Playing with dice became a popular activity. The dices were apparently made of Vibhidaka nuts. From the Rigveda, it appears that the Vedic Aryans knew the art of boxing.

Education in the Epics

Takshashila was a noted centre of learning. The story is told of one of its teachers named Dhaumya who, had three disciples named Upamanyu, Aruni, and Veda.

Hermitages

The Mahabharata tells of numerous hermitages where pupils from distant parts gathered for instruction round some far-famed teachers. A full-fledged Asrama is described as consisting of several Departments which are enumerated as following:

1. Agnisthana, the place for fire-worship and prayers
2. Brahma-sthana, the Department of Veda
3. Vishnusthana, the Department for teaching Raja-Niti, Arthaniti, and Vartta
4. Mahendrasthana, Military Section
5. Vivasvata-sthana, Department of Astronomy
6. Somasthana, Department of Botany
7. Garuda-sthana, Section dealing with Transport and Conveyances
8. Kartikeya-sthana, Section teaching military organization, how to form patrols, battalions, and army.

The most important of such hermitage was that of the Naimisha, a forest which was like a university, the presiding personality of the place was Saunaka, to whom was applied the designation of Kulapati, sometimes defined as the preceptor of 10,000 disciples.

The hermitage of Kanva was another famous centre of learning, of which a full description is given. It is situated on the banks of the Malini, a tributary of the Sarayu River. It was not a solitary hermitage, but an assemblage of numerous hermitages round the central hermitage of Rishi Kanva, the presiding spirit of the settlement. There were specialists in every branch of learning cultivated in that age; specialists in each of the four Vedas; in sacrificial literature and art; Kalpa-Sutras; in the Chhanda (Metrics), Sabda (Vyakarana), and Nirukta. There were also Logicians, knowing the principles of Nyaya, and of Dialectics (the art of establishing propositions, solving doubts, and ascertaining conclusions). There were also specialists in the physical sciences and art. There were, for example, experts in the art of constructing sacrificial altars of various dimensions and shapes (on the basis of a knowledge of Solid Geometry); those who had knowledge of the properties of matter (dravyaguna); of physical processes and their results of causes and their effect; and zoologists having a special knowledge of monkeys and birds. It was thus a forest University where the study of every available branch of learning was cultivated.

The hermitage of Vyasa was another seat of learning. There Vyasa taught the Vedas to his disciples. Those disciples were highly blessed Sumantra, vaisampayana, Jamini of great wisdom, and Paila of great ascetic merit." They were afterwards joined by Suka, the famous son of Vyasa.

True Value of Education

The real difficulty is that people have no idea of what education truly is. We assess the value of education in the same manner as we assess the value of land or of shares in the stock-exchange market. We want to provide only such education as would enable the student to earn more. We hardly give any thought to the improvement of the character of the educated. The girls, we say, do not have to earn; so why should they be educated? As long as such ideas persist there is no hope of our ever knowing the true value of education.

Not Mere Literacy

In Western countries education is so highly valued that senior teachers are treated with much respect. There are at present in England, schools that have been running for hundreds of years and have turned out many renowned men. One of these famous schools is Eton. A few months ago the Old Boys of Eton presented an address to the Head Master, Dr. Weir, who is well known throughout the British Empire. Writing about the occasion, *The Pall Mall Gazette*, a well-known journal in England, has explained the nature of real education. Its comments deserve the attention of us all. The writer in *The Pall Mall Gazette* says:

> *We hold that real education does not consist merely in acquainting oneself with ancient or modern books. It consists in the habits which one knowingly or unknowingly imbibes from the atmosphere, one's surroundings and the company one keeps and above all in work. It is all very well to acquire a stock of knowledge from good books or from other sources. But the more important thing is to learn humanity. The primary function of teachers is, therefore, not to teach the alphabet, but to inculcate humanity. Aristotle said that virtue is not learnt by reading big volumes. It is by doing good deeds that we learn virtue. Another great writer also says that it is well for one to know what is good, but one will be considered a happy person only if one acts upon that knowledge.*

Judged by these standards, English schools will not be found wanting. If we think of English schools as places for turning out human beings, we shall see that they give us statesmen and administrators. Those educated in German schools may have greater knowledge, but if they become also men of action like the pupils of Eton, it is not by virtue of their training in the schools. Despite the defects that may exist in English schools, it is these that produce true men. They are men who are ever ready to meet an enemy threatening at the gates of England.

We can readily realize how a country that invests education with such a noble purpose becomes prosperous. India's star will shine bright when Indian children receive such education.

Parents, teachers and pupils ought to ponder over the passage quoted above. It would not do merely to know it, it is necessary to act upon it. That is to say, parents should provide for excellent education, teachers should discharge their responsibility and pupils should recognize that mere literacy is not education.

Education as Training

Now I have read a great deal in the prison. I have been reading Emerson, Ruskin and Mazzini. I have also been reading the *Upanishads*. All confirm the view that education does not mean a knowledge of letters but it means character building, it means a knowledge of duty. Our own word literally means 'training'. If this be the true view and it is to my mind the only true view, you are receiving the best education—training—possible.

Education as Service

True education lies in serving others, oblige them without the least feeling of one-uppishness. The more mature you grow, the more you will realise this. A great deal of religious obligations on us are fulfilled when we nurse the sick. I am not worried about your bookish learning so long as you perform your duties and observe solemn ethical conduct. For me carrying out the fundamentals of ethics is *duty*.

I shall support you if you want to study further out of your love for it or for excellence. But I won't scold you if you do not do it. Try your best to carry out the decisions you have made. Write to me what you do at the press, at what time do you get up and about your work at the farm.

Service before Self

I was extremely glad to read your letter of the 21st (ultimo) about Mr. West. I read the letter twice. I felt proud of you and thanked God that I had such a son.

I wish you to remain such for ever. To do good to others and serve them without any sense of egoism—this is real education. You will realize this more and more as you grow up. What better way of life can there be than serving the sick? Most of religion is covered by it.

Moral Path

The true occupation of man is to build his character. It is not quite necessary to learn something special for earning [one's livelihood]. He who does not leave the path of morality never starves, and is not afraid if such a contingency arises.

Living a Good Life

The service you are rendering to Mr. West and others is the best study for you. He who does his duty is all the while studying. You say that you had to leave your studies; but it is not so. You are certainly studying when you are serving. It would be correct to say that you had to give up reading books. There is no harm in thus leaving studies. One can get academic education later on. One cannot say that one will get an opportunity of serving others later on...' Let this be inscribed in your heart that, since your mind is pure, you will not fall ill while serving others. And even if you fall ill, I will not worry. You and I, all of us, will achieve perfection only by being moulded in this manner. Learning to live a good life is in itself education. All else is useless. *(Letter to Manilal Gandhi, 12 October 1909 (CW 9, p. 475))*

Laying Strong Foundation

What is the meaning of education? It simply means a knowledge of letters. It is merely an instrument, and an instrument may be well used or abused. The same instrument that may be used to cure a patient may be used to take his life, and so may a knowledge of letters. We daily observe that many men abuse it and very few make good use of it; and if this is a correct statement, we have proved that more harm has been done by it than good.

The ordinary meaning of education is a knowledge of letters. To teach boys reading, writing and arithmetic is called primary education. A peasant earns his bread honestly. He has ordinary knowledge of the world. He knows fairly well how he should behave towards his parents, his wife, his children and his fellow villagers. He understands and observes the rules of morality. But he cannot write his own name. What do you propose to do by giving him a knowledge of letters? Will you add an inch to his happiness? Do you wish to make him discontented with his cottage or his lot? And even if you want to do that, he will not need such an education. Carried away by the flood of Western thought we came to the conclusion, without weighing pros and cons, that we should give this kind of education to the people.

Now let us take higher education. I have learned Geography, Astronomy, Algebra, Geometry, etc. What of that? In what way have I benefited myself or those around me? Why have I learned these things? Professor Huxley has thus defined education:

> *That man, I think, has had a liberal education who has been so trained in youth that his body is the ready servant of his will and does with ease and pleasure all the work that as a mechanism it is capable of; whose intellect is a clear, cold, logic engine with all its parts of equal strength and in smooth working order;... whose mind is stored with a knowledge of the fundamental truths of nature;... whose passions are trained to come to heel by a vigorous will, the servant of a tender conscience;... who has learnt to hate all vileness and to respect others as himself. Such a one and no other, I conceive, has had a liberal education, for he is in harmony with nature. He will make the best of her and she of him.*

If this is true education, I must emphatically say that the sciences I have enumerated above I have never been able to use for controlling my senses. Therefore, whether you take elementary education or higher education, it is not required for the main thing. It does not make men of us. It does not enable us to do our duty.

Reader: If that is so, I shall have to ask you another question: What enables you to tell all these things to me? If you had not received higher education, how would you have been able to explain to me the things that you have?

Editor: You have spoken well. But my answer is simple: I do not, for one moment, believe that my life would have been wasted, had I not received higher or lower education. Nor do I consider that I necessarily serve because I speak. But I do desire to serve and in endeavouring to fulfil that desire, I make use of the education I have received. And, if I am making good use of it, even then it is not for the millions, but I can use it only for such as you, and this supports my contention. Both you and I have come under the bane of what is mainly false education. I claim to have become free from its ill effect, and I am trying to give you the benefit of my experience and in doing so, I am demonstrating the rottenness of this education.

Moreover, I have not run down a knowledge of letters in all circumstances. All I have now shown is that we must not make of it a fetish. It is not our *Kamadhuk*. In its place it can be of use and it has its place when we have brought our senses under subjection and put our ethics on a firm foundation. And then, if we feel inclined to receive that education, we may make good use of it. As an ornament it is likely to sit well on us. It now follows that it is not necessary to make this education compulsory. Our ancient school system is enough. Character-building has the first place in it and that is primary education. A building erected on that foundation will last. *(Hind Swaraj, Chapter XVIII, 21 November 1909 (CW 10, pp. 54–55))*

The Three R's

But although much good and useful work can be done without a knowledge of the three R's, it is my firm belief that we cannot always do without such knowledge. It develops and sharpens one's intellect, and it increases our capacity of doing good. I have never placed an unnecessarily high value on the knowledge of the three R's. I am only attempting to assign its proper place to it.

Again, the true knowledge of self is unattainable by the millions who lack such education. Many a book is full of innocent pleasure, and this will be denied to us without education. It is no exaggeration to say that a human being without education is not far removed from an animal. Education, therefore, is necessary for women as it is for men. *(Speech at Bhagini Samaj, Bombay, 20 February 1918 (CW 14, p. 206))*

Education as Liberation

"That is true education which leads to freedom." That alone is true education which enables us to preserve our dharma.

This is the motto accepted by our university. The idea has appealed to me very much: "That is true education which leads to freedom." That which liberates is education. Liberation is of two kinds. One form of liberation consists in securing the freedom of the country from foreign rule. Such freedom may prove short-lived. The other kind of liberation is for all time. In order to attain *moksha*, which we describe as our *paramadharma*, we should have freedom in the worldly sense as well. He who is ridden with many fears cannot attain the ultimate *moksha*. If one would attain this, would achieve the highest end of human effort, one has no choice but to attain that *moksha* which is nearest to one. That education which delays our freedom is to be shunned, it is Satanic, it is sinful. Whatever the quality of the education given in Government schools and colleges, it is to be shunned because the Government which imparts it is Satanic and deserves to be shunned. *(Speech to students, Ahmedabad, 18 November 1926 (CW 18, p. 471))*

Education as Assimilation

But I must advise you, students, to read these prize-books carefully, to reflect over their real import and, keeping in mind all the profound truths set out in them, follow the path enjoined by religion. Whether you are a girl or a boy, you will grow up one day and have to carry a heavy burden of worldly duties; give some thought, therefore, to the future. Truth is revealed not only in our scriptures but in the scriptures of other religions as well.

It is the duty of students to assimilate whatever they have learnt. They should have religious and moral instruction, as much of it as they can usefully apply. They need education in such measure that it would not become too much of a useless burden on them. I should like to address a few words exclusively to students. Men and women students, you will benefit from what you have learnt only to the extent that you have assimilated it. That should be the object of this institution too. You should ponder over the element of truth in whatever books of religion you read. If you cling to truth, success is yours. I would advise you from my experience, to profit well from your education. That will be to your advantage and to your country's as well.

(Speech to students in Bombay, 14 February 1915 (CW 13, p. 23))

Overcoming Fear

Speaking about the timidity induced by their education, Gandhiji said: We may feel in our heart any measure of devotion for Tilak Maharaj, but where is the student who will express it freely?

For us, fear has become synonymous with life. What is the use of that education which does not help us to overcome fear, but which, on the contrary, strengthens it? What kind of an education is it which does not teach us to follow truth and to cultivate devotion for the country? *(Speech at students' meeting, Agra, 23 November 1920 (CW 19, p. 16))*

Culture of the Heart

There is one thing which, as I am speaking to you occurs to me, which comes to me from my early studies of the Bible. It seized me immediately. I read the passage:

> *But seek ye first the Kingdom of God, and his righteousness; and all these things shall be added unto you.*

I tell you that if you will understand, appreciate and act up to the spirit of this passage, you won't even need to know what place Jesus or any other teacher occupies in your heart. If you will do the proper scavenger's work, clean and purify your hearts and get them ready, you will find that all these mighty teachers will take their places without invitation from us.

That, to my mind, is the basis of all sound education. Culture of the mind must be subservient to the culture of the heart. May God help you to become pure! *(Speech at Central College, Jaffna, The Hindu, 2 December 1927 (CW 35, p. 343))*

Learning and Courage

Let them (students) realize that learning without courage is like a waxen statue beautiful to look at but bound to melt at the least touch of a hot substance. (*Young India*, 12 July 1928, p. 236).

Character vs Knowledge

In brief, formation of character should have priority over knowledge of the alphabet. If this order is reversed, the attempt would be like putting the cart before the horse and making it push the cart with its nose, and would meet with the same success as the latter course. *(9 January 1924 (CW 37, p. 248))*

Education as Contemplation

Education, character and religion should be regarded as convertible terms. There is no true education which does not tend to produce character, and there is no true religion which does not determine character. Education should contemplate the whole life. Mere memorizing and book-learning is not education. I have no faith in the so-called systems of education which produce men of learning without the backbone of character. *(Interview with W.W. Hall, October 1928 (CW 37, p. 320))*

Education of the Whole Child

Education does not mean a knowledge of the alphabet. This type of knowledge is only a means to education. Education implies a child's learning how to put his mind and all his senses to good use. That is to say, he really learns how to use his hands, feet and other organs of action and his nose, ear and other organs of sense. A child who has acquired the knowledge that he should not use his hands for stealing or for killing flies nor for beating up his companions or younger brothers and sisters has already begun his education. He has started it, we can say, when he understands the necessity of keeping his body, his teeth, tongue, ears, head, nails, etc., clean and keeps them clean. That child has made good progress in education who does not indulge in mischief while eating and drinking, eats and drinks alone or in society in a proper manner, sits properly and chooses pure foodstuffs knowing the difference between pure and impure foodstuffs, does not eat like a glutton, does not clamour for whatever he sees and remains calm even if he does not get what he wants.

Even that child has advanced on the road to education whose pronunciation is correct, who can recount to us the history and geography of the country surrounding him without knowing those terms and who understands what his country means. That child has made very good progress in his education who can understand the difference between truth and untruth, worth and worthlessness and chooses the good and the true, while rejecting the bad and the untrue. *(Navajivan, 2 June 1929 (CW 41, p. 6))*

Education as Self-discipline

All your scholarship, all your study of Shakespeare and Wordsworth would be vain if at the same time you do not build your character, and attain mastery over your thoughts and actions. When you have attained self-mastery and learnt to control your passions you will not utter notes of despair. You cannot give your hearts and profess poverty of action. To give one's heart is to give all. You must, to start with, have hearts to give. And this you can do if you will cultivate them. *(Speech to students, Agra, 19 September 1929 (CW 41, p. 391))*

Right Learning

I have been all this time looking at the motto in front of me: "Learning owes its worth to dharma." What the motto says is true. I have discovered in the course of my travels in India that, without dharma, learning is barren. This raises the question: "What is right learning?" I have given my reply often enough. We shall settle afterwards the issue of what manner of learning to provide. For the present, we may follow one definite method and include religious instruction in it. Religion is not a matter for reflection but of conduct..It is not a subject for talking about, be it noted. Teachers can create the thing only by their conduct. Gurjarat itself should produce such teachers; it is shameful to go looking for them outside. *(Speech at foundation laying of Vanita Vishram, Ahmedabad, 13 July 1919; (CW 15, p. 410) (Translated from Gujarati))*

Becoming Strong

In the circumstances in which you pursue your studies, you can only learn to fear man. I would say, on the other hand, that he alone is a real M.A. who has given up the fear of man and has learnt to fear God. Any education you receive will have justified itself only when you have become so strong that you will not beg of anyone for your living. It will have justified itself when the feeling has grown in you that, so long as you are strong of limb, you need not humble yourselves before anyone for a livelihood. *(Speech at students' meeting, Banaras; Navajivan, 5 December 1920 (CW 19, p. 27))*

Literary Training

Literary training by itself adds not an inch to one's moral height and that character-building is independent of literary training. *(Young India, 1 June 1921, p. 172)*

Development of Body, Mind and Spirit

The English word 'education' etymologically means 'drawing out'. That means an endeavour to develop our latent talents. The same is the meaning of *kilavani*, the Gujarati word for education. When we say that we develop a certain thing, it does not mean that we change its kind or quality, but that we bring out the qualities latent in it. Hence 'education' can also mean 'unfoldment'. In this sense, we cannot look upon knowledge of the alphabet as education. This is true even if that knowledge gains us the M.A. degree or enables us to adorn the place of a Shastri in some *pathshala* with the requisite knowledge of Sanskrit. It may well be that the highest literary knowledge is a fine instrument for education or unfoldment, but it certainly does not itself constitute education.

True education is something different. Man is made of three constituents, the body, mind and spirit. Of them, spirit is the one permanent element in man. The body and the mind function on account of it. Hence we can call that education which reveals the qualities of spirit. That is why the seal of the Vidyapith carries the dictum 'Education is that which leads to *moksha*'.

Education can also be understood in another sense; that is, whatever leads to a full or maximum development of all the three, the body, mind and spirit, may also be called education. The knowledge that is being imparted today may possibly develop the mind a little, but certainly it does not develop the body and spirit. I have a doubt about the development of the mind too, because it does not mean that the mind has developed if we have filled it with a lot of information. We cannot therefore say that we have educated our mind. A well-educated mind serves man in the desired manner. Our literate mind of today pulls us hither and thither. That is what a wild horse does. Only when a wild horse is broken in can we call it a trained horse. How many 'educated' young men of today are so trained?

Now let us examine our body. Are we supposed to cultivate the body by playing tennis, football or cricket for an hour every day? It does, certainly, build up the body. Like a wild horse, however, the body will be strong but not trained. A trained body is healthy, vigorous and sinewy. The hands and feet can do any desired work. A pickaxe, a shovel, a hammer, etc. are like ornaments to a trained hand and it can wield them. That hand can ply the spinning-wheel well as also the ring and the comb while the feet work a loom. A well trained body does not get tired in trudging 30 miles. It can scale mountains without getting breathless. Does the student acquire such physical culture? We can assert that modern curricula do not impart physical education in this sense.

The less said about the spirit the better. Only a seer or a seeker can enlighten the soul. Who will awaken that dormant spiritual energy in us all? Teachers can be had through an advertisement. Is there a column for spiritual quest in the testimonials which they have to produce? Even if there is one, what is its value? How can we get through advertisements teachers who are seekers after self-realisation? And education without such enlightenment is like a wall without a foundation or, to employ an English saying, like a whited sepulchre. Inside it there is only a corpse eaten up or being eaten by insects. *(Navajivan Education Supplement, 28 February 1926 (CW 30, pp. 58-59))*

Science and Responsibility

At the time when emphasis in education is put more upon literary knowledge than upon character building, the following from the article of Principal Jacks in the *Sunday School Chronicle* will be read with profit:

Our life presents itself as an endless movement, in which the march of science never quite overtakes the final problem of its own application. The point where responsibility rests upon us all is always just ahead of the last point reached by advancing science. The more the pursuer quickened his pace the more the fugitive quickens his. This inability of science to overtake responsibility is what I mean by its limitations. Applied science will tell you how to make a gun, but it will not tell you when to shoot nor whom to shoot at. You say that moral science will look after that. I answer that moral science in revealing the right use of my gun, inevitably reveals the wrong use also, and since the wrong will often serve my selfish purpose better than the right, my neighbours run a new risk of being shot at and plundered. A bad man armed with moral science is another name for the devil. If Mephistopheles had been examined in moral science in the University of London, he would have carried off all the prizes. At that point moral science and natural science are both in the same boat. How shall we name this fugitive thing which science never catches? I have called it life, others call it spirit or soul or sense, or perhaps the will. I do not think it matters greatly what we call it, so long as we recognize that it exists and that it carries in its arms the fortunes of mankind. Let education look to that. This is the point where all the enterprise of education and all the activities of religion come to their focus—the point of responsibility. If we do it at all other points and leave the point of responsibility uncared for, we shall inevitably come to grief. (Young India, 30 September 1926)

Against Atheism

My association with the students of our country dates back to 10 years, since my return to India. I know the hardships and the difficulties of the students. I have been seeing them every day. I also know their weak points. It has been my privilege to have a corner in their hearts. They have not hesitated to open their hearts to me, to tell me even what they had concealed from their parents. I do not know how I could bring them peace, or what message I could give them. I share in their sorrows, and I have been striving to alleviate their hardships. But in this world, we have to look only to God for help. None other could render any effectual help.

There is no sin equal to that of disbelieving in Him, in denying Him. Amongst the students of today the spirit of atheism is gaining ground. I am deeply grieved that things should be so. Whenever I see Hindu students, I ask them to think of God, to pray, to repeat Ramanama. They ask me where is God, where is Rama and such other questions. When I see Musalman youths and ask them to read the Koran, and to live the life enjoined therein, they also ask me similar questions. The education which leads to the negation of God cannot make for the service of the country nor of humanity. In your address, you have referred to my service to my country. Whatever I have been doing is done with a sense of my duty to God. And this I consider to be the right thing. God is not seated in the skies, in the heavens, or elsewhere. He is enshrined in the heart of everyone—be he a Hindu, Mohammedan, Christian or Jew, man or woman. *(Speech to students, Mysore—The Hindu, 21 July 1927 (CW 34, pp. 203–04))*

Education and Culture

"Culture" means refinement of feelings and "education" means knowledge of literature. Education is a means and culture is the end. The latter is possible even without education. For instance, if a child is brought up in a truly cultured family, it will unconsciously imbibe culture from its environment. In our country at any rate, present-day education and culture have no connection with each other. If the educated still retain some culture, that is in spite of their education. This fact shows that the roots of our culture are deep. *(Letter to Premabehn Kantak—5 January 1931 (CW 45, pp. 63–64))*

Strengthening of Character

In my wanderings among the students I made the discovery at an early stage of the movement that in order to conduct a movement of this kind character must be the foundation. We also found that real education consists not in packing the brain with so many facts and figures, not in passing examinations by reading numerous books but in developing character. I do not know to what extent you students of France lay stress upon character rather than upon intellectual studies, but I can say this that if you explore the possibilities of nonviolence you will find that without character it will prove a profitless study. *(Speech at meeting of students, Marseilles—Young India, 1 October 1931 (CW 47, p. 422))*

Knowledge of the Self

True education is that which helps us to know the *atman*, our true self, God and Truth. To acquire this knowledge, some persons may feel the need for a study of literature, some for a study of physical sciences and some others for art.

But every branch of knowledge should have as its goal knowledge of the self. That is so in the Ashram. We carry on numerous activities with that aim in view. All of them are, in my sense of the term, true education.

Those activities can also be carried on without any reference to the goal of knowledge of the self. When they are so carried on, they may serve as a means of livelihood or of something else, but they are not education. In an activity carried on as education, a proper understanding of its meaning, devotion to duty and the spirit of service are necessary. *(10 July 1932 (CW 50, p. 182))*

Ideal Education

When it is remembered that the primary aim of all education is, or should be, the moulding of the character of pupils, a teacher who has a character to keep need not lose heart. *(Harijan, 1 December 1933, p. 3 (CW 56, p. 296))*

Real Education

Real education has to draw out the best from the boys and girls to be educated. This can never be done by packing ill-assorted and unwanted information into the heads of the pupils. It becomes a dead weight crushing all originality in them and turning them into mere automata. *(Harijan, 1 December 1933 (CW 56, p. 295))*

Book of Humanity

Real education consists in drawing the best out of yourself. What better book can there be than the book of humanity? *(Harijan, 30 March 1934, p. 55)*

Education of the Hand

Literary education should follow the education of the hand—the one gift that visibly distinguishes man from beast. It is a superstition to think that the fullest development of man is impossible without a knowledge of the art of reading and writing. That knowledge undoubtedly adds grace to life, but it is in no way indispensable for man's moral, physical, or material growth. *(Harijan, 8 March 1935, p. 28)*

Fighting Social Evils

All this means education of a character that will revolutionize the mentality of the youth of the nation. Unfortunately the system of education has no connection with our surroundings which therefore remain practically untouched by the education received by a microscopic minority of the boys and girls of the nation. Whilst, therefore, whatever can be done to abate the evil must be done, it is clear to me that this evil and many others which can be named can only be tackled if there is education which responds to the rapidly changing conditions of the country. How is it that so many boys and girls who have even passed through colleges are found unable or unwilling to resist the manifestly evil custom which affects their future so intimately as marriage does? Why should educated girls be found to commit suicide because they are not suited? Of what value is their education if it does not enable them to dare to defy a custom which is wholly indefensible and repugnant to one's moral sense? The answer is clear. There is something radically wrong in the system of education that fails to arm girls and boys to fight against social or other evils. That education alone is of value which draws out the faculties of a student so as to enable him or her to solve correctly the problems of life in every department. *(Harijan, 23 May 1936 (CW 62, p. 436))*

Buddhist Education

Buddhism as a Phase of Hinduism

Buddhist education can be rightly regarded as a phase of the ancient Hindu system of education. Buddhism, itself, especially in its original and ancient form, is, as has been admitted on all hands, rooted deeply in the pre-existing Hindu systems of thought and life. Max Muller in Chips from a German Workshop i 434), "To my mind, having approached Buddhism after a study of the ancient religion of India, the religion of the Veda, Buddhism has always seemed to be, to a new religion, but a natural development of the Indian mind in its various manifestations, religious, philosophical, social, and political."

Auguste Barth (1834-1916) in The Religions of India, p. 101 calls Buddhism: "a Hindu phenomenon, a natural product, so to speak, of the age and social circle that witnessed its birth", and "when we attempt to reconstruct its primitive doctrine and early history we come upon something so akin to what we meet in the most ancient Upanishads and in the legends of Hinduism that it is not always easy to determine what features belong peculiarly to it."

T. W. Rhys Davids (1843-1922) in Buddhism p. 34 calls Gautama Buddha "the creature of his times", of whose philosophy it must not be supposed that "it was entirely of his own creation." He wrote: "The fact we should never forget is that Gautama was born and brought up and lived and died a Hindu. On the whole, he was regarded by the Hindus of that time a Hindu. Without the intellectual work of his predecessors, his work, however, original, would have been impossible. He was the greatest and wisest and best of the Hindus and, throughout his career, a characteristic India."

Edward Washburn Hopkins (1857-1932) goes so far as to assert (The Religions of India p. 298) that "the founder of Buddhism did not strike out a new system of morals; he was not a democrat; he did not originate a plot to overthrow the Brahminic priesthood; he did not invent the order of monks."

Hermann Oldenberg (1854-1920): "For hundreds of years before Buddha's time, movements were in progress in Indian thought which prepared the way for Buddhism."

The Buddha was a Product of the Hindu System

The thesis also receives a most conclusive confirmation from the details of the Buddha's own career as preserved in the traditional texts. The details show how largely Buddha was himself the product of the then prevailing Hindu educational systems. We see how in the very first step that he takes towards the Buddhahood, the renunciation of the home and the world, the world of riches to which he is born, he was not at all singular but following the path trodden by all seekers after truth in all ages and ranks of society. Our ancient literature is full of examples of the spirit of acute, utkata, vairagya under which the rich, the fortunate, and the noble not less than the poor, the destitute and the lowly, the young with a distaste for life before tasting it as much as the old who have had enough of it, even women and maidens, as eagerly leave their homes and adopt the ascetic life as a positive good as their dear ones entreat them to desist such a step.

The Buddha's next step was to place himself under the guidance of two successive gurus. The first was the Brahmin, Alara Kalama, at Vesali, having a following of 300 disciples who taught him the successive stages of meditation and the doctrine of the Atman, from which the Buddha turns back dissatisfied on the ground that it "does not lead to aversion, absence of passion, cessation, quiescence, knowledge, supreme wisdom and Nirvana, but only as far as the realm of nothingness". Next he attaches himself to the sage of Rajagaha with 700 pupils, Uddaka, the disciple of Rama but "he gained no clear understanding from his treatment of the soul." As Rhys David points out "Gautama, either during this period or before must have gone through a very systematic and continued course of study in all the deepest philosophy of the time." .

2

BASIC PRINCIPLES OF THE EDUCATION

Introduction

For many years past, several friends and I have felt that our present education is not national and that in consequence people do not get from it the benefit they ought to. Our children languish as a result of this education. They become incapable of any great achievement and the knowledge they acquire does not spread among the masses—not even in their families. Nor do the young people have any aim in mind in taking this modern education except to get a job and make money. It is one of the fundamental principles of education that it should be planned with a view to the needs of the people. This idea finds no place at all in our schools. Wherever I have travelled in India, I have discussed this question with the leaders and, without exception, almost every one has admitted that our educational system must change.

To look to the Government for this will be sheer waste of time. The Government will wait on public opinion and, being foreign, move very timidly; it cannot understand our needs, its advisers may be ill-informed or they may have interests of their own to serve. For a variety of such reasons, it will probably be quite long before there is any serious change in the present system; the time that passes meanwhile is so much loss to the people.

It is, however, not intended to suggest here that we should not try to get the Government to move. Let petitions be made to it and let public opinion be ascertained. But the best petition to the Government will be an actual demonstration by us and this will also be the easiest way of cultivating public opinion. It has accordingly been decided, in consultation with some educated gentlemen, to start a national school.

Basic principle: The education will be physical, intellectual and religious.

For physical education, there will be training in agriculture and hand-weaving and in the use of carpenter's and blacksmith's tools incidental to these. That will provide sufficient exercise for the pupils. In addition, they will be given drill, which is both an entertainment [and a practical utility] and, as part of this, they will be taught how to march in squads and how each one may work with quiet efficiency in case of accidents such as fire.

They will have instruction on how to preserve health and on home remedies for ordinary ailments, with as much of physiology and botany as may be necessary for the purpose.

For intellectual training, they will study Gujarati, Marathi, Hindi and Sanskrit as compulsory subjects. Urdu, Tamil and Bengali will also be taught.

There will be no teaching cf English during the first three years.

In addition, the pupils will be taught Mathematics (Arithmetic, Algebra and Geometry). Instruction in multiplication tables, Indian book-keeping and the measures, weights, etc., currently in use will begin at once and the rest of the curriculum will be covered progressively.

There will be instruction in History, Geography, Elements of Astronomy and Elements of Chemistry.

By way of instruction in religion, pupils will be taught general ethical principles and we are hopeful that the teachers will demonstrate by their conduct that the essence of religion is good character.

All teaching will be through Gujarati, right up to the highest stage, and most of it will be oral during the first few years. The intention is to put across to the children, before they learn to read and write, quite a few things orally by way of stories, as was the practice in old days, and so help their minds to grow, and to give them some general knowledge as they play about, rather than repress them by doing nothing more than remarking, "Oh dear, dear! How dirty", and so on.

Explanation

The aim at present is that after a few years of such education, the student's equipment will approximate to that of a well-informed graduate. That is, he will have a reduced load by way of learning English and, during the time so saved, he will be given all the useful knowledge a graduate acquires. He will be freed from the fear of examinations. All the students will be tested from time to time, but that will be by the teachers of the school itself. The use to which the student puts his abilities after leaving school will be the true measure of the worth of his education.

Every opportunity will be taken to rid his mind of the fallacious notion that the aim of education is to get employment. And, finally, every pupil joining this school is likely to develop such self-confidence in a few years that he will not be troubled with doubts or fears about how he will make a living.

A pupil who has been in the school for five years will be fixed up, if he so desires, in some work in the school itself and be paid for it. The school will make arrangements with some factories, etc., so that they provide training in vocations and give a start to those who wish to set themselves up independently. If, after ten years of study, anyone wants to pursue a subject further, necessary arrangements for the purpose are left to the future.

Free Education

No fees will be charged in this school, the expenses being met from donations received.

Teachers

Paid teachers will be engaged and will be, all of them, grown-up men who have reached the college level or possess equivalent attainments. The idea is that children should have the best teachers in the early stages.

Objects of School

1. To adopt a new method of education.
2. To pay special attention to character-building, the aim being that ten per cent of the pupils at any rate get trained for national service.
3. To raise the status of the Gujarati language.
4. To work for the spread of the national language, Hindi.
5. To open schools of the new pattern in every place, and make this school a model for them, and for Government as well, to copy. The aim is to have teachers trained in this school who will then go to villages and run schools there.
6. To get the new pattern adopted by the Government.

Requirements for Teachers

1. Knowledge of Hindi and Marathi
2. Proficiency in weaving
3. Well-preserved health
4. Travel in India
5. Readiness for other work besides that in the school, that is, for work in the Ashram or as secretary to Bapu

Work to be Attended to by Teachers, Apart from Teaching

1. Textbooks
2. Vocabulary of technical terms

Co-Education

I am myself in favour of coeducation, but I don't insist on it if the teachers hold a different opinion.

I am not in favour of common residence. Girls should not be kept in a hostel. I am of the view that they must live under the constant supervision of their mothers and nowhere else.

There should be holidays in summer and the school should be shifted to a cooler place. This, I believe, will enable the teachers and the pupils to work very much better at other times. The teachers and the pupils should spend the holidays together.

English should be an optional subject. One should know good, at any rate correct, English. It would be excellent if we could get an English teacher for the purpose, but I can think of no one at present except Miss Schlesin. If only she would come, we could want nothing better. She is a very capable person. A pupil of the school should be able to talk in English with any Englishman without being nervous. Drawing will be taught not as a fine art but because the pupil should be able to draw for practical purposes, draw maps, for instance, and straight lines, have a good handwriting and should know memory drawing.

Rules should be framed for discipline in the school, but no compulsion should be used to enforce obedience to them; they [the pupil] should feel inclined to obey them on their own. One should keep a watch on them whether they do. If any of them does not, we should express our disapproval and advise him. To start with, 100 pupils should be admitted to the school, all of whom can pay for their own expenses. Nothing may be spent from the School Fund for any of the pupils. If there is a good but poor student, we may secure help for him from one of our friends and beg of another for his fees; but the School Fund cannot be used for the purpose.

History, Geography, Science and Hygiene can be part of Gujarati.

We have necessarily to come into contact with people from the South, and this is to our benefit too; everyone should, therefore, know Marathi. *(After 18 January 1917; 23 June 1917 (CW 13, pp. 332–34, 447–48))*

True National Education

Our teachers must be men of high moral character. Conditions must be created to enable the poorest Indian to receive the best possible education. There must be a happy union of literary knowledge and Dharma. Education must be related to the conditions of life in our country. And the heavy burden on the minds of our young men resulting from the use of an alien language as the medium of instruction must be removed. Unless we reshape our education so as to fulfil the foregoing the level of the life of our people cannot be raised.

True national education should be imparted through the language of each province. The teachers must be men of high ability. The school should be located at a place where students would get clean drinking water, pure air and a peaceful atmosphere. The surroundings must be perfectly healthy. The scheme of education must provide for securing to the students a knowledge of the main occupations and religions of India.

[Except]... the first five years of a child's life, the rest of his education is given through a foreign language. Besides, in the first five years, which are in some respects the most useful and of the greatest importance, education is usually imparted by the most ordinary type of teachers. Then begins English. At this stage the boys pass as if into a different world altogether. The education which is given to them has no relation to the life at home. The boys who till then were quite happy to do their lessons sitting on the ground now have benches. At home, even today, the prevailing custom in most homes is to sit on the floor. Until then, the boy, if he was a Hindu, was content to wear a dhoti, a kurta and the angarakha and, if a Muslim, to wear the payjamas instead of the dhoti; but now he uses a coat and trousers.

Until then, he could do with the homely kalam, but now he has a pen with a steel nib. Thus, many significant changes take place in his outer living and a wide gulf divides the home and the school. Gradually, but definitely, this change begins to enter his inner life too. How are these changes in the outer life and the inner mental make-up of the boy going to affect his home and the way his people live at home? His parents have no idea at all as to what sort of education the boy is getting and their faith in that education is negligible.

Parents only know that it will help the boy to earn money. And this satisfies them. If this situation lasts long, we might all become foreigners! What is worse even the Swaraj for which we are struggling may become foreign in character when we finally get it, with the result that the very burden under which we are crushed today may continue even after Swaraj. There is only one way to escape this danger. It is to change and overhaul our system of education. In the national education to be evolved:

1. Education must be imparted through the mother-tongue.
2. There must be accord between the education a child receives at school and the environment of the home.
3. It must be so planned as to meet the needs of the majority of the people.
4. The teachers in primary classes must be competent men of good character right from the first class.
5. Education must be free.
6. Overall control must be in the hands of the people.

Education must be imparted through the mother-tongue. It is a pity that we are required to prove this self-evident truth. If we had not been dazzled by the lure of English, there should have been no need to prove this most obvious truth. The advocates of English say:

1. It is through English that an awakening has been created in the country.
2. English literature is so rich and vast that to give it up would be a great misfortune. It is not possible to translate it all into our language.
3. We can achieve unity only through English. To try to encourage and promote the different languages of India would amount to disrupting this unity and retarding the growing feeling that we are one nation.
4. English is the language of the rulers.

These are the main arguments of the advocates of English. They have many other things to say, but they have no more substance or importance than is included in the above.

To say that all the awakening we see in the country has been brought about through English is only a half-truth. The fact is that all the education in the country is being imparted through English. And because the Hindus are not absolute blockheads they have imbibed and utilized the good they have found in it. And yet the overall result which this education has yielded has been disappointing. Everybody admits that the present system of education suffers from some grave defects. We have not received from it the results which we are entitled to expect of an education which has now lasted for more than fifty years. Why is it so?

If it had been imparted from the beginning through the mother-tongue it would have produced much good by this time. What only a few English-knowing people know at present would have spread and reached crores of our people—who would have shown the spirit and the strength which is now shown only by the English-knowing handful. At present, our young men, when they pass out of the college, appear to be devoid of all energy and just wander about in search of jobs. Instead, if they had been educated through the mother-tongue, then having been spared the strain of cramming, they would have been stronger both in body and mind and would have therefore rejected Government service as something inferior.

No one suggests that English literature should be given up. We should have translated what is precious in it into our different languages. Japan and South Africa have done it. In Japan, they taught German and French to some who then translated good books from German and French into Japanese. It is not that German has nothing to borrow from English. Even so, not all Germans learn English. No German receives his education through English. Only a few Germans learn English and then translate into German whatever they think will be of value to their nation, and thus serve their mother-tongue. We should do the same.

As to the assumption that we have received a sense of unity by using English, the fact is that we become sharply aware of the illusion of our separateness from one another only after this alien language was introduced into our country, though it may be admitted that once we had seen through that illusion we strove to throw it off and regain our national solidarity. We observe that in many countries the oneness of the people is not always due to the oneness of the language. There are two languages in South Africa. But the people are striving to achieve unity because their interests are the same. Similar is the case with Canada. In England, Scotland and Wales they still speak three different languages. Mr. Lloyd George is making great efforts to revive Welsh, the language of Wales. And, yet, in all the three parts of Great Britain there is a strong feeling that they are one nation. Development of the regional languages of our country will produce social, political and economic awakening amongst our people.

They will have a better appreciation of their condition and position in the picture of the wider whole of the country. They will know that though belonging to different provinces they are sailing in the same boat.

Thus they will forget differences of language, appreciate the unity of their interests and be ready to fight for it, and protect it from dangers. Besides, the better educated amongst us will have to learn Hindi—as the common medium of speech. The effort required to learn Hindi is as nothing compared to that needed to learn English.

That English is the language of the rulers proves nothing beyond the fact that some of us have to master this alien tongue. I do not dislike English; I am only pleading that it be put in its proper place. Then, we can truly appreciate its merits, and derive such benefit as we can. It cannot, however, continue to be the medium of our education; nor can it be the language of interprovincial communication. In our schools and colleges we must provide for imparting even the highest education through the mother-tongue.

There must be accord between the education given in the school and the home. The reason for this is obvious. Today, there is no such accord between the two. In national education, we must see that such accord is achieved and maintained.

We will now pass on to the third attribute of national education, namely, that it should be so designed as to meet the needs of the majority of the people. The great bulk of our people are peasants. So, if our boys had been given, from the very beginning, a knowledge of agriculture and weaving and if they had cultivated an appreciation of the needs of these two classes, and if these classes had received the scientific training in these vocations, our peasants today would have been happy and prosperous. Our cattle would not have been weak and diseased as they are today. Our peasants would not have been crushed with the weight of debt—incurred by poverty.

Our produce would not have first gone to foreign countries as raw material and then brought back to us in the shape of finished goods to drain us of wealth. Today, we feel ashamed of such a state of affairs. We could not have paid England 85 crores rupees a year for cotton cloth. The prevailing system of education has made slaves of us instead of masters.

In the lower stages of primary education teachers must be men of high character. There is a proverb in English: 'The child is the father of the man.' We have a similar proverb: 'A child, even while in the cradle, shows signs of what he is going to be in the future.' If we entrust our children, in their most impressionable years, to incompetent teachers, we have no right to expect that they will grow to be men of good and strong character. That would be as absurd as to sow the seeds of kauvach and expect from them the flowers of mogra. We must procure the best teachers for our children whatever it may cost. In ancient times, our children received their education from learned and wise Rishis and Munis.

The fifth requirement of national education is that it should be free. Education should not be made to depend on money. Just as the sun gives light to all equally and rain pours down for all, even so learning must be made available to all.

Lastly, the people themselves must have control over the planning and carrying out of education. In the exercise of this control lies education too. People will then have faith in the education meted out to their children, and feel their responsibility towards it. When this stage is reached and education occupies an important place in the life of our people, it will be possible for us to obtain Swaraj with no trouble at all. Therefore, it is our duty to initiate such education. It is also our right to ask the Government for it. But we can approach the Government about this matter only after we start the ball rolling ourselves. However, it is beyond the scope of this article to discuss the steps we should take for organizing such a type of national education. Let people first accept the view expressed herein. *(Atmoddhar—a Marathi Monthly, True Education, pp. 39–44)*

National Higher Education

I have done a good many things in my life; some of them I feel proud of, though some others I regret. A few of them were very responsible undertakings. But I should like to state here—

I am sure I am guilty of no exaggeration—that nothing I have done so far can stand comparison with what we are about to do today. I am aware of a great risk in this undertaking, but not because I fear that it may prove harmful to the nation; what pains me, or rather the incongruity I feel, is this that I am not fit for the task I have undertaken. I do not say this as a matter of formality, I speak from the heart.

If I knew that the present undertaking related to education in the real sense of the term, this preface would not have been necessary. This Mahavidyalaya is not being established with the sole object of imparting education; it [also] aims at helping the student to acquire a means of livelihood and when, in this respect, I compare it with Gujarat College and other similar institutions, I simply shudder.

In this, too, I am not exaggerating. What comparison is possible between Gujarat College and other similar colleges, on the one hand, and this small Mahavidyalaya of ours? To my mind, of course, it is great, but I am afraid that in your eyes, as you compare this Vidyalaya with the colleges you have in India, this Mahavidyalaya probably appears an Anuvidyalaya. You are very likely thinking in terms of brick and mortar. Of this, to be sure, I see more in Gujarat College.

Today, not an inch of the ground is ours. Everything belongs to the Government. This land, these trees, everything belongs to Government, even this body, and I have now begun to doubt whether our soul also is ours. Placed in this pitiable condition, why go looking for good buildings to house our Mahavidyalaya? How can we afford to wait till we had found men of great learning? Even if the most ignorant of ignorant men, a mere simpleton, were to come forward and could succeed in convincing us that our atman had been starved, that this country had lost its light—its knowledge of things of the spirit—I would appoint him as the principal. I am not sure that you would be ready to appoint a shepherd as principal and so we have had to find Shri Gidwani. I have not been attracted by the position he occupied. Perhaps you do not know him apart from that position. I should, however, like you to adopt a different criterion, some another touchstone, for judging the worth of this Vidyalaya if you test it on the common touchstone, it will seem to be brass but it will be found to be gold if you test it on the touchstone of character.

The coming together of [talented] men for educational work here is like the holy confluence of rivers. We have men of character assembled here. Fine men from Sind, Maharashtra and Gujarat have banded together here. How could we have, ordinarily, secured this?

I shall first address my prayer to the sisters and brothers who have come here for the function. You are witnesses to the establishment of this Mahavidyalaya. If there are any among you who feel that what is taking place is a farce, I would ask them not to be so conscientious and sit through the function. They should remain only if they wish to give their blessings. With the blessings of you all, the Mahavidyalaya will earn a name as a great institution. But they should not be blessings merely uttered with the lips; bless it from your heart. This you can do only by offering your sons and daughters to the institution. People in India have plenty of capacity to contribute money. In no field is progress held up for lack of funds. It is held up for want of men—of teachers or leaders, or if a leader is forthcoming, for want of pupils, *i.e.*, soldiers. It is my belief that, if the leader is worthy, there will be no lack of soldiers. A carpenter will not quarrel with his tools, however bad they may be. He will handle the bluntest of them with the utmost ease. Likewise, if the leader is a real artisan, whatever the quality of the material, he will produce gold from it, will produce gold from the country's clay. This is my prayer to the principal.

You, principal and teachers, have been inspired by one ideal only in joining this institution. You have undertaken to secure freedom through the miracle not of learning but of character, secure it not by meeting the Government, sword against its shining sword, but with peaceful, spiritual effort—howsoever imperfect it be—against its aggressive, Satanic way. We want just now to sow the seed of freedom and afterwards we will water the plant and rear it into a tree. This tree can be raised only through character, with pure, spiritual strength.

So long as the principal and the teachers go on working with their eyes on this one aim, we shall never be put to shame. May God justify in your experience the faith which is mine.

Were it not for this unshakable faith of mine, I would not at all have accepted the sacred position of chancellor. I am ready to live and die for this cause, thinking that to die in this cause is to live; it is because I know that this is also true of you that I live among you and have accepted this exalted position.

We are establishing this Vidyalaya, not with an educational, but with a national aim in view. Advising that students be taught to cultivate strength and character, I have been saying everywhere that in the measure we succeed with them we shall make ourselves fit for Swaraj in the country. Swaraj cannot be secured in any other way. No amount of money we can spend or strength of character we can employ to ensure the success of such colleges will be enough.

This is a time not for words but for action. I have placed my thoughts before you as they came. I asked of you what you could give. Now I shall ask something of the students as well. There is no doubt at all that they have in them the courage which takes risks. I shall not look upon them-upon those who have already joined—as mere students and, therefore, I will not treat them as being free from responsibility. Those who have registered their names here are half teachers. It is they who have provided the foundation for the Mahavidyalaya.

It is on them that the structure of the institution has been raised. Had they not joined, this Mahavidyalaya could not have been started. They also, therefore, share equal responsibility. You are equal partners in this and, if you do not play your part well, no efforts on the part of the teachers will succeed or, at any rate, succeed completely. Students who have left their colleges should understand why they have joined here and what they should expect to gain. May God grant them the strength to go on with their work, no matter how long this grim war continues. If they do, I am sure that, even if they are a mere handful, this Mahavidyalaya will shine forth and be a model institution for the whole country.

The reason will not be that Gujarat has wealth or that it has learning; it will be rather, that noncooperation had its origin here. The seed was sown and watered here, the required tapascharaya was performed here. Do not think from this that I am a conceited man to speak in this manner, or that all the tapascharaya has been mine and the seed was sown by me. I merely gave the mantra, I fulfilled the function of a rishi, if a Vanik's son can do so.

I have done nothing more than this. The planting was done by my co-workers. It is because their faith was greater than mine that we have succeeded. I claim the knowledge which comes from direct perception. Even if the gods came down and tried to persuade me to the contrary, my faith would not be shaken. As surely as I see, with my eyes, the trees in front of me, so surely I know that there is no salvation for India except through nonviolent noncooperation. As for my co-workers, however, they have believed this through logic or reasoning or accepted it on faith.

My co-workers have laid the foundation. Many of them are Gujaratis; there are Maharashtrians, too, but having been in Gujarat, they have become half or three-quarters Gujaratis or, perhaps, more Gujaratis than the Gujaratis themselves. They have made this a weapon of shining strength. We have not yet seen all its miraculous power. Within six months, you will see more of the miraculous power of this programme for which young girls handed over their bangles to me. But the source of it all—the visible image—is this Mahavidyalaya. Hindus are worshippers of images and we are proud of being so. This image has its various limbs: one of them is the chancellor and that is myself. The teachers, the principal and the students are other limbs. I am, myself, an old man, a withering leaf, and busy with other work. The falling away of such a leaf as I am can do no harm to a tree. The principal and the teachers, too, are no more than leaves, though green leaves as yet. In a short while, they also will grow old and, perhaps, fall off. The students, however, are the branches of this beautiful tree and it is on them that principals and teachers will grow as leaves.

I request them to put the same faith in their teachers as they do in me. Should they, however, see that the principal or any of the teachers is weak, let them burn him to ashes with the fire which was Prahlad's and go ahead with their work. This is my prayer to God and my blessings to the students.

I shall end with a prayer to God and I want you all to say "amen" to it. Join me in my prayer, all of you, with a pure heart,

"God! Make this Mahavidyalaya of such worth that through it we may win the freedom for which we offer prayers day and night and grant it that, through that freedom, not only India but the entire world, in which India is but a dot, may be happy." *(Inaugural speech at the setting up of Gujarat Vidyapith, 15 November 1920 Navajivan, 18 November 1920 (CW 18, pp. 463–68) (Translated from Gujarati))*

National Institutions

Since some of the staunchest supporters of noncooperation have lost faith in it and since the numbers attending national institutions are dwindling, what is the use of holding on to these tottering schools and colleges and wasting good money after bad institutions?

My believing eye detects a flaw in this argument. My faith in noncooperation remaining as staunch as ever, I can find it possible to reconcile myself to the existing national institutions even though the attendance may be reduced to half a dozen. For the half a dozen will be the makers of Swaraj whenever it comes. When virgins are required to perform certain sacred ceremonies, others are not accepted as substitute if no virgin is found. And even one virgin if found is enough to save the situation. So will it be with the planting of the Swaraj flag-post. The flags will be unfurled with the unsullied hands of those, be they ever so few, who have remained true to their original creed.

I do not therefore regard it as waste of money to continue the national institutions. They are so many oases in the desert. They give the water of life to the souls thirsting for freedom. In writing this I cast no reflection upon those who attend or otherwise support Government schools. They are entitled to hold the view if they choose that theirs is the only way or also a way to freedom.

National institutions are meant for those whose thirst for freedom is not satisfied by the ones managed or patronized by the Government. Few as they are, insignificant though they may appear, they supply a felt want and contain in them the seeds, as it appears to non-co-operators, of true and lasting freedom.

The final success of these institutions depends upon the worth of the teachers. "But they are deserting the national schools and colleges," says the critic. So some of them are. It tries the faith of the survivors. Have they the courage to stand alone? Are there enough monied men to support the surviving national institutions? On the correct answer to these questions depends the future of the national institutions and with them the freedom of the country, and so far as I can judge, there are teachers enough to stand the severest test and there are monied men enough to support them. I know no organisation that has died for want of funds. Organisations die always for want of men, *i.e.*, honesty, efficiency and self-sacrifice. And it is my certain knowledge that where there are teachers, pupils are not wanting.

But the pupils have perhaps the largest share of responsibility on their shoulders. The future depends upon their ability, integrity, application, and patriotism. The teachers cannot give what the pupils have not. The teachers can help to 'draw out' in the pupils what they have. If it were otherwise, if the teachers were capable of putting something into their pupils, all the latter receiving instruction under them will be alike, whereas we know as a matter of fact that no two pupils have been yet known to be alike. The pupils must therefore have initiative. They must cease to be mere imitators. They must learn to think and act for themselves and yet be thoroughly obedient and disciplined. The highest form of freedom carries with it the greatest measure of discipline and humility. Freedom that comes from discipline and humility cannot be denied; unbridled licence is a sign of vulgarity injurious alike to self and one's neighbours. *(Young India, 3 June 1926 (CW 30, pp. 519–20)*

Non-Co-operation Movement's First University

Kakasaheb is writing about what Gujarat Vidyapith has done and what it is trying to achieve. There is one bit of criticism, however, to which he cannot reply. Some say that the Vidyapith has met with disaster since he took charge of it. If it has been ruined, I am responsible for it, not Kakasaheb. This is because so long as the people are enamoured of me or are fond of me and largely accept my advice, I am responsible for the changes that have been made in the Vidyapith. I was primarily responsible for the boycott of Government schools and for formulating a policy for national education. This I must humbly say or admit.

It was I who brought over Acharya Gidwani and it is I who asked him to step down. Kakasaheb was connected with the Vidyapith ever since its inception. Again, it was I who took him away from the Vidyapith. During Acharya Gidwani's term of office, the Vidyapith attracted students, land was bought for it and buildings were erected. Perhaps the Vidyapith would not be there if there were no Acharya Gidwani. He had promised me twice that he would readily come over whenever I summoned him. I received Vallabhabhai's telegram in Bhiwani in which he had suggested that Acharya Gidwani should take charge of the Vidyapith. He immediately agreed to do so. And in a few days, the first noncooperation university in India was launched.

The treaty that was made between Gujarat and Sind by bringing him over to the former place is still there. I withdrew Acharya Gidwani because of a difference of opinion that arose in the Vidyapith. That did not imply any slur on anyone. It is my conviction that even today, Acharya Gidwani belongs to Gujarat. He went over to Prem Mahavidyalaya because Gujarat sent him there. And today he is in Karachi, only as a delegate from Gujarat. At all the three places, it is hoped, the national viewpoint will be fostered. At all the three places, there will certainly be propaganda for Khadi.

Acharya Kripalani was borrowed from the Kashi Ashram, which is his own creation. I relieved him as I had promised to do so. Under his leadership, too, the Vidyapith has not taken a retrograde step. At the time of the students' strike, we saw that he had stolen the hearts of the students. Acharya Kripalani was a second gift that Sind gave to Gujarat. Even today, he belongs to Gujarat. In my opinion, under his leadership also the Vidyapith has progressed. Although all may have a common ideal, there is naturally a difference in the work and character of every man.

And, it is in accordance with this that an institution which is in charge of a particular person develops and takes on a distinct colour. However, in regard to the Vidyapith, I have felt that this variety has been as beautiful as the variety in the colours of a rainbow. Whereas one principal has strengthened one aspect of it, another has done the same for another aspect of it. The result has only been good. At present the rudder is in the hands of Kakasaheb. He has been moulding the Vidyapith.

The Vidyapith has not crumbled; it is going ahead. So long as Kakasaheb is at the helm, all that needs to be said with regard to it is that anyone who has any doubts about it should go there and inspect it. Just as all the three principals have been complementary to one another, the periods to which they belonged also stand in the same relationship to one another. As all the three are fruits of the same tree, there is a continuity hidden behind their work. Not even one of them has wiped out what had been achieved before, but has added to the sum total of its achievements. The present state of the Vidyapith, itself bears testimony to this. At the very inception of the Vidyapith, I had suggested a test for judging it; that holds good even today.

The Vidyapith is going to be judged neither by its buildings nor by the number of its students, nor again by the knowledge of English that its students possess. It is going to be judged by the patriotism of its students, by their capacity to give to others the knowledge of the subjects which they have learnt, by their knowledge of Hindi by their knowledge of the science of the spinning-wheel, by the strength of character of its students and teachers, and by their turning towards the villages. Judged by these standards, it is my confirmed belief that the Vidyapith has taken forward strides and anyone who wishes to ascertain this can do so by going over to examine it. Just as a tree is judged by its fruit, the Vidyapith can be examined in a similar manner. It is not a distant institution about which an investigator would need a testimonial from me or from anyone else. Moreover, it is fair to scrutinize a thing personally, wherever this is possible and where such a scrutiny is necessary. After conducting this inquiry if it is felt that the Vidyapith has made continuous progress and has augmented its capacity to serve, it is only fitting that contributions should flow in to its doors. *(Navajivan, 29 December 1929 (CW 42, pp. 327–29) (Translated from Gujarati))*

Salt Satyagraha

It has been often said that the money spent on national education in general and the Gujarat Vidyapith in particular has been so much waste. In my opinion the Gujarat Vidyapith by its supreme sacrifice has more than justified its existence, the hopes entertained by its authors and the grants made to it by donors. For the Vidyapith has suspended its literary activities save for boys under 16 who are already under training there. The teachers and students of over 15 years of age have offered their services as volunteers and nearly forty students with the teachers are already in the field. A class for giving fifteen days' emergency training in connection with Satyagraha has been opened for the sake of those who may need such training. I congratulate the students and the teachers on the promptitude with which they have acted. I may state that twenty of these are with me on the march. They are divided into two parties, both preceding the 80 pilgrims to make preparations in advance and assisting the villagers. They are under orders not to offer civil resistance till the 80 are arrested and immediately to replace them as soon as they are arrested.

I am sure that every national educational institution will copy the noble example of the Gujarat Vidyapith which was the first to come into being in response to the call of noncooperation in 1920. And I hope that the Government and aided institutions will also copy the example. Every revolution of modern times has found students in the forefront. This, because it is peaceful, ought not to offer less attraction to the students. *(Young India, 20 March 1930 (CW 43, pp. 109–10))*

Freedom Struggle

I learnt what happened in India after my arrest in Karadi only through the newspapers. Later on, after my release, I also heard about it from the people. I have heard so much about the part that the Vidyapiths—our national schools and colleges—have played in the movement that I am really overwhelmed with joy. I have come to know more about the Gujarat Vidyapith as also of the Bihar and Kashi Vidyapiths. It is no small matter that the teachers and students from all these three institutions cast aside their books and came to join the fight for freedom.

When the history of this fight comes to be written the world will be glad to know of the great part played in it by the students and the national Vidyapiths. While in jail, whenever I read anything in the newspapers about the students and the teachers, I would at once make a comparison between them and those in Government schools. As a result of which it became clear to me how correct we were in launching the programme of the boycott of Government schools in 1920.

It is true that the Government schools are yet as crowded with students as they used to be. And it is even more tragic that the students are so eager to enter them that they ask for pardon, pay fines and somehow secure admission into them. This so far emboldens the heads of the colleges, or the authorities of the education department, that they send circulars that before admitting the students who have taken a direct or indirect part in the fight or who have gone to jail the matter should first be referred to the head of the education department. It is he who is to permit their admission after studying their cases. What are we to think of students who thus seek entrance into Government schools and colleges at the cost of their self-respect, and what of the authorities of the education department who insist on such conditions?

So much about the achievement of our college section. Let me now draw your attention to Appendix III of the Report of the Vidyapith. It mentions the names of the teachers and students who had gone to jail. Kakasaheb has said that what the students have learnt in the past one year, they had never learnt before, though the Vidyapith was the same; it was no less national then, and yet we did not then achieve as much as in the past year. And in future too whenever there is a call for the fight and we fill the jails, we will again have the satisfaction of having done our duty which is the greatest gift of knowledge. We believe that when we do so we shall be true teachers and students.

The point is that the Snataka and Gramseva-Dikshitas should not think that they are the product of any ordinary school. What can we do; we too have to earn a living; fate has brought us to the Vidyapith, so willy-nilly we must act as we are asked to! You should never entertain such thoughts in your mind even for a moment. Even though superficially you may appear to be only a handful, really you are like a sea, while the others, though they may appear to be as big as a sea, are really a phantom which has no existence. It is difficult, if not impossible, to instil in them the courage and the power to win Swaraj. As to the cultivation of that power in national schools, we can see it in these students. Those who have seen their work will bear witness to the fact that we have not lost anything in setting up these Vidyapiths. On the contrary, we have fully recovered with interest the money gifted for it. *(Navajivan, 3 May 1931 (CW 45, pp. 407–08))*

The Spinning Wheel Message

The real work of the Vidyapith lies in the villages. I have been stressing this point ever since the inception of the Vidyapith, but until a couple of years ago, when it was declared an illegal organisation and most of our professors and boys were imprisoned, we laboured under the impression that the work could be carried on only through a central institute situated in the capital town of Gujarat.

But under the altered conditions and now that we have some breathing time to put our heads together and to collect our thoughts, we shall do well to hark back to the original conception and think of our future work in its terms. Each member of a live institution must be a living embodiment of the ideals of the institution, wherever he may be, and when such a state of things is brought about, it is the same thing whether the institution has a habitation and a corporate existence or not.

I would, therefore, expect every one of you who has cherished the ideals of the Vidyapith and who is pledged to serve it to go straight to the villages and start living those ideals there. Each one of you will thus be a peripatetic Vidyapith, teaching the ideals by means of his own personal example. It is quite conceivable that a host of workers, after having lived the life in the villages according to the ideals of the Vidyapith, re-establish the central institute in a village. But we are not in that position today. We have yet to gain all that experience on which alone you can build the new Vidyapith.

The centre of this village worker's life will be the spinning-wheel. I am sorry I have not been able yet to bring home to anyone the message of the spinning-wheel in all its implication. The reason is that my life itself is not a true echo of the message. But it came home to me again and again during my nine months' peregrinations in India. We have not yet sufficiently realized that hand-spinning is a supplementary industry of universal application and scope in India. The village weaver cannot live but for the spinning-wheel. He gets his yarn no doubt from the mills, but he is doomed to destruction, if he is to remain for ever dependent on the mills. Today, the spinning-wheel has established itself in our economic life only to the extent that it is needed to minister to the clothing needs of the new class of khadi weavers that has sprung up during the past decade.

But a large body like the Spinners' Association cannot justify its existence to fulfil that limited object. The idea at the back of khadi is that it is an industry supplementary to agriculture and coextensive with it, that it is the life-breath of millions of Harijan weavers who derive their sustenance from it. The spinning-wheel cannot be said to have been established in its own proper place in our life, until we can banish idleness from our villages and make every village home a busy hive. Unemployment and idleness of millions must lead to bloody strife. Khadi is the only alternative to this and not the so called socialism, which presupposes industrialism. The socialism that India can assimilate is the socialism of the spinning-wheel. Let the village worker, therefore, make the wheel the central point of his activities.

The worker will not be spinning regularly but will be working for his bread with the adze or the spade or the last, as the case may be. All his hours minus the eight hours of sleep and rest will be fully occupied with some work. He will have no time to waste. He will allow himself no laziness and allow others none. His life will be a constant lesson to his neighbours in ceaseless and joy-giving industry. Bodily sustenance should come from body labour, and intellectual labour is necessary for the culture of the mind. Division of labour there will necessarily be, but it will be a division into various species of body labour and not a division into intellectual labour to be confined to one class and body labour to be confined to another class. Our compulsory or voluntary idleness has to go. If it does not go, no panacea will be of any avail, and semi-starvation will remain the eternal problem that it is. He who eats two grains must produce four. Unless the law is accepted as universal, no amount of reduction in population would serve to solve the problem. If the law is accepted and observed, we have room enough to accommodate millions more to come.

The village worker will thus be a living embodiment of industry. He will master all the process of khadi, from cotton-sowing and picking to weaving, and will devote all his thought to perfecting them. If he treats it as a science, it won't jar on him, but he will derive fresh joy from it everyday, as he realizes more and more its great possibilities. If he will go to the village as a teacher, he will go there no less as a learner. He will soon find that he has much to learn from the simple villagers. He will enter into every detail of village life, he will discover the village handicrafts and investigate the possibilities of their growth and their improvement. He may find the villagers completely apathetic to the message of khadi, but he will, by his life of service compel interest and attention. Of course, he will not forget his limitations and will not engage in, for him, the futile task of solving the problem of agricultural indebtedness.

Sanitation and hygiene will engage a good part of his attention. His home and his surroundings will not only be a model of cleanliness, but he will help to promote sanitation in the whole village by taking the broom and the basket round.

He will not attempt to setup a village dispensary or to become the village doctor. These are traps which must be avoided. I happened during my Harijan tour to come across a village where one of our workers who should have known better had built a pretentious building in which he had housed a dispensary and was distributing free medicine to the villages around. In fact, the medicines were being taken from home to home by volunteers and the dispensary was described as boasting a register of 1,200 patients a month! I had naturally to criticize this severely. That was not the way to do village work, I told him. His duty was to inculcate lessons of hygiene and sanitation in the village folk and thus to show them the way of preventing illness, rather than attempt to cure them. I asked him to leave the palace-like building and to hire it out to the Local Board and to settle in thatched huts. All that one need stock in the way of drugs is quinine, castor oil and iodine and the like. The worker should concentrate more on helping people realize the value of personal and village cleanliness and maintaining it at all cost.

Then he will interest himself in the welfare of the village Harijans. His home will be open to them. In fact, they will turn to him naturally for help in their troubles and difficulties. If the village folk will not suffer him to have the Harijan friends in his house situated in their midst, he must take up his residence in the Harijan quarters.

A word about the knowledge of the alphabet. It has its place, but I should warn you against a misplaced emphasis on it. Do not proceed on the assumption that you cannot proceed with rural instruction without first teaching the children or adults how to read and write. Lots of useful information on current affairs, history, geography and elementary arithmetic, can be given by word of mouth before the alphabet is touched. The eyes, the ears and the tongue come before the hand. Reading comes before writing and drawing before tracing the letters of the alphabet. If this natural method is followed, the understanding of the children will have a much better opportunity of development than when it is under check by beginning the children's training with the alphabet.

The worker's life will be in tune with the village life. He will not pose as a literature buried in his book, loath to listen to details of humdrum life. On the contrary, the people, whenever they see him, will find him busy with his tools—spinning-wheel, loom, adze, spade, etc.—and always responsive to their meanest inquiries. He will always insist on working for his bread. God has given to everyone the capacity of producing more than his daily needs and, if he will only use his resourcefulness, he will not be in want of an occupation suited to his capacities, however poor they may be. It is more likely than not that the people will gladly maintain him, but it is not improbable that in some places he may be given a cold shoulder. He will still plod on. It is likely that in some villages he may be boycotted for his pro-Harijan proclivities. Let him in that case approach the Harijans and look to them to provide him with food. The labourer is always worthy of his hire and, if he conscientiously serves them, let him not hesitate to accept his food from the Harijans always, provided that he gives more than he takes. In the very early stages of course, he will draw his meagre allowance from a central fund where such is possible.

I have deliberately left out the question of the cow. The village worker will find it difficult to tackle the question and will not attempt it, except to the extent of educating the people in the theory of it. We have not yet hit upon the best way of curing dead cattle's hide and dyeing it, as also the best means of protecting the cow. In Gujarat the buffalo problem complicates the situation. We have got to make people realize that to encourage the buffalo is to allow the cow to die. But more of this some other time.

Remember that our weapons are spiritual. It is a force that works irresistibly, if imperceptibly. Its progress is geometrical rather than arithmetical. It never ceases so long as there is a propeller behind. The background of all your activities has therefore, to be spiritual. Hence the necessity for the strictest purity of conduct and character.

You will not tell me that this is an impossible programme, that you have not the qualifications for it. That you have not fulfilled it so far should be no impediment in your way. If it appeals to your reason and your heart, you must not hesitate. Do not fight shy of the experiment. The experiment will itself provide the momentum for more and more effort. *(Harijan, 31 August 1934 (CW 58, pp. 305–9))*

Village Schools

"The cruelest irony of the new Reforms lies in the fact that we are left with nothing but the liquor revenue to fall back upon in order to give our children education," said Gandhiji in one of the numerous talks he has been giving on the subject, ever since the Congress Ministers took up office. "That is the educational puzzle but it should not baffle us. We have to solve it and the solution must not involve the compromise of our ideal of prohibition cost whatever else it may. It must be shameful and humiliating to think that unless we got the drink revenue, our children would be starved of their education. But if it comes to it, we should prefer it as a lesser evil. If only we will refuse to be obsessed by the figures and by the supposed necessity of giving our children the exact kind of education that they get today, the problem should not baffle us." That explains Gandhiji's emphasis on our educationists putting their heads together in order to evolve a system of education which is at once inexpensive and also in consonance with the needs of our vast rural population.

"Then you would really abolish what is called secondary education and give the whole education up to matriculation in the village schools?" asked a questioner in great surprise.

"Certainly. What is your secondary education but compelling the poor boys to learn in a foreign language in seven years what they should learn in the course of a couple of years in their own mother-tongue? If you can but make up your minds to free the children from the incubus of learning their subjects in a foreign tongue, and if you teach them to use their hands and feet profitably, the educational puzzle is solved. You can sacrifice without compunction the whole of the drink revenue. But you must resolve to sacrifice this revenue first, and think of the ways and means about education later. Make the beginning by taking the big step." *(Harijan, 21 August 1937 (CW 66, p. 57))*

Self-supporting Education

In spite of the weak state of his health and the quantities of rest that he needs, Gandhiji has shown his readiness to discuss his theory of self-supporting education with anyone who has thought about the subject and wants to contribute his share to making the new experiment a success. The discussions have been, in view of his health, necessarily few and brief, but every now and then something new has emerged, and whenever he has talked, he has had some fresh suggestion to make and fresh light to throw. Thus on one occasion he sounded a warning against the assumption that the idea of self-supporting education sprang from the necessity of achieving total prohibition as soon as possible. "Both are independent necessities," he said. "You have to start with the conviction that total prohibition has to be achieved revenue or no revenue, education or no education. Similarly, you have to start with the conviction that looking to the needs of the villages of India our rural education ought to be made self-supporting if it is to be compulsory."

"I have the first conviction deep down in me," said an educationist who carried on the discussion. "Prohibition to me is an end in itself, and I regard it as a great education in itself. I should, therefore, sacrifice education altogether to make prohibition a success. But the other conviction is lacking. I cannot yet believe that education can be made self-supporting."

"There, too, I want you to start with the conviction. The ways and means will come as you begin to work it out. I regret that I woke up to the necessity of this at this very late age. Otherwise I should have made the experiment my self. Even now, God willing, I shall do what I can to show that it can be self-supporting. But my time has been taken up by other things all these years, equally important perhaps; but it is this stay in Segaon that brought the conviction home to me.

We have up to now concentrated on stuffing children's minds with all kinds of information, without ever thinking of stimulating and developing them. Let us now cry a halt and concentrate on educating the child properly through manual work, not as a side activity, but as the prime means of intellectual training."

"I see that too. But why should it also support the school?"

"That will be the test of its value. The child at the age of 14, that is, after finishing a seven years' course, should be discharged as an earning unit. Even now the poor people's children automatically lend a helping hand to their parents—the feeling at the back of their minds being, what shall my parents eat and what shall they give me to eat if I do not also work with them? That is an education in itself. Even so the State takes charge of the child at seven and returns it to the family as an earning unit. You impart education and simultaneously cut at the root of unemployment. You have to train the boys in one occupation or another. Round this special occupation you will train up his mind, his body, his writing, his artistic sense, and so on. He will be master of the craft he learns."

"But supposing a boy takes up the art and science of making Khadi. Do you think it must occupy him all the seven years to master the craft?"

"Yes. It must, if he will not learn it mechanically. Why do we give years to the study of history or to the study of languages? Is a craft any the less important than these subjects which have been up to now given an artificial importance?"

"But as you have been mainly thinking of spinning and weaving, evidently you are thinking of making of these schools so many weaving schools. A child may have no aptitude for weaving and may have it for something else."

"Quite so. Then we will teach him some other craft. But you must know that one school will not teach many crafts. The idea is that we should have one teacher for twenty-five boys, and you may have as many classes or schools of twenty-five boys as you have teachers available, and have each of these schools specializing in a separate craft—carpentry, smithy, tanning or shoe-making. Only you must bear in mind the fact that you develop the child's mind through each of these crafts. And I would emphasize one more thing. You must forget the cities and concentrate on the villages. They are an ocean. The cities are a mere drop in the ocean. That is why you cannot think of subjects like brick-making. If they must be civil and mechanical engineers, they will after the seven years' course go to the special colleges meant for these higher and specialized courses.

"And let me emphasize one more fact. We are apt to think lightly of the village crafts because we have divorced educational from manual training. Manual work has been regarded as something inferior, and owing to the wretched distortion of the varna we came to regard spinners and weavers and carpenters and shoemakers as belonging to the inferior castes, the proletariat. We have had no Cromptons and Hargreaves because of this vicious system of considering the crafts as something inferior, divorced from the skilled. If they had been regarded as callings having an independent status that learning enjoyed, we should have had great inventors from among our craftsmen. Of course the 'Spinning Jenny' led on to the discovery of water-power and other things which made the mill displace the labour of thousands of people. That was, in my view, a monstrosity. We will by concentrating on the villages see that the inventive skill that an intensive learning of the craft will stimulate will subserve the needs of the villages as a whole." *(Harijan, 18 September 1937 (CW 66, pp. 137–9))*

The Best System

At the end of the Educational conference held at Wardha, (1937), Gandhiji remarked in the course of a talk with the members of the Executive Committee," I have given many things to India. But this system of education together with its technique is, I feel, the best of them. I do not think I will have anything better to offer to the country.".*(Problem of Education, 'Introduction', p. v.)*

Nayee Taleem

This work of basic education is the last work of my life. If, by the grace of God, it is completed, Hindustan will be totally transformed. The present system of education is useless. Those boys who get their education in schools and colleges, they get only literacy, but over and above literacy something more is needed. If that literacy renders our other parts of the body inactive, I would say I don't need such literacy. We need blacksmiths, carpenters, oil millers, masons, carders, spinners and labourers. In essence, we need persons ready to do all sorts of physical work and along with that literacy for all is also necessary. Knowledge that is confined to a handful of individuals is not useful to me. Now the question is, how could that knowledge be available to all? Nai Taleem has emerged from this consideration. I say that Nai Taleem should start with the conception by the mother rather than at the age of seven years. Please try to understand its mystery. If mother would be the one inclined to do physical labour, be thoughtful, be systematic, be under self-restraint, her child would inherit her qualities from the time of his very conception.

My definition of Nayee Taleem is that if the person who has received Nayee Taleem, is enthroned, he would not feel vanity of power, on the other hand, if he is given a broom, he will not feel ashamed. For him both the jobs will be of equal importance. There would be no place to vain rejoicing in his life. None of his actions will be unproductive or useless. No student of Nayee Taleem shall be dull, because each part of his body would be active and he would have nice neuromuscular coordination. When the people would do manual labour, there would be no unemployment or starvation. My Nayee Taleem and the village industries are mutually complementary. When they both will be a success, we will attain true Swaraj. *(Bapuni Chaayaman, pp. 157–158 (Translated from Gujarati))*

Newness and Originality

It is necessary to understand the newness or originality in the Nai Taleem. Whatever good there is in the old education will of course, be retained in the Nayee Taleem; but there will be enough of the new element besides. If Nayee Taleem is really new it should lead to the following results: Our sense of frustration should give place to hope; our penury and starvation to a sufficiency of means to maintain ourselves; unemployment to industry and work; discord to concord. It should enable our sons and daughters to learn to read and write and know along with it a craft through which they will acquire knowledge. *(Utmanzai, 14 October 1938 (CW 67, p. 438))*

Education Through Craft

Speaking about education through a craft Gandhiji said:

"If such education is given, the direct result will be that it will be self-supporting. But the test of success is not its self-supporting character, but that the whole man has been drawn out through the teaching of the handicraft in a scientific manner. In fact I would reject a teacher who would promise to make it self-supporting under any circumstances. The self-supporting part will be the logical corollary of the fact that the pupil has learnt the use of every one of his faculties. If a boy who works at a handicraft

for three hours a day will surely earn his keep, how much more a boy who adds to the work a development of his mind and soul!" (Harijan, 11 June 1938 (CW 67, p. 115))

Basic Education

This Basic Education has grown out of the atmosphere surrounding us in the country and is in response to it. It is, therefore, designed to cope with that atmosphere. This atmosphere pervades India's seven hundred thousand villages and its millions of inhabitants. Forget them and you forget India. India is not to be found in her cities. It is in her innumerable villages.

The following are the fundamentals of Basic Education:

1. All education to be true must be self-supporting, that is to say, in the end it will pay its expenses excepting the capital which will remain intact.
2. In it the cunning of the hand will be utilized even up to the final stage, that is to say, hands of the pupils will be skilfully working at some industry for some period during the day.
3. All education must be imparted through the medium of the provincial language.
4. In this there is no room for giving sectional religious training. Fundamental universal ethics will have full scope.
5. This education, whether it is confined to children or adults, male or female, will find its way to the homes of the pupils.
6. Since millions of students receiving this education will consider themselves as of the whole of India, they must learn an interprovincial language. This common interprovincial speech can only be Hindustani written in Nagari or Urdu script. Therefore, pupils have to master both the scripts. *(Harijan, 2 November 1947 (CW 89, pp. 404–05))*

Intellectual Development

During my recent wanderings in Travancore and Madras I found that most of the students and 'intellectuals' who came into touch with me were an instance of intellectual dissipation rather than intellectual development. The fault lies in the modern system of education which encourages this vicious tendency, misdirects the mind, and thereby hinders its development instead of helping it. My experiments in Segaon have only confirmed this impression. But they are as yet too incomplete to be cited as evidence. The views on education that I am now going to set forth have been held by me right from the time of the founding of the Phoenix Settlement in South Africa in the year 1904.

I hold that true education of the intellect can only come through a proper exercise and training of the bodily organs, *e.g.* hands, feet, eyes, ears, nose, etc. In other words, an intelligent use of the bodily organs in a child provides the best and quickest way of developing his intellect. But unless the development of the mind and body goes hand in hand with a corresponding awakening of the soul, the former alone would prove to be a poor lopsided affair. By spiritual training I mean education of the heart. A proper and all-round development of the mind, therefore, can take place only when it proceeds pari passu with the education of the physical and spiritual faculties of the child. They constitute an indivisible whole. According to this theory, therefore, it would be a gross fallacy to suppose that they can be developed piecemeal or independently of one another.

The baneful effects of absence of proper coordination and harmony among the various faculties of body, mind and soul respectively are obvious. They are all around us; only we have lost perception of them owing to our present perverse associations. Take the case of our village folk. From their childhood upward they toil and labour in their fields, from morning till night, like their cattle in the midst of whom they live.

Their existence is a weary endless round of mechanical drudgery unrelieved by a spark of intelligence or higher graces of life. Deprived of all scope for developing their mind and soul, they have sunk to the level of the beast. Life to them is a sorry bungle which they muddle through anyhow. On the other hand, what goes by the name of education in our schools and colleges in the cities today is in reality only intellectual dissipation.

Intellectual training is there looked upon as something altogether unrelated to manual or physical work. But since the body must have some sort of physical exercise to keep it in health, they vainly try to attain that end by means of an artificial and otherwise barren system of physical culture which would be ridiculous beyond words if the result was not so tragic. The young man who emerges from this system can in no way compete in physical endurance with an ordinary labourer. The slightest physical exertion gives him a headache; a mild exposure to the sun is enough to cause him giddiness. And what is more, all this is looked upon as quite 'natural'. As for the faculties of the heart, they are simply allowed to run to seed or to grow anyhow in a wild undisciplined manner. The result is moral and spiritual anarchy. And it is regarded as something laudable!

As against this, take the case of a child in whom the education of the heart is attended to from the very beginning. Supposing he is set to some useful occupation like spinning, carpentry, agriculture, etc., for his education and in that connection is given a thorough comprehensive knowledge relating to the theory of the various operations that he is to perform and the use and construction of the tools that he would be wielding. He would not only develop a fine healthy body but also a sound, vigorous intellect that is not merely academic but is firmly rooted in and is tested from day to day by experience. His intellectual education would include a knowledge of mathematics and various other sciences that are useful for an intelligent and efficient exercise of his avocation.

If to this is added literature by way of recreation, it would give him a perfect well-balanced, all-round education in which the intellect, the body and the spirit have all full play and develop together into a natural, harmonious whole. Man is neither mere intellect, nor the gross animal body, nor the heart of soul alone. A proper and harmonious combination of all the three is required for the making of the whole man and constitutes the true economics of education. To say that this kind of education can only be given after we have attained our independence would, I am afraid, be like putting the cart before the horse.

The advent of independence would be incredibly hastened if we could educate millions of our people through an intelligent exercise of their respective vocations like this and teach them that they live for the common good of all. *(Harijan, 8 May 1937 (CW 65, pp. 73–75))*

Just Social Order

What kinds of vocations are the fittest for being taught to children in urban schools? There is no hard and fast rule about it. But my reply is clear. I want to resuscitate the villages of India. Today our villages have become a mere appendage to the cities.

They exist, as it were, to be exploited by the latter and depend on the latter's sufferance. This is unnatural. It is only when the cities realize the duty of making an adequate return to the villages for the strength and sustenance which they derive from them, instead of selfishly exploiting them, that a healthy and moral relationship between the two will spring up.

And if the city children are to play their part in this great and noble work of social reconstruction, the vocations through which they are to achieve their education ought to be directly related to the requirements of the villages. So far as I can see, the various processes of cotton manufacture from ginning and cleaning of cotton to the spinning of yarn, answer this test as nothing else does.

Even today the cotton is grown in the villages and is ginned and spun and converted into cloth in the cities. But the chain of processes which cotton undergoes in the mills from the beginning to the end constitutes a huge tragedy of waste in men, materials and mechanical power.

My plan to impart primary education through the medium of village handicrafts like spinning and carding, etc. is thus conceived as the spearhead of a silent social revolution fraught with the most far-reaching consequences. It will provide a healthy and moral basis of relationship between the city and the village and thus go a long way towards eradicating some of the worst evils of the present social insecurity and poisoned relationship between the classes. It will check the progressive decay of our villages and lay the foundation of a juster social order in which there is no unnatural division between the 'haves' and the 'have-nots' and everybody is assured of a living wage and the right to freedom.

And all this would be accomplished without the horror of a bloody class war or a colossal capital expenditure such as would be involved in the mechanisation of a vast continent like India. Nor would it entail a helpless dependence on foreign imported machinery or technical skill. Lastly, by obviating the necessity for highly specialized talent, it would place the destiny of the masses, as it were, in their own hands. But who will bell the cat? Will the city-folk listen to me at all? Or, will mine remain a mere cry in the wilderness? Replies to these and similar questions will depend more on lovers of education like my correspondent living in cities than on me. *(Harijan, 9 October 1937)*

Manual Labour

"One of the complaints that has been made by one of you," Gandhiji remarked, "is that too much emphasis is laid here on manual work. I am a firm believer in the educative value of manual work. Our present educational system is meant for strengthening and perpetuating the imperialist power in India. Those of you who have been brought up under it have naturally developed a taste for it and so find labour irksome. No one in Government schools or colleges bothers to teach the students, how to clean the roads or latrines. Here, cleanliness and sanitation form the very alpha and omega of your training. Scavenging is a fine art you should take pains to learn. Persistent questioning and healthy inquisitiveness are the first requisite for acquiring learning of any kind. Inquisitiveness should be tempered by humility and respectful regard for the teacher. It must not degenerate into impudence. The latter is the enemy of the receptivity of mind. There can be no knowledge without humility and the will to learn.

"Useful manual labour, intelligently performed, is the means par excellence for developing the intellect. One may develop a sharp intellect otherwise too. But then it will not be a balanced growth but an unbalanced, distorted abortion. It might easily make of one a rogue and a rascal. A balanced intellect presupposes a harmonious growth of body, mind and soul. That is why we give to manual labour the central place in our curriculum of training here. An intellect that is developed through the medium of socially useful labour will be an instrument for service and will not easily be led astray or fall into devious paths. The latter can well be a scourge. If you grasp that essential point, the money spent by your respective governments in sending you here for training will have been well-spent." *(Harijan, 8 September 1946 (CW 85, pp. 199–200))*

Basic School Product

Shri Aryanayakam brought nine boys of the 7th class to meet Gandhiji. These had all practically completed their seven years' course in the Sevagram Basic School. They were village lads from Sevagram and the neighbouring villages. Compared to those whom one sees working in the fields and who have never been to school, they were a heartening result of a first endeavour. They were clean, well-groomed, disciplined well-mannered. Gandhiji cracked a few jokes with them which they entered into with merry laughter. One of them had the temerity to ask Gandhiji what type of boys of fourteen he expected to be turned out after a seven years' course at a Basic School? Gandhiji seized the opportunity of telling them that if the school had done its duty by them, boys of fourteen should be truthful, pure and healthy. They should be village-minded. Their brains and hands should have been equally developed. There would be no guile in them. Their intelligence would be keen but they would not be worried about earning money. They would be able to turn their hands to any honest task that came their way. They would not want to go into the cities. Having learnt the lessons of cooperation and service in the school, they would infect their surroundings with the same spirit. They would never be beggars or parasites. *(Harijan, 8 September 1946 (CW 85, pp. 199–200))*

Craft and Curriculum

This is a libel on me. It is true I have said that all instruction must be linked with some basic craft. When you are imparting knowledge to a child of 7 or 10 through the medium of an industry, you should, to begin with, exclude all those subjects which cannot be linked with the craft. By doing so from day to day you will discover ways and means of linking with the craft many things which you had excluded in the beginning. You will save your own energy and the pupils' if you follow this process of exclusion to begin with. We have today no books to go by, no precedents to guide us. Therefore we have to go slow. The main thing is that the teacher should retain his freshness of mind. If you come across something that you cannot correlate with the craft, do not fret over it and get disheartened. Leave it and go ahead with the subjects that you can correlate. May be another teacher will hit upon the right way and show how it can be correlated. And when you have pooled the experience of many, you will have books to guide you, so that the work of those who follow you will become easier.

How long, you will ask, are we to go on with this process of exclusion? My reply is, for the whole lifetime. At the end you will find that you have included many things that you had excluded at first, that practically all that was worth including has been included, and whatever you have been obliged to exclude till the end was something very superficial that deserved exclusion. This has been my experience of life. I would not have been able to do many things that I have done if I had not excluded an equal number.

Shrimati Asha Devi asked Gandhiji to explain to them how the mind could be trained through the hands.

The old idea was to add a handicraft to the ordinary curriculum of education followed in the schools. That is to say, the craft was to be taken in hand wholly separately from education. To me that seems a fatal mistake. The teacher must learn the craft and correlate his knowledge to the craft, so that he will impart all that knowledge to his pupils through the medium of the particular craft that he chooses.

Take the instance of spinning. Unless I know arithmetic I cannot report how many yards of yarn I have produced on the takli, or how many standard rounds it will make, or what is the count of the yarn that I have spun. I must learn figures to be able to do so, and I also must learn addition and subtraction and multiplication and division. In dealing with complicated sums I shall have to use symbols and so I get my algebra. Even here, I would insist on the use of Hindustani letters instead of Roman.

Take geometry next. What can be a better demonstration of a circle than the disc of the takli? I can teach all about circles in this way, without even mentioning the name of Euclid.

Again, you may ask how I can teach my child geography and history through spinning. Some time ago I came across a book called Cotton—The Story of Mankind. It thrilled me. It read like a romance. It began with the history of ancient times, how and when cotton was first grown, the stages of its development, the cotton trade between the different Countries, and so on. As I mention the different countries to the child, I shall naturally tell him something about the history and geography of these countries. Under whose reign the different commercial treaties were signed during the different periods? Why has cotton to be imported by some countries and cloth by others? Why can every country not grow the cotton it requires? That will lead me into economics and elements of agriculture. I shall teach him to know the different varieties of cotton, in what kind of soil they grow, how to grow them, from where to get them, and so on. Thus takli-spinning leads me into the whole history of the East India Company, what brought them here, how they destroyed our spinning industry, how the economic motive that brought them to India led them later to entertain political aspirations, how it became a causative factor in the downfall of the Moguls and the Marathas, in the establishment of the English Raj, and then again in the awakening of the masses in our times. There is thus no end to the educative possibilities of this new scheme. And how much quicker the child will learn all that, without putting an unnecessary tax on his mind and memory.

Let me further elaborate the idea. Just as a biologist, in order to become a good biologist, must learn many other sciences besides biology, the basic education, if it is treated as a science, takes us into interminable channels of learning. To extend the example of the takli a pupil teacher, who rivets his attention not merely on the mechanical process of spinning, which of course he must master, but on the spirit of the thing, will concentrate on the takli and its various aspects. He will ask himself why the takli is made out of a brass disc and has a steel spindle.

The original takli had its disc made anyhow. The still more primitive takli consisted of a wooden spindle with a disc of slate or clay. The takli has been developed scientifically, and there is a reason for making the disc out of brass and the spindle out of steel. He must find out that reason. Then, the teacher must ask himself why the disc has that particular diameter, no more and no less. When he has solved these questions satisfactorily and has gone into the mathematics of the thing, your pupil becomes a good engineer. The takli becomes his Kamadhenu—the 'Cow of plenty'. There is no limit to the possibilities of knowledge that can be imparted through this medium. It will be limited only by the energy and conviction with which you work. You have been here for three weeks. You will have spent them usefully if it has enabled you to take to this scheme seriously, so that you will say to yourself, 'I shall either do or die.'

I am elaborating the instance of spinning because I know it. If I were a carpenter, I would teach my child all these things through carpentry, or through cardboard work if I were a worker in cardboard.

In training pupil teachers, would it not be better if they are first taught a craft separately and then given a sound exposition of the method of teaching through the medium of that craft? As it is, they are advised to imagine themselves to be of the age of 7 and relearn everything through a craft. In this way it will take them years before they can master the new technique and become competent teachers.

No, it would not take them years. Let us imagine that the teacher when he comes to me has a working knowledge of mathematics and history and other subjects. I teach him to make cardboard boxes or to spin. While he is at it I show him how he could have derived his knowledge of mathematics, history and geography through the particular craft. He thus learns how to link his knowledge to the craft. It should not take him long to do so. Take another instance. Suppose I go with my boy of 7 to a basic school. We both learn spinning and I get all my previous knowledge linked with spinning. To the boy it is all new. For the 70-year-old father it is all repetition but he will have his old knowledge in a new setting. He should not take more than a few weeks for the process. Thus, unless the teacher develops the receptivity and eagerness of the child of 7, he will end up by becoming a mere mechanical spinner, which would not fit him for the new method.

A boy who has passed his matriculation can go to college if he wishes to. Will a child who has gone through the basic education syllabus too be able to do so?

Between the boy who has passed his matriculation and the boy who has gone through basic education, the latter will give a better account of himself because his faculties have been developed. He would not feel helpless when he goes to college as matriculates often do. Seven has been put down as the minimum age for admission of children to a basic education school. Is it to be a chronological or mental age?

Seven should be the average minimum age, but there will be some children of a higher and some of a lower age as well. There is physical as well as mental age to be considered. One child at the age of 7 may have attained sufficient physical development to handle a craft. Another one may not be able to do so even at 7. One cannot therefore lay down any hard and fast rules. All the factors have to be taken into consideration.

Many questions show that many of you are filled with doubts. This is the wrong way of going about the work. You should have robust faith. If you have the conviction that I have, that Wardha education is the thing required to give training for life to millions of our children, your work will flourish. If you have not that faith, there is something wrong with those in charge of your training. They should be able to imbue you with this faith, whatever else they may or may not give you.

The basic education scheme is supposed to be for the villages. Is there no way out for the city-dwellers? Are they to go along the old rut?

This is a pertinent question and a good one, but I have answered it already in the columns of Harijan. Sufficient for the day is the good thereof. As it is, we have a big enough morsel to bite. If we can solve the educational problem of seven lakhs of villages, it will be enough for the present. No doubt educationists are thinking of the cities too. But if we take up the question of the cities along with that of the villages, we will fritter away our energies.

Supposing in a village there were three schools with a different craft in each, the scope for learning may be wider in one than in the other. To which school out of these should the child go?

Such overlapping should not occur. For the majority of our villages are too small to have more than one school. But a big village may have more. Here the craft taught in both should be the same. But I should lay down no hard and fast rule. Experience in such matters would be the best guide. The capacity of various crafts to become popular, their ability to draw out the faculties of the student, should be studied. The idea is that whatever craft you choose, it should draw out the faculties of the child fully and equally. It should be a village craft and it should be useful.

Why should a child waste 7 years on learning a craft when his real profession is going to be something else, *e.g.*, why should a banker's son, who is expected to take to banking later on, learn spinning for 7 years?

The question betrays gross ignorance of the new scheme of education. The boy under the scheme of basic education does not go to school merely to learn a craft. He goes there to receive his primary education, to train his mind through the craft. I claim that the boy who has gone through the new course of primary education for seven years, will make a better banker than the one who has gone through the seven years of ordinary schooling.

The latter when he goes to a banking school will be ill at ease because all his faculties will not have been trained. Prejudices die hard. I will have done a good day's work if I have made you realize this one central fact that the new education scheme is not a little of literary education and a little of craft. It is full education up to the primary stage through the medium of a craft.

Would it not be better to teach more than one craft in every school? The children might begin to feel bored of doing the same thing from month to month and year to year.

If I find a teacher who becomes dull to his students after a month's spinning, I should dismiss him. There will be newness in every lesson such as there can be new music on the same instrument. By changing over from one craft to another a child tends to become like a monkey jumping from branch to branch with abode nowhere. But I have shown already in the course of our discussion that teaching spinning in a scientific spirit involves learning many things besides spinning. The child will be taught to make his own takli and his own winder soon. Therefore, to go back to what I began with, if the teacher takes up the craft in a scientific spirit, he will speak to his pupils through many channels, all of which will contribute to the development of all his faculties.

Shantiniketan

From Rajkot I proceeded to Shantiniketan. The teachers and students overwhelmed me with affection. The reception was a beautiful combination of simplicity, art and love.

The Phoenix family had been assigned separate quarters at Shantiniketan. Maganlal Gandhi was at their head, and he had made it his business to see that all the rules of the Phoenix Ashram should be scrupulously observed. I saw that, by dint of his love, knowledge and perseverance, he had made his fragrance felt in the whole of Shantiniketan.

Andrews was there, and also Pearson. Amongst the Bengali teachers with whom we came in fairly close contact were Jagadanandbabu, Nepalbabu, Santoshbabu, Kshitimohanbabu, Nagenbabu, Sharadbabu and Kalibabu.

As is my wont, I quickly mixed with the teachers and students, and engaged them in a discussion on self-help. I put it to the teachers that, if they and the boys dispensed with the services of paid cooks and cooked their food themselves, it would enable the teachers to control the kitchen from the point of view the boys' physical and moral health, and it would afford to the students an object-lesson in self-help. One or two of them were inclined to shake their heads. Some of them strongly approved of the proposal. The boys welcomed it, if only because of their instinctive taste for novelty. So we launched the experiment.

When I invited the Poet to express his opinion, he said that he did not mind it provided the teachers were favourable. To the boys he said, ' The experiment contains the key to Swaraj.'

Pearson began to wear away his body in making the experiment a success. He threw himself into it with zest. A batch was formed to cut vegetables, another to clean the grain, and so on. Nagenbabu and others undertook to see the sanitary cleaning of the kitchen and its surroundings. It was a delight to me to see them working spade in hand.

But it was too much to expect the hundred and twenty-five boys with their teachers to take to this work of physical labour like ducks to water. There used to be daily discussion. Some began early to show fatigue. But Pearson was not the man to be tired.

One would always find him with his smiling face doing something or other in or about the kitchen. He had taken upon himself the cleaning of the bigger utensils. A party of students played on their sitar before this cleaning party in order to beguile the tedium of the operation. All alike took the thing up with zest and Shantiniketan became a busy hive.

Changes like these when once begun always develop. Not only was the Phoenix party's kitchen self-conducted, but the food cooked in it was of the simplest. Condiments were eschewed. Rice, dal, vegetables and even wheat flour were all cooked at one and the same time in a steam cooker.

And Shantiniketan boys started a similar kitchen with a view to introducing reform in the Bengali kitchen. One or two teachers and some students ran this kitchen.

The experiment was, however, dropped after some time. I am of opinion that the famous institution lost nothing by having conducted the experiment for a brief interval, and some of the experiences gained could not but be of help to the teachers. *(An Autobiography Vol. II, p. 565)*

Satyagraha Ashram, Kochrab

The Ashram experiment in education was a trial for us as nothing else was.

We saw at once that the women and children in the Ashram should be taught to read and write, and a little later on that there should be similar facilities for even the illiterate men that came to the Ashram. Those who had already joined the Ashram could not undertake to teach.

If capable teachers were to be attracted to the Ashram, the rule of Brahmacharya had to be relaxed in their case. The Ashram was therefore divided into two sections, the 'teachers' quarters and the Ashram proper.

Human beings cannot overcome their weakness all at once. As soon as the two sections came into being, a feeling of superiority and inferiority poisoned the Ashram atmosphere in spite of all our efforts to scotch it. The Ashramites developed spiritual pride, which the teachers could not tolerate. This pride was an obstacle in the attainment of the Ashram ideal and therefore an aspect of untruth as well.

If Brahmacharya was to be observed in its perfection, the division was inevitable. But the brahmacharis had no reason to think too highly of themselves. It may be that the brahmacharis who sinned mentally in spite of themselves were retrogressing while those who did not claim to be brahmacharis but liked Brahmacharya were making progress. This was clear to the intellect but it was not easy for all of us to put it into practice.

Then again there were differences of opinion as regards the method of education which gave rise to difficulties in administration. There were bitter discussions, but at last all calmed down and learned the lesson of forbearance. This was in my view a triumph of truth, the goal of all Ashram endeavour. Those who held divergent views harboured no evil intentions in their minds, and were indeed grieved at the divergence. They wished to practise truth as they saw it. Their partiality for their own standpoint came in the way of their giving due weight to the arguments of their opponents. Hence the quarrels which put our charity to a severe test.

I have my own perhaps peculiar views on education which have not been accepted by my colleagues in full, and here they are:

1. Young boys and girls should have coeducation till they are eight years of age.
2. Their education should mainly consist in manual training under the supervision of an educationist.
3. The special aptitudes of each child should be recognized in determining the kind of work he or she should do.
4. The reasons for every process should be explained when the process is being carried.
5. General knowledge should be imparted to each child as he begins to understand things. Learning to read or write should come later.
6. The child should first be taught to draw simple geometrical figures, and when he has learnt to draw these with ease, he should be taught to write the alphabet. If this is done he will write a good hand from the very first.
7. Reading should come before writing. The letters should be treated as pictures to be recognized and later on to be copied.
8. A child taught on these lines will have acquired considerable knowledge according to his capacity by the time he is eight.
9. Nothing should be taught to a child by force.
10. He should be interested in everything taught to him.
11. Education should appear to the child like play. Play is an essential part of education.
12. All education should be imparted through the mother tongue.
13. The child should be taught Hindi-Urdu as the national language, before he learns letters.
14. Religious education is indispensable and the child should get it by watching the teacher's conduct and by hearing him talk about it.

15. Nine to sixteen constitutes the second stage in the child's education.
16. It is desirable that boys and girls should have coeducation during the second stage also as far as possible.
17. Hindu children should now be taught Sanskrit, and Muslim children Arabic.
18. Manual training should be continued during the second stage. Literary education should be allotted more time according to necessity.
19. The boys during this stage should be taught their parents' vocation in such a way that they will by their own choice obtain their livelihood by practising the hereditary craft. This does not apply to the girls.
20. During this stage the child should acquire a general knowledge of world history and geography, botany, astronomy, arithmetic, geometry and algebra.
21. Each child should now be taught to sew and to cook.
22. Sixteen to twenty-five is the third stage, during which every young person should have an education according to his or her wishes and circumstances.
23. During the second stage (9–16) education should be self-supporting; that is, the child, all the time that he is learning, is working upon some industry, the proceeds of which will meet the expenditure of the school.
24. Production starts from the very beginning, but during the first stage it does not still catch up with the expenditure.
25. Teachers should be paid not very high salaries but only a living wage. They should be inspired by a spirit of service. It is a despicable thing to take any Tom, Dick or Harry as a teacher in the primary stage. All teachers should be men of character.
26. Big and expensive buildings are not necessary for educational institutions.
27. English should be taught only as one of several languages. As Hindi is the national language, English

is to be used in dealing with other nations and international commerce.

As for women's education I am not sure whether it should be different from men's and when it should begin. But I am strongly of opinion that women should have the same facilities as men and even special facilities where necessary.

There should be night schools for illiterate adults. But I do not think that they must be taught the three R's; they must be helped to acquire general knowledge through lectures, etc., and if they wish, we should arrange to teach them the three R's also.

Experiments in the Ashram have convinced us of one thing, *viz.*, that industry in general and spinning in particular should have pride of place in education, which must be largely self-supporting as well as related to and tending to the betterment of rural life.

In these experiments we have achieved the largest measure of success with the women, who have imbibed the spirit of freedom and self-confidence as no other class of women have done to my knowledge. This success is due to the Ashram atmosphere.

Women in the Ashram are not subject to any restraint which is not imposed on the men as well. They are placed on a footing of absolute equality with the men in all activities. Not a single Ashram task is assigned to the women to the exclusion of the men. Cooking is attended to by both. Women are of course exempted from work which is beyond their strength; otherwise men and women work together everywhere. There is no such thing as purdah or laj in the Ashram. No matter from where she has come, a woman, as soon as she enters the Ashram, breathes the air of freedom and casts out all fear from her mind. And I believe that the Ashram observance of Brahmacharya has made a big contribution to this state of things. Adult girls live in the Ashram as virgins. We are aware that this experiment is fraught with risk but we feel that no awakening among women is possible without incurring it.

Women cannot make any progress so long as there are child marriages. All girls are supposed to be in duty bound to marry and that too before menstruation commences, and widow remarriage is not permitted. Women, therefore, when they join the Ashram, are told that these social customs are wrong and irreligious. But they are not shocked as they find the Ashram practising what it preaches.

Not much of what is usually called education will be observed in the Ashram. Still we find that the old as well as the young, women as well as men are eager to acquire knowledge and complain that they have no time for it. This is a good sign.

Real education begins after a child has left school. One who has appreciated the value of studies is a student all his life. His knowledge must increase from day to day while he is discharging his duty in a conscientious manner. And this is well understood in the Ashram.

The superstition that no education is possible without a teacher is an obstacle in the path of educational progress. A man's real teacher is himself. And nowadays there numerous aids available for self-education. A diligent person can easily acquire knowledge about many things by himself and obtain the assistance of a teacher when it is needed. Experience is the biggest of all schools. Quite a number of crafts cannot be learnt at school but only in the workshop. Knowledge of these acquired at school is often only parrotlike. Other subjects can be learnt with the help of books. Therefore what adults need is not so much a school as a thirst for knowledge, diligence and self-confidence.

The education of children is primarily a duty to be discharged by the parents. Therefore the creation of a vital educational atmosphere is more important than the foundation of numerous schools. When once this atmosphere has been established on a firm footing the schools will come in due course. *(History of the Satyagraha Ashram, 11 July 1932 (CW 50, pp. 232–36))*

3

ESTABLISH SPIRITUAL RELATIONSHIP

Introduction

The suggestion which the writer has made to teachers is certainly sound. But where there are forty to fifty children in a class and the relationship of the teacher with the pupils is confined to class-work lessons, how will it be possible for the teacher, even if he so wishes, to establish any spiritual relationship with so many children? Again, when six or seven teachers teach six or seven different subjects, which of them can assume the responsibility to give them moral instruction? Lastly, how many teachers can we come across who will guide the children along the path of morality or win their confidence? This indeed raises the whole question of education, but it cannot be discussed here.

Make Schools Ideal

To teachers, Gandhiji said that they must not make any use of books for imparting education, as books spoiled eyes and blunted the intellect. He himself had experienced that. He understood that in Russia they were conducting one thousand schools for peasants and that they were giving education without the aid of books by making all possible use of the senses. He asked them to clean their own houses and streets themselves and not to depend on others for doing the same. Concluding, Mahatmaji asked them to make their schools ideal in every way, so that the boys and girls of the mill-owners might envy them and the mill-owners might be tempted to send their children to the labour schools. On truth depended the foundation of education, and they must always resort to truth.

Develop Motherly Love

I have made no use in this article of the word 'teacher'. A teacher is a mother. She who cannot take the place of a mother can never become a teacher. A child should not feel that it is receiving education. The child whose mother's eyes follow it everywhere is receiving education all the twenty-four hours. A child who sits six hours in a school may not be receiving any education at all. In this topsy-turvy life, perhaps we may not find women-teachers. It may well be that child education is practicable at present only through men-teachers. Then the men-teachers will have to acquire the noble status of a mother and ultimately the mothers will have to get ready for this job. But if my concept is right, any mother if she has love in her heart can become fit with a little assistance. And while preparing herself she will prepare the children as well.

Develop Proper Relationship

If a student develops contempt for national education whom would you hold responsible? Generally, the teachers and the students both are responsible, but more often the teachers. Should a teacher marry a girl who is his student? Likewise, should a boy marry a girl studying in his class?

I at any rate would consider both very improper. A girl who is my student should be as safe (with me) as my daughter, and a girl in my class as safe as a sister. That pure brother-and-sister relationship is the only proper relationship between boys and girls studying together. This is all I should like to say in reply to this question, but it is an important enough question for a fuller discussion. I have no doubt in my mind about the correctness of my reply to the first question. With regard to the second, however, I see some difficulties in these modern times when thousands of boys and girls attend the same school. In any case, in every institution that I have managed I have insisted on the foregoing rule being followed and the results have always been happy.

Teaching for the Love of It

However, the teachers have asked for advice and I can but place it before them so that each may then respond to the best of his ability. The unfortunate position is that educated Indians take to teaching not for the love of it, but because they have nothing better and nothing else for giving them a livelihood. Many of them even enter the teaching profession with a view to preparing for what they regard as a better thing. The wonder is that in spite of this self-imposed initial handicap so many teachers are not worse than they are. By well-ordered agitation, no doubt they may better their pecuniary prospects, but I see no chance even under a swaraj government of the scale of salary being raised much higher than it is today. I believe in the ancient idea of teachers teaching for the love of it and receiving the barest maintenance.

The Roman Catholics have retained that idea and they are responsible for some of the best educational institutions in the world. The *rishis* of old did even better. They made their pupils members of their families, but in those days that class of teaching which they imparted was not intended for the masses. They simply brought up a race of real teachers of mankind in India. The masses got their training in their homes and in their hereditary occupations. It was a good enough ideal for those times. Circumstances have now changed. There is a general insistent demand for literary training. The masses claim the same attention as the classes. How far it is possible and beneficial to mankind generally cannot be discussed here. *(Young India, 6 August 1925 (CW 28, pp. 34–35))*

Be Affectionate

Students must not be given corporal punishment. But there should be such a rapport between the teacher and the taught that if the teacher punishes himself in some way the children, because of their affection for him, should feel sorry, their hearts should melt and they should change for the better. I am not talking in the air. This has been my personal experience. Mothers also can reform their children in the same way. In South Africa I had looked after Hindu, Muslim and Parsi boys and girls. During those days I remember having only once beaten a pupil.

But it was my experience that my nonviolent method was more successful. If the children have affection for their teacher they are bound to feel sorry when they find the teachers suffering on their account. That would soften them. But if in spite of that there is a difficult pupil, we should non-co-operate with him. But that is another method. The former is the better method. *(Letter to a Teacher, 15 April 1947—Biharni Komi Agman, pp. 202–03 (CW 87, pp. 283–84) (Translated from Gujarati))*

Strive Continuously to Improve

I am a teacher in a school. I have not as much character, love of truth and *Brahmacharya* as a teacher should have, though I am striving to achieve them. Under the circumstances, would you advise me to resign?

I believe that in the absence of sufficient strength of character it is well to resign your post as teacher. But, discrimination is necessary. Resignation is not necessary if the defects are likely to be overcome. No one is perfect. Character in teachers is not much in evidence today. One may well feel satisfied if one remains watchful in one's work and continuously strives to improve oneself. But there can be no single rule which would cover all such cases. Everyone must think for himself and do what is best.

Inculcate Sense of Honour

We have to fall back upon the voluntary assistance of teachers, but when I look for teachers, they are very few, especially, teachers of the type wanted, in order to draw the best from the children through understanding, through studying their individuality and then putting the child on its own resources, as it were, on its own honour. And believe me from my experience of hundreds, I was going to say thousands, of children—I know that they have perhaps a finer sense of honour than you and I have. The greatest lessons in life—if we would but stoop and humble ourselves, we would learn not from grown-up learned men, but from the so-called ignorant children. Jesus never uttered a loftier or a grander truth than when he said that wisdom cometh out of the mouths of babes. I believe it, I have noticed it in my own experience that, if we would approach babes in humility and in innocence, we would learn wisdom from them.

Follow Golden Rule

If the teachers have secret relations with their girl students and later when such relations can no longer be kept concealed legalize them with marriage, this cannot be said to have sanctified those relations. It is my firm belief that just as a brother and a sister cannot have a husband–wife relation even so a teacher and his girl-student too cannot have a husband–wife relation. This is a golden rule and its non-observance can only result in the destruction of the institution. This rule serves as guarantee for the protection of the girls from their teachers. The teacher's is a high office and it enables him to exercise great influence upon the boys and girls in his charge. They regard what he says as gospel truth. They are not likely to suspect him of any illicit designs and he must, therefore, observe these essential rules. Where the welfare of the soul as distinct from the body is of greater importance such relations (as marriage between the teacher and his girl-student) are inadmissible and must be so regarded. *(Harijanbandhu, 29 November 1936 (CW 64, p. 91))*

Be a Student of Students

A teacher who establishes rapport with the taught, becomes one with them, learns more from them than he teaches them. He who learns nothing from his disciples is, in my opinion, worthless. Whenever I talk with someone I learn from him. I take from him more than I give him. In this way, a true teacher regards himself as a student of his students. If you will teach your pupils with this attitude, you will benefit much from them.

Students' Dharma

Many students feel that it is not necessary to pay much attention to the body. This is a great mistake. Regular exercise for the body is absolutely necessary. What can be expected of a student who has not the wealth of the body? Just as milk cannot be kept for long in a paper or cardboard container, so also education is not likely to remain for long in the paper-like (delicate) bodies of our students.

The body being the abode of the spirit, is holy. We must protect it. Walking regularly and zestfully for an hour and a half in the morning and for the same period in the evening keeps it healthy, and the mind fresh. The time thus devoted is not wasted. Exercise and rest invigorate both the body and the intellect, enabling one to learn things more quickly. I think expensive games like hockey and cricket are not advisable for a poor country like India. We have a number of inexpensive and interesting games of our own.

The daily life of the student also should be above reproach. He alone can experience true delight whose mind is pure. Indeed, to ask him to seek delight in worldly pleasures is to deprive him of the real delight which is his. He who has resolved to rise higher does indeed rise higher. Ramachandra wished for the moon and he got it because his mind was pure.

Looked at in one way the world appears illusory; in another, quite solid and real. Students should regard it as the latter because they have to use their energy for the good of humanity and do brave deeds in this world. He who declares the world to be illusory without getting at the real truth, claims to have renounced it and then acts as he likes in disregard of moral laws, is not a *jnani;* he is merely a self-deluded fool even though he may be a Sannyasi.

Now I come to *Dharma*. Where there is no *dharma,* there can be no knowledge, wealth, health, etc. Where there is no *dharma*, life is totally barren. There can be no progress. In our present scheme of education there is no place for the teaching of *dharma*. It is like a *barat* (wedding party) without the bridegroom. Students cannot experience pure joy without a knowledge of *dharma.* In order to have this experience it is necessary to study the *shastras,* to reflect over their teaching and to act thoughtfully. Smoking a cigarette or indulging in useless gossip as soon as one gets up in the morning does good to nobody. Nazir has said that even the birds sing the name of the Lord morning and evening, but we waste our time in sleeping.

It is the duty of every student to somehow acquire the knowledge of *dharma*. Whether this is taught in schools or not, it is my prayer that students will try to introduce the substance of *dharma* in their life. What exactly is *dharma?* What should be the concrete method of imparting knowledge concerning it? We cannot discuss these questions here for lack of time. However, from experience, let me tell you to read the Gita and Ramayana with understanding, for you have a real jewel in the latter. Make use of its teachings. But remember that you have to study these two books in order to learn the secret of *dharma*.

The seers who wrote these works had no intention of writing history. They desired only to impart teaching of *dharma* and *neeti*, *i.e.*, the rules of good conduct. Crores of people read these books and try to pattern their lives upon them. They study them with a pure heart and carry on their work sustained by the strength and joy which they derive from these two books. For Muslim students, the Koran is the best book in this respect. They should study it in a spirit of religious humility, and try to understand its message. I also recommend that both Hindus and Muslims study each other's religious scriptures with humility and try to understand them, for this in turn will create a better understandings of one community by the other.

From this most absorbing question I shall pass on to topics of more worldly interest. I have often been asked whether students should take part in politics or not. I will let you know my opinion about it without going into the reasons. Politics may be divided into two parts; first, the study of its science; second, political action. It is certainly necessary for students to study the former, but dangerous to embark on the latter. Students may attend political meetings or the sessions of the Congress in order to learn the science of politics, since they are useful in giving them object-lessons in the subject of their study. Students should have complete freedom to attend such meetings and conferences, and efforts should be made to remove the bans which have recently been placed on attending these. Students should, however, refrain from speaking or giving their opinion on the questions discussed at such assemblies.

But they may serve as volunteers if this does not interfere with their studies. No student can afford to miss the opportunity of serving Malaviyaji if it comes his way. Students should avoid party politics. They should observe neutrality and not align themselves with this or that group, and should also cultivate respect for all leaders without any distinction. It is not for students to discuss their merits and demerits, and assess their comparative worth and importance. Students are concerned only with seeking and acquiring virtues wherever they can find them; they have to learn to worship the virtues.

It is the duty of students to respect elders, to consider what they say, and follow their advice whenever possible. He who has not learnt to respect others cannot hope for respect from them. An attitude of insolence ill becomes students. Here, I should like to point out a phenomenon which is taking place in the India of today. Older folk are disregarding the standard of conduct expected of them. They seem to be oblivious of the fact that in their behaviour and conduct they set a model for the younger generation. What are the students to do in the circumstances? I cherish the hope that they will cultivate and acquire the spirit of *dharma*.

When confronted with a clash between their loyalty to *dharma* and obedience or respect to elders, students should remember Prahlad. Placed in certain circumstances which were distasteful to him, this boy respectfully disobeyed the commands of his father. In the same way, we can also respectfully refuse to obey the elders if the circumstances warrant it. But any disrespect shown to them beyond this will be wrong. Disrespect to elders leads to the ruin of the community. The right of the elders to respect does not depend merely on age, but also on knowledge, experience and wisdom. Where the latter are absent the right depends simply on age. But nobody worships mere age.

Another question is: How can students serve the country? First, by carefully acquiring knowledge and, while doing so, keeping up their health, for both these will be needed in the service of our country. If a student does this he certainly serves his country. We can easily do much useful work without any great effort on our part if we would just try to live a good and useful life. I shall now tell you of one job which all of you can do quite easily. You must have seen my letter in the newspapers about the difficulties of the third class passengers. I suppose most of you travel third.

You must have then noticed that these passengers spit in the compartment; they also expectorate betel leaves and tobacco which they go on chewing; throw the skins of oranges and bannanas and other leavings on the floor of the carriage; do not use the latrine carefully and foul it, and smoke *bidis* and *cigarettes* without any regard for the inconvenience of fellow-passengers. Students should explain to such passengers, when they travel, that doing these things is not only bad manners, but also unhygienic. You can explain the ill effect of creating this filth. Most passengers respect students and listen to what they have to say with attention.

They should not then miss these opportunities of explaining the rules of hygiene to our masses. The eatables sold at stations by vendors are often dirty. It is the duty of students, when they see any such uncleanliness, to draw the attention of the traffic manager to it. And take care that you write to him in Hindi. It may be that the traffic manager will ignore your request. But when he receives many such letters, he will be forced to pay attention to it. This can be done without much effort, but it will yield important results.

I have spoken about the habits of chewing betel leaves and tobacco. In my opinion, both are harmful and unclean. Large numbers of Indian men and women have become the slaves of these evil habits. We have to get rid of this slavery. A stranger visiting India would surely feel that we go on eating some thing or the other throughout the day. That the betel leaf, possibly, helps to digest food may be conceded, but food taken in accordance with the laws of health gets digested without any help from it. Moreover, there is hardly any agreeable taste in the betel leaf. And tobacco-chewing must be given up as well. Students should always practise self-control.

The problem of smoking is a difficult one to tackle. Our rulers have set a bad example in this matter. They are used to smoking irrespective of time and place. This has led us to consider it a fashion, and to turn our mouths into chimneys for ejecting the smoke. There are many books by competent writers to show that smoking of tobacco does great harm. We call this age Kaliyuga. Christians believe that Christ will reincarnate Himself when such evils as selfishness, immorality, addiction to drugs and drink, etc. becomes rife in the life of human beings. I do not say how far we can concur in this belief. Yet, I do feel that the world is suffering a great deal from such evils as drink, tobacco, opium, *ganja, bhang (hemp)*, etc. We cannot exactly assess the harm which these are doing to us, because almost all of us are caught in their widespread snares. It is my fervent prayer that you, the students, keep away from them.

The purpose in my making and your hearing these speeches is that you should learn something from them and put it into practice. How many of you following Smt. Besant's advice, have adopted the Indian mode of dress, simplified your food and given up unclean habits? Or acting on Prof. Jadunath Sirkar's advice, how many of your have spent your summar vacation in teaching poor students without any charge? Many such questions may be asked. I do not want a reply now. But you may reply these questions to your conscience.

The value of your learning is judged not by what you know intellectually but how you act. You may receive some monetary reward for filling your mind with book learning, but the value of the good work you do will be many times greater than that. The value of the learning you have acquired is really equal only to that of the work you do. The rest is an useless burden. My request to you is that you practise what you learn and what appears to you to be right. That is the only way to progress. *(Presidential Speech, 17th Session of the Bihar Students' Conference, Bhagalpur, 1917, (CW 14, pp. 137–39))*

Students' Life

The life of students is similar to that of *Sannyasis*. You must therefore live in complete purity and celibacy as befits a *Brahmachari*. The two civilizations—the old and the modern—are at present vying with each other or for supremacy over the student community. The old civilization lays stress on self-control. It proclaims that the more a man reduces his wants consciously and with full understanding of what it means, the greater is his progress towards higher living. Whereas modern civilization holds that progress lies in increasing one's wants.

There is the same difference between control and abandonment as between *dharma* and *adharma* or the right and wrong way of living. The method advocating control accords an inferior status to the trappings of material living, and rightly gives more importance to the quality of our thoughts and emotions or spiritual and mental well-being. There is the danger, at present, of our people being carried away by the lure of the newer civilization and throwing away the older one. Students can do a lot in warding off this danger. For instance, the students of this University will be judged not by what they know but by what they do.

Therefore, teaching and practice of *dharma* should be given prior consideration in the scheme of education at this University. Students should offer their wholehearted cooperation in achieving this object. I, personally, feel that we shall not derive any real benefit from political reforms unless we first arrive at a clear conception of *dharma*, or the right way of individual and social life for us in India. For it is not these reforms which will create and establish *dharma* but *dharma* which will show up the defects of the former and help us in removing them. *(Speech delivered before the students of the Hindu University, Navajivan, 29 January 1920 (True Education, pp. 208–09))*

Students' Faith

I have come in contact with thousands of students during the last ten years. They have confided their innermost secrets to me and have given me the right to enter their hearts. I know therefore all your difficulties and every one of your weaknesses. I do not know whether I can render any effective help to you. I can but be your friend and guide, attempt to share your sorrows and give you the benefit of my experience, though you must know that the only help of the helpless is God. There is no greater punishment or misery for man than that his faith in God should be blasted. And I confess to a deep sense of sorrow that faith is gradually disappearing in the student world. When I suggest to a Hindu boy to have recourse to *Ramanama,* he stares at me and wonders who Rama may be; when I ask a Musalman boy to read the Koran and fear God, he confesses his inability to read the Koran and Allah is a mere lip-profession. How can I convince such boys that the first step to a true education is a pure heart? If the education you get turns you away from God, I do not know how it is going to help you and how you are going to help the world. *(Young India, 4 August 1927 (True Education, p. 225))*

No Intoxicants Please

In response to the request of a Calicut professor I shall now proceed to say something about cigarette smoking and coffee and tea drinking. These are not necessities of life. There are some who manage to take ten cups of coffee a day. Is it necessary for their healthy development and for keeping them awake for the performance of their duties? If it is necessary to take coffee or tea to keep them awake, let them not drink coffee or tea but go to sleep. We must not become slaves to these things. But the majority of the people who drink coffee or tea are slaves to them. Cigars and cigarettes, whether foreign or indigenous, must be avoided. Cigarette smoking is like an opiate and the cigars that you smoke have a touch of opium about them. They get to your nerves and you cannot leave them afterwards. How can a single student foul his mouth by converting it into a chimney? If you give up these habits of smoking cigars and cigarettes and drinking coffee and tea you will find out for yourselves how much you are able to save. A drunkard in Tolstoy's story is hesitating to execute his design of murder so long as he has not smoked his cigar. But he puffs it, and then gets up smiling and saying, 'What a coward am I,' takes the dagger and does the deed. Tolstoy spoke from experience. He has written nothing without having had personal experience of it. And he is much more against cigars and cigarettes than against drink. But do not make the mistake that between drink and tobacco drink is a lesser evil. No, if cigarette is Beelzebub, then drink is Satan. *(Young India, 15 September 1927 (True Education, pp. 234–35))*

Gain Courage to Ask Questions

Three students write: "We desire to serve the country. Kindly tell us through the columns of the *Navajivan* how we can do so without having to leave our native place or our studies." These students have given their names, age and addresses. They say, "Please do not disclose our names and addresses. Nor should you write to us direct to our addresses. The conditions in which we are living are such that we cannot even send for letters." I consider it difficult to give any advice to such students. What can I say to those who have not the freedom even to receive replies to their letters?

However, I can say this much: Self-purification is the best service one can render to the country. Have these students attempted such self-purification? Are their hearts pure? Have they been able to keep away from the evils prevailing amongst students? Do they observe the vow of truth? Seeing that they are afraid even to get a reply to their letters, there appears to be something gravely wrong in this situation.

The students should cast out fear. They must learn to put their views to their elders firmly and courageously. Do they use Khadi? Do they spin? If they spin and use Khadi they may be said to be taking part in the service of the country. Do they attend on an ailing neighbour in their leisure hours? Do they, if things are messy about them, or streets dirty around their home, snatch time from their work and clean them with their own hands? Many more such questions could be asked and if they can answer them satisfactorily, they may be said to be serving the country even now. *(Navajivan, 8 July 1928 (True Education, pp. 238–39))*

Utilize Vacations for Social Service

As to the use of the vacation by students, if they will approach the work with zeal, they can undoubtedly do many things. I enumerate a few of them:

1. Conduct night and day schools with just a short course, well-conceived, to last for the period of the vacation.
2. Visit Harijan quarters and clean them, taking the assistance of Harijans if they would give it.
3. Taking Harijan children for excursions, showing them sights near their villages and teaching them how to study nature, and generally interesting them in their surroundings, giving them by the way a working knowledge of geography and history.

4. Reading to them simple stories from the Ramayana and the Mahabharata.
5. Teaching them simple *bhajans*.
6. Cleaning the Harijan boys of all the dirt that they would find about their persons and giving both the grown-ups and the children simple lessons in hygiene.
7. Taking a detailed census in selected areas of the condition of Harijans.
8. Taking medical aid to the ailing Harijans.

This is but a sample of what is possible to do among the Harijans. It is a list hurriedly made, but a thoughtful student will, I have no doubt, add many other items. I have so far confined my attention to the service of Harijans, but there is a service no less necessary to be rendered to caste-Hindus. The students can often in the gentlest manner possible carry the message of anti-untouchability to them in spite of themselves. There is so much ignorance which can be easily dispelled by a judicious distribution of clean authentic literature. The students can make a survey of those who are for abolishing untouchability and who are against and, whilst they are making this survey, they may take note of wells, schools, ponds and temples open to Harijans and of those closed to them.

If they will do all these things in a methodical and persistent manner, they will find the results to be startling. Every student should keep a log-book in which he should enter the details of his work, and at the end of the vacation a comprehensive but brief report of the results of their labours could be prepared and sent by them to the Servants of Untouchables Society of their province. Whether other students accept all or any of the suggestions made here, I shall expect my correspondent to give me a report of what he and his associates have done. *(Harijan, 1 April 1933 (True Education, pp. 246–47))*

Be Humble

The first thing the students had to learn was humility, without which they could not make a good use of their attainments. They might achieve academic distinction and secure high office, but if they would devote their learning to the service of man, humility was absolutely necessary. There was a vast number of bright students among them but they scarcely existed for the poor long-suffering Indian villager. The ideal all the world over was that man's intellectual and spiritual gifts were designed for service and that he should use his hands and feet in order to obtain his livelihood.

In ancient times, jurisconsults charged their clients nothing for their advice, and even now barristers could not sue a client for fees, which were called their honorarium. If the students wished to serve the country, it would not do for them to become imitation *sahebs,* like the jackdaw in the fable, dressed up in peacock's feathers. They should realize that they had to serve a nation whose average income per head was 40 rupees, according to Lord Curzon. They could render this service only if they were satisfied with a coarse piece of Khadi and gave up all ambition of living in expensive European style. They should, as men of culture, also be ashamed of exacting large sums of money as dowry from their prospective father-in-law. *(Speech delivered to students at Karachi—Harijan, 27 July 1934)*

Pay for Your Own Education

When it is difficult for millions even to make the two ends meet, when millions are dying of starvation, it is monstrous to think of giving our relatives a costly education. Expansion of the mind will come from hard experience, not necessarily in the college or the school-room. When some of us deny ourselves and ours the so-called Higher Education, we shall find the true means of giving and receiving a really Higher Education. Is there not, may there not be, a way of each boy paying for his own education? There may be no such way. Whether there is or there is not such a way is irrelevant.

But there is no doubt that when we deny ourselves the way of expensive education, seeing that aspiration after Higher Education is a laudable end, we shall find out a way of fulfilling it more in accord with our surroundings. The golden rule to apply in all such cases is resolutely to refuse to have what millions cannot. This ability to refuse will not descend upon us all of a sudden. The first thing is to cultivate the mental attitude that will not have possessions or facilities denied to millions, and the next immediate thing is to rearrange our lives as fast as possible in accordance with that mentality. *(Young India, 24 June 1926 (Towards New Education, pp. 100–01))*

Self-study

It is a gross superstition to suppose that knowledge can be obtained only by going to schools and colleges. The world produced brilliant students before schools and colleges came into being. There is nothing so ennobling or lasting as self-study. Schools and colleges make most of us mere receptacles for holding the superfluities of knowledge. Wheat is left out and mere husk is taken in. I do not wish to decry schools and colleges as such. They have their use. But we are making altogether too much of them. They are but one of the many means of gaining knowledge. *(Young India, 25 May 1931 (Towards New Education, pp. 101–02))*

Dignity of Labour

A student asks:

> *What should a matriculate or an undergraduate who is unfortunately father of two or three children do in order to produce a living wage, and what should he do when he is forced to marry against his will and before even the age of twenty-five?*

The simplest answer that occurs to me is that a student who does not know how to support his wife or children or who marries against his will has studied to no purpose. But that is past history for him. The perplexed student deserves a helpful answer. He does not say what his requirement is. If he does not pitch it high because he is a matriculate and will put himself in level with an ordinary labourer, he should have no difficulty in earning a livelihood. His intelligence should help his hands and feet and enable him to do better than the labourer who has had no opportunity of developing his intelligence.

This is not to say that the labourer who has never learnt English is devoid of intelligence. Unfortunately labour has never been helped to develop the mind, and those who pass through schools do have their minds opened even though under a handicap not to be found in any part of the world. Even this mental equipment is counterbalanced by false notions of dignity inculcated during school and college days. And so students think that they can earn their living only at the desk. The inquirer has therefore to realize the dignity of labour and seek the maintenance of himself and his family in that field.

And there is no reason why his wife should not add to the family income by utilizing her spare hours. Similarly if the children are at all able to do any work, they too should be inspanned for productive work. The utterly false idea that intelligence can be developed only through book reading should give place to the truth that the quickest development of the mind can be achieved by the artisan's work being learnt in a scientific manner. True development of the mind commences immediately the apprentice is taught at every step why a particular manipulation of the hand or a tool is required. The problem of the unemployment of students can be solved without difficulty, if they will rank themselves among the common labourers. *(Harijan, 9 January 1937)*

Foreign Studies

I have never been an advocate of our students going abroad. My experience tells me that such, on return, find themselves to be square pegs in round holes. That experience is the richest and contributes most to growth which springs from the soil. *(Harijan, 8 September 1946)*

Help Educational Reconstruction

If there is one compact students' organization, it can become a mighty instrument of service. Their objective can only be one: Never for the purpose of finding a lucrative career but fitting themselves for the service of the motherland. If they were to do so, their knowledge would attain a great height. Agitation is only for those who have completed their studies. While studying, the only occupation of students must be to increase their knowledge. The education, as it is prescribed today, is detrimental, conceived in terms of masses of India. It is possible to show that the present education has been of some use to the country. I regard it as negligible. Let no one be deceived by it. The acid test of its usefulness is this: Does it make, as it should, an effective contribution to the production of food and clothing? What part does the student world play in allaying the present senseless slaughter? All education in a country has got to be demonstrably in promotion of the progress of the country in which it is given.

Who will deny that education in India has not served that purpose? Hence, one purpose of the organization should be to discover the defects of the present education and seek to remove them, so far as possible in their own persons. By their correct conduct they will be able to convert to their view the heads of education. If they do so, they will never be entangled in party politics. In the revised scheme, constructive and creative programme will naturally have its due place. Indirectly, their action will keep the politics of the country free of the spirit of exploitation. *(Harijan, 7 September 1947)*

No Party Politics

Gandhiji referred to a letter by some students saying that the proposed students' strike on the 9th was being organized by the Communist students, not Congress students. Gandhiji said that while he congratulated the Congress students who had dissociated themselves from the proposed strike, he would reiterate what he had already said about such strikes, *viz.* that for students there should be no party politics. There should be no Socialist, Communist, Congress and other groups among students. They should be all students first and last determined to gather as much knowledge as possible and that for the sake of the service of the people, not for the sake of getting jobs. *(Harijan, 18 January 1948)*

Improve Teaching Methods

My ideas about education are very exacting. If we want to pour our souls into the pupils, we should constantly exercise our mind on how to teach them. We should not get angry with them. Passing on to them in the best possible language from day to day whatever we wish to give them, will take up much of our time. Moreover, we must for the present think of teaching methods as well. Everything will have to be taught in a new way.

The teachers will have to come together at least once a week to exchange ideas and make such changes as may be called for. The intelligent students should be consulted and their suggestions invited about methods of teaching.

The students' health is the collective responsibility of the teachers; the main responsibility, however, will rest on the teacher in charge of hygiene.

The teachers should read up the subjects in the curriculum which they do not know. Especially Hindi. I can see from my work here how very essential Hindi is. I find that I shall have to ask for volunteers from other places. Difficulties will arise about those of them who do not know Hindi. I see it proved every day that education is altogether incomplete without Hindi. *(Letter to Narahari Parikh, 17 May 1917 (CW 13, p. 399))*

Build National Education

So long as education in the country is not imparted by persons of integrity and conditions are not created in which the highest knowledge will be available to the poorest of Indians, so long as a perfect confluence of education and *dharma* has not taken place and education has not been brought into relation with conditions in India, so long as the intolerable burden imposed on the minds of the young by imparting education through a foreign medium has not been lifted, so long will there be no upsurge of national life; there is no denying this.

Purely national education should be imparted in the regional language. The teachers must be of a high calibre. The school should be situated in surroundings where the student has fresh air and water, where he enjoys peace, where the building and the adjoining land are object lessons in healthful living; and the educational pattern must be one which will instruct (the pupil) in the main professions and religions of India. *(Navajivan, 21 September 1919 (CW 16, p. 156))*

Cultivate the Spirit of Sacrifice

As the second condition for the success of national education we need teachers of good character. I congratulate the head master and other teachers of this high school who have made a sacrifice for the sake of their *dharma* and their country, and I ask of them that in their work henceforth they show the same spirit which has prompted their self-sacrifice. Once you are absorbed in your work, money will come in of itself. Your executive committee will be able to raise funds with ease. Even if they have nothing else than clean ground to sit on, the boys of national schools will be able to hold their own against other boys and, if their teachers are men of character, will acquire a greater spirit of manliness than the pupils of the more pretentious Government schools. *(Navajivan, 10 November 1920 (CW 18, p. 419))*

Be Makers of New India

You are embarking upon a new career. You are turning over a new leaf. You are shouldering a great responsibility. You are counting yourselves among the makers of India of the future. And if you realize this responsibility, I have no doubt, you will dispel all these fears which have been expressed in other parts of India. Those who know Bengal well are in the position also to testify that Bengalis on many an occasion have not been found wanting; and for my part I shall certainly decline to believe that those students who have responded and who will join this institution will be found wanting. I shall hope also that the professors and the teachers will prove true to their trust.

What I said in all humility to the professors and teachers at the time of performing the opening ceremony of the Gujarat National College, I am tempted to repeat here; that the success and failure of this institution will very largely depend upon the honest exertion that the professors and teachers may put forth. At this critical moment in the history of our dear country every one of us, who intends to mould the young mind of the country, has a serious responsibility, and if the professors and the teachers are found asleep, if they are overtaken with doubt, if they are overtaken with fear as to the future, God help the students who come under their charge. And I shall pray to the Almighty that he may bless the professors and teachers with wisdom, with courage, with faith and hope. *(Young India, 9 February 1921 (CW 19, p. 320))*

Develop Positive Outlook

This conference was held and is now over. It should be regarded as an important conference from the point of view of teachers and the general public too. But these are not days when either of them would attach importance to it. The value of teachers is recognized neither by the public nor by the teachers themselves. They are valued according to their salary. A teacher is paid less than an ordinary clerk. Hence, in practice, a teacher is valued less than a clerk. Is it for this reason that we refer to a teacher as *Mehtaji?*

If it is so, how can we expect that the teachers' worth will ever rise? Can anyone raise the salaries of seven lakh teachers in seven lakh villages? If the salaries of so many teachers do not rise and if it is considered necessary to raise them, we should rest content with employing high-paid teachers in a few villages and allowing the rest to go without education. We have been doing this since the establishment of British rule. We realize that this practice is wrong. Hence let us find out a scheme which can cover all villages.

Under this scheme, teachers will not be valued according to their salaries and work. Teachers themselves will place more value on their teaching work than on their salaries. In short, teaching should be regarded as the teachers' *dharma*. The teacher who takes his food without performing the sacrifice should be looked upon as a thief.

If that is done, there will be no shortage of teachers and yet they will be valued a million times higher than millionaires. By changing his outlook, every teacher can enjoy that position even today.

It is up to the teachers to make a success or failure of this conference. The key to success lies in the teachers' pledge.

If the teachers would forget the question of their livelihood and think only of their duty, the schools will come to have new vitality and become truly national, and then alone will they be of use to the national movement. It is the first lesson for the young and the old, for men and women, that they should remain loyal to a pledge once they have accepted it. *(Navajivan, 10 August 1924 (CW 24, p. 542) (Translated from Gujarati))*

Make Teaching Absorbing

Experience shows that students' interest in a subject is sustained not by the subject-matter but by the teacher. My own experience has been that one teacher used to bore me to sleep while teaching chemistry, whereas another teacher kept me wide awake and interested in the same subject.

The former, who talked and talked without clarifying the topic, was not liked while, as the other teacher elucidated the theme, one wished that his period should never end. The topic was the same as well as the students. Instruction by one, however, was absorbing and by the other insipid. The spinning-wheel holds a jar or nectar. In the Dakshinamurti Bhavan, it appears, there are teachers who can reveal this. *(Navajivan, 17 August 1924 (CW 25, p. 5) (Translated from Gujarati))*

Working for Livelihood

As this teacher has answered his own questions, my task is simplified. What I had said could not possibly mean that ten teachers or a single teacher should rest after teaching only one child. My contention is that not merely ten but even twenty teachers should not forsake a solitary student or leave a school but should try to increase their number.

When plenty of students are available, the teacher should draw an allowance sufficient for his living, but his true test lies in his ability to accept nothing and starve to death if the need arises, and let his dependents also starve to death. Such a teacher sacrifices his relations, his parents, his children, his all for his work. What do those who practise other professions do when they incur heavy losses?

If a person does not find a job despite all possible efforts, he lets his dependents starve along with himself; this should be the case with the teachers in national schools. This would make our dependents work for their livelihood.

When teachers are idle for want of students, they should, of course, take up some other activity, but even while doing so, they must try to revive the school.

Build Heart to Heart Contact

I ask their teachers to cultivate their hearts and establish with the students a heart-contact. I have felt that the teachers' work lies more outside than inside the lecture-room. In this workaday life where teachers and professors work for the wages they get they have no time to give to the students outside the classroom, and that is the greatest stumbling-block in the development of the life and character of students today. But unless the teachers are prepared to give all their time outside the classroom to their students, not much can be done. Let them fashion their hearts rather than their brains. Let them help them to erase every word out of their dictionary which means disappointment and despair. *(Young India, 4 April 1929 (CW 40, p. 120)).*

Freedom for All-round Growth

The students' minds must not be caged nor for that matter those of the teachers. The teachers can only point to their pupils what they or the State considers is the best way. Having done so they have no right to curb their pupils' thoughts and feelings. This does not mean that they are not to be subject to any discipline. No school can be run without it. But discipline has nothing to do with artificial restraint upon the students' all-round growth. This is impossible where they are subjected to espionage. The fact is that hitherto they have been in an atmosphere subtly anti-national where it has not been openly that. This should now be dispelled. The students should know that the cultivation of nationalism is not a crime but a virtue. *(Harijan, 18 September 1937 (CW 66, p. 141)).*

Use all Resources to be Constructive and Creative

What we need is educationists with originality, fired with true zeal, who will think out from day to day what they are going to teach their pupils. The teacher cannot get this knowledge through musty volumes. He has to use his own faculties of observation and thinking and impart his knowledge to the children through his lips, with the help of a craft. This means a revolution in the method of teaching, a revolution in the teachers' outlook. Up till now you have been guided by inspector's reports. You wanted to do what the inspector might like, so that you might get more money yet for your institutions or higher salaries for yourselves. But the new teacher will not care for all that. He will say, 'I have done my duty to my pupil if I have made him a better man and in doing so I have used all my resources. That is enough for me. *(Harijan, 18 February 1939 (CW 68, pp. 374–75)).*

Develop Sense of Belonging

How to teach in the best possible manner?

You can teach best by identifying yourself with your students. In order to do so, the teacher must prepare himself fully in the subject he has to teach.

4

RELATED QUESTIONS AND DIFFERENT STAGES OF THE EDUCATION

Introduction

Educating children should be normally the easiest of things; but somehow it has become, or been made, the most difficult. Experience shows that the children are always learning one thing or another whether we notice it or not and whether what they learn is good or bad. This may seem strange to some readers. But if we would consider carefully—who is a child; what is education and who is best qualified to teach the children?—the observation made above would not seem strange and might even appear quite correct.

By children we mean young boys and girls not more than 10 years of age. Then, education does not mean simply the knowledge of letters—the capacity to read and write. The knowledge of letters is only one of the means to education. Really speaking, education consists in learning to use in the right way all one's sense-organs, including the mind. In other words, the child should know how to use his organs of action such as hands and feet, etc. as also his organs of knowledge such as the nose, the eyes, etc. A boy who knows that he should not use his hands in stealing things or killing flies or beating the younger brothers, sisters and playmates has already made a good beginning on his way to education.

The same may be said of the boy who understands the need for keeping his teeth, tongue, ears, eyes, nails,-etc. clean and does so. A boy who does not indulge in pranks while eating or drinking, who has learnt to eat and drink in the right manner whether alone or in company, who knows the distinction between wholesome and unwholesome food and chooses the former, who does not overeat, who does not ask for every new thing that he sees and who, when he asks for it and does not get it, remains quiet, may be said to have progressed quite a great deal in his education.

Whose pronunciation is good, who can tell the history and geography of his region—even though he may not know these terms,—who knows what is meant by the motherland, he has traversed a fairly good distance on the road to education. Similarly with him who has learnt to distinguish between truth and untruth, between good and evil and who invariably chooses what is true and good, there is no need to further elaborate the point. The readers can fill in the picture themselves. Only I should make one thing clear: there is no need of the knowledge of reading and writing in order to learn the things I have spoken of above. To make the boys to learn the alphabet is to put an undue burden on their young minds and to misuse their eyes and hands. A rightly educated boy gets to learn reading and writing almost without any effort and, what is more, gladly at the proper time. At the present time, however, this thing becomes a heavy burden upon him.

Much of the valuable time which could be put to better use goes to waste and in the end, instead of producing shapely letters or acquiring a finely articulated pronunciation, all that they succeed in doing is to produce misshapen letters and cultivate a bad handwriting. As for reading, they read much which had better been left unread and read it indifferently without any sense of pronunciation. To call it education is to abuse that august term. The boy must first get elementary knowledge before learning to read and write. If this is done our poor country would be saved from much unnecessary expense incurred on various readers and children's books and many other evils. If children's readers are at all thought necessary they should be written for use by the teachers and not for boys of my conception. But for our drifting with the current vogue this thing should be as clear to us as daylight.

The boys can get the education I have spoken of only at home and that too only through the mother. In a way, all boys do get some sort of an education from the mother. But seeing that the home has disintegrated, so to say, and seeing that most parents are not equal to the task, the boys should be placed in surroundings where they will get the same atmosphere as they do at home. Since of all persons the mother is the most competent to undertake the duty of educating the children, this particular task should be entrusted only to women. As a rule men are far behind women in respect of love and patience. If this is true the question of the education of children cannot be solved unless efforts are made simultaneously to solve the women's education. And I have no hesitation in saying that as long as we do not have real mother-teachers who can successfully impart true education to our children they will remain uneducated even though they may be going to schools.

Let me now set forth in brief an outline of the children's education. Suppose that a mother-teacher is entrusted with five children. These children have no training in manners. They do not speak distinctly. They do not know how to walk or even to sit in the right manner. The nose, eyes, ears, and nails are dirty. Asked to sit, they stretch out their legs and when they speak, they mumble. They have no knowledge of directions. The clothes are untidy and the pockets are filled with dirty titbits which they are always taking out and putting in their mouths. The border of the cap on the head has turned black and sticky and it gives out a foul odour. Now the teacher in question can train them only if she has the heart of a mother.

The first lesson she has to give them would be that of cleanliness. She will drench them with her love and amuse them in various ways as only mothers know how to do and as did Kaushalya her Rama and thus she will bind them to herself with the ties of love and so will be in a position to secure from them willing compliance to all that she wants. She will know no rest until these boys have learnt to keep neat and tidy, until their teeth, ears, hands and feet are clean, until they learn to take care of their clothes and have improved their pronunciation. Having accomplished this she will first teach them *Ramanama*—the name of Lord God. He has many names and it does not matter by which name He is called.

The next in order after *dharma* is *artha, i.e.*, the temporal knowledge. So she will now set out to teach them arithmetic. She will get them to learn the multiplication tables and teach them addition and subtraction—as much of it as can be managed orally. The boys must know the place where they live. So she will tell them of the rivers and rivulets, hills, buildings of interest, etc. and in the process give them the knowledge of directions. She will improve her own knowledge for the sake of the children. History and geography are not to be treated as separate subjects in this method. Both will be taught by way of stories. She will not however be content with this. A Hindu mother will recite Sanskrit verses to her children from their infancy, so that they get used to the pronunciation of Sanskrit words. She will get them to learn Sanskrit verses in praise of God. A patriotic mother will of course teach them Hindi too.

She will therefore converse with them in Hindi. She will read out to them selected passages from Hindi books and thus make them bilingual. She will not teach them the alphabet yet, but she will certainly give them the brush. She will get them to trace the geometrical figures—to draw straight lines and circles. A boy who cannot draw a flower or a water-jug or a triangle cannot be said to be educated. Again, she will not but introduce them to good music.

She will not tolerate the children being unable to sing in unison the national song or hymns, etc. She will teach them to sing to the accompaniment of time. If possible, she will give them *ektara,* or *jhanjh.* To make them physically fit she will get them to do physical exercises, to practise running and jumping. Then, the boys should also be taught the love of service and various skills. She will therefore teach them spinning with all the ancillary processes beginning from the picking of cotton pods. And these boys will willingly spin for at least half an hour every day.

Most of the textbooks which we have today are useless for this purpose. The mother-teacher therefore will find out or produce new ones and her love for the children will help her in this task. Every village has its own history and geography; naturally it will have its own history-book and geography-book.

The arithmetical exercises too will be new. The mother-teacher will prepare the lessons she wants to teach the children herself everyday. She will produce new sums and will always have many new things to say to the boys—which she will note down in her notebook when she prepares the lesson. Her lesson in the class will thus be not a mechanical performance but something lively and creative. The syllabus will vary according to the progress of the children. It should therefore be drawn up after every three months. The children constituting the class come from different homes—each has his own different background of nurture. We cannot therefore have the same syllabus for all of them.

At times it may be necessary even to induce them to unlearn what they have learnt. For example, if a six or seven year old child has learnt to trace letters in a slovenly way or has picked up the habit of reading without trying to understand what he reads, the mother-teacher will see that he unlearns all that. She must cast out the illusion that the child can acquire knowledge only through reading.

It is easy enough to understand that even one who never had any training in reading can be wise. I have not used the word teacher in this article; I have throughout used the word 'mother-teacher' in its place. Because the teacher must really be a mother to the children she teaches. One who cannot take the place of a mother cannot be a teacher. The child should never feel that he is being taught. Let her simply keep her eye upon him and guide him. A child who spends six hours in the school will possibly be wasting his time while the former will be learning something or the other all the time in terms of real education.

It is likely that we may not get good women-teachers in the existing conditions. That being so we may make use of men for the purpose. In that case these men-teachers will have to fill the place of the mother. But eventually it is the mother who will have to undertake the task. But if I am right any mother who has love for children can easily prepare herself for it. And she can also prepare the children at the same time that she is preparing herself. *(Navajivan, 2 June 1929 (CW 41, pp.5–9))*

Montessori Education

I have no difficulty in agreeing with the scientific views of Madame Montessori. However, if they are propagated in their Western garb in Indian villages they are more likely to prove useless and might even prove harmful, because in that garb they will be too expensive for Indian villages and ill-adapted to the village atmosphere.

It is possible the cities may not feel the expense so much and women influenced by Western ways may be receptive to the ideas presented in Western garb; but even so it will be of no use because India lives not in cities but in its seven lakh villages. Besides, scientific education with Western trappings might prove poisonous to the city dwellers because here education begins the moment the child is conceived and ends no one knows when. These days the cities are created by the foreigners to serve their ends and so they do not represent the villages. They do not protect the interests of the villagers but are becoming their exploiters. *(Letter to Saraladevi Sarabhai, 12 April 1945 (CW 71, pp. 370–71))*

Nursery Education

I saw the work done by teachers trained under Madame Montessori, and carefully observed the working of the Nursery School. Of course the things were foreign and the poor teacher had not digested what she had been taught. What to speak of the children? They could not even observe normal discipline. I am not criticising anyone.

I have given the gist of my experience just for your information. Imbibe whatever you find useful and discard the rest. The conclusion I have drawn from this experience is that we shall be able to propagate scientific knowledge of child education only when our teachers are competent. They should have the will to become one with children. I am afraid I am not saying anything new in this. These things are certainly not beyond your range of experience but since I have come to know you and also love you I hope you will not find fault with me for saying the things you already know. *(Letter to Tarabehn Modak, 16 October 1945 (CW 81, p. 364))*

Primary Education

After a great deal of reflection and experimentation I have come to the conclusion that primary education should be given for at least a year without books and even after that the use of books should be restricted to the minimum.

If books are introduced from the very start and the children made to master the alphabet, the development of their various abilities are arrested and their intelligence stunted, although this is the time when it should grow rapidly. A child begins to learn immediately after its birth, but mostly through the eyes and ears or through the senses. And, as soon as he has learnt to speak, *i.e.*, to imitate the sound of words, he begins rapidly to acquire the use of language. Naturally he picks up the same language as that of his parents. If the parents have taste and refinement, he also develops those qualities. He pronounces the words correctly and copies their good manners and conduct. This is his real education. And if our culture and traditions had not fallen apart, children would still be receiving the best kind of education in their homes.

But looking at the deplorable conditions in which we are living at present this cannot be and there is no alternative save to send our boys to schools. But if the child has to go to a school, we must see that it looks like a home to him and the teachers like parents, and the education provided should be such as would be provided in a cultured home. This means that all preliminary teaching should be oral. A child educated in this way would learn in a year ten times more than the boy taught in the other way, *i.e.*, through the alphabet.

Oral teaching would enable the children to know the usual rudiments of history and geography much in the same way as they get to know stories, quite easily, in the very first year. They would commit to memory a fairly good number of poems; and they would learn the counting of numbers almost automatically without any effort. And because they would not be subjected to the burden of recognizing and learning the alphabet, the growth of their minds would not be stopped and their eyes would not be misused.

They would use their hands not in tracing different letters—a practice which spoils their handwriting for good—but in drawing the figures of geometry and simple pictures. This would be good preliminary training for the hand, as it would develop both coordination and skill.

And if we want to provide education to the crores of children of Gujarat and of India, this is the only way in which primary education should be imparted to them.

Under the conditions existing in the country it is impossible to give books to children. I admit that if it is necessary to give books to children in the primary stage also, then attempts must be made to do so whatever the expenditure, but if they are considered unnecessary and even harmful then this plea for stopping the use of books in the initial years. The idea should be given a fair trial. A thing which is unnecessary from the moral point of view is always found to be impermissible also from the practical point of view. In an ideal civilization morality and what is called practical policy are not two contradictory things.

Lastly, it is clear that the present group of teachers cannot be expected to give effect to the scheme of education presented here. They may manage to teach the boys the alphabet and also simple arithmetic. But they themselves are ignorant of the type of knowledge which, according to the scheme I have sketched, should be made available to the boys in the very first year of the school. Since they themselves do not speak correctly, how can they then help the boys to form the habit of correct speech?

We will consider this difficulty in the next article. *(Navajivan, 13 May 1928 (Problem of Education, pp. 147–49))*

Secondary Education

A system of education has to be so conceived as to be an instrument of protection of the freedom of a nation.

Hence, we must make our own experiments in education. It may well be that in the course of these experiments we get to know the experiences which Europe has had; but we should never give credence to the idea that everything European is good, or that what is good for Europe under the conditions obtaining there will also be good for us here in India. Granting that this line of reasoning is correct, one of the conclusions it leads us to is that we should evaluate what goes on in the Government schools critically. Knowing as we do that Government education is detrimental to Swaraj and destructive of our civilization, we are likely to get at the right solution for us if we do just the opposite of what is done in the Government schools. Let us now study examples:

> *There, the medium of education is English. We should know from this that it should never be permitted in national education.*
>
> *There, they have big expensive buildings. We should know that this is undesirable. The buildings of our school should be simple— as befit the poor.*
>
> *There, they concentrate on mere literacy and the study of language and literature and neglect the indigenous crafts. Evidently this is not right.*

There they leave out the teaching of religion—I mean the basic principles common to all religions and not any particular creed. We know that this has the effect of nullifying the good that the rest of the education might ordinarily do to students. History, as taught in Government schools, if not wholly untrue, is presented essentially from the point of view of the British Government. German, French and American historians would treat and interpret the same material in a different way. Even recent events, as for example, the Punjab Massacre is presented by Government writers in one way and by nationalist writers in quite another light. Economics, as taught in Government schools, approves of the policies of the Government, while we look at them from a totally different point of view.

While in Government primary schools, the teachers are appointed without any consideration of their character, in our schools they must be men of the highest character. The former have only the minimum qualifications for the work they are expected to do and are paid the lowest salaries. The latter, on the other hand, should be highly qualified men and though they will also be paid low salaries, the reason would be their selflessness and not their helplessness.

This, I think, should give you some idea of the type of education which should be given in our city schools.

Our students should be men who will work for the stabilisation and revitalisation of our rural civilization. They would study the needs of the villagers, try to remove the defects they may discover in them and train their children to become good farmers and good villagers and not to be lured by the dazzle of the cities. Thus, as long as we do not set about to make a radical change in the form and content of the education now going on in the cities, we cannot fulfil one of the important aims of the Vidyapith. Take only one example: We are running three institutions in Ahmedabad—the Mahavidyalaya or the college, the New Gujarati Pathashala, and the Vinaya Mandir or the secondary school. We have the right to run these institutions only if we mean to try to make good villagers of the students studying in them. They should have a thorough knowledge of village life and develop a love for it. Eventually, those of them who pass out of the Mahavidyalaya or the Vinaya Mandir, after having completed their studies, should spread out in the villages and immerse themselves in the service of the people there.

As to how this could be done, we shall consider it in the next article. *(Navajivan, 20 May 1928 (CW 36, pp. 327–29))*

Rural Education

The problem of primary education, *i.e.*, of rural education, can be tackled and solved only if the teachers appreciate and accept the point of view presented by me, and we agree to overhaul and change the curriculum in the Vinaya Mandir and Mahavidyalaya.

Today, we hesitate to make any changes out of fear for what people might say, or because the number of students might go down and the institution may suffer in the estimate of the people. But if we could make bold and introduce the necessary changes there would pass out from these schools a group of workers pledged to the service of the villages who would atone in some degree at least for the sin of the cities.

The students passing out of these schools should be first class carders, spinners and weavers. They should be experts in the cultivation of cotton. They should know enough carpentry for the purposes of the village, that is, they should be able to manufacture good Charkhas and should be able if not to manufacture at least to repair the carts and ploughs, etc. Then they should know enough sewing for village-life. Their handwriting must be good, and they should be able to write good simple prose, as also to work out simple arithmetical problems.

They should be intimately conversant with old religious books like the *Ramayana* and *Mahabharata,* and have the ability to interpret them in terms of today. They should know village games and the rules of health. They should be able to recognize simple diseases and cure them through simple home remedies. They should know the art of cleaning the village-wells, tanks and dust-heaps. I could recount many other things. But the point is that our schools should provide such training to the boys as would enable them to serve the villages in every way. And the expenditure incurred on this training should be regarded as having been incurred on education. Such training alone would qualify us to enter and reform village-life.

I am aware that some of you fear that as soon as we introduce these changes and clarify our aim as above our schools would be empty. But even if this fear proves true I would be ready to face it for the sake of truth. But as long as it is the object of the Vidyapith to work out a suitable system of education for the villages, it will be a betrayal of our trust not to do so.

But it is my experience and conviction that if we stick to our aims with undivided loyalty, the people will come to recognize their importance in the end and cooperate with us in their propagation. If we try to discover the reasons of this real or supposed failure we will find that the workers were either not loyal to their aims or only half-hearted in carrying them out. A man who wavers in his faith, as says the *Gita,* is doomed to failure.

It is my firm belief that if there were in our schools teachers who have faith and the spirit of sacrifice, they would be filled with students. People do recognize and appreciate fundamental values. It may seem that this takes an unusually long time to come about in many cases. But this is merely an illusion. The fact is that the right path is also always the shortest.

How does it profit anyone if a school which encourages the desire for sensual pleasures and panders to the weaknesses of people attracts large numbers? Mere numbers do not prove the usefulness of an institution or its success in its chosen task. I am aware that the acceptance of my scheme may lead to but one result, *i.e.*, the students who have come here in the hope of getting the same sort of education as they do in Government school or of acquiring the equipment for a comfortable city-life, will leave our schools. But that would be good. It will save both us and them from an undesirable situation and enable both to serve each other in a disinterested way.

I think I have said enough to have explained my viewpoint in regard to the problem of primary education which was the purpose in writing the present series. I have to add only a little more and then I will close it. And then I hope to discuss a few questions put to me on the subject. If the idea of not introducing the teaching of the alphabet in the first year of primary education is correct, some of its good result should also be visible in our Vinaya Mandirs or secondary schools and the Mahavidyalaya.

There is a great increase in the number of books being brought out today. Books are being published daily. Whoever has or thinks he has a certain command of the language or believes to have studied or reflected a little over a certain thing, becomes impatient to express his ideas in writing and have them printed, and actually thinks that he thereby serves the country. The result is that there is a great strain on the minds of the students and the pockets of the parents! The intellectual growth of the students is paralyzed. The minds become storehouses of strange and unrelated facts and there is no room left in them for original ideas. And those facts too do not fall each into its right place as in a well-arranged plan but lie scattered as the things in the house of a lazy man. Neither can they make any worthwhile use of them nor do they yield any good to the people.

Therefore, if I could have my way, I would not put the large number of books that are being published today into the hands of the people. Even the students who know reading and writing receive most of what they get to learn from the teacher's mouth. So I would advise the students to read only a few selected books. But they should think over what they read and put into practice what appears worthwhile. If they do so, it will make their lives beautiful and pure as also full of strength and energy. They will have learnt to think and discriminate—the hallmark of real education. This is the education which will suit and profit our poor people. It will do good to both the students and the people.

The solution of the difficult problem which faces Vidyapith depends upon the capacity of its present teachers to sincerely reflect upon and accept the aims of the Vidyapith and to try to implement them in practice. *(Navajivan, 3 July 1928 (CW 36, pp. 343-45))*

Teacher–Taught Relationship

I believe in *guru-bhakti.* But every teacher cannot be a *guru.* The *guru–shishya*—the teacher–disciple—relation in this sense is something spiritual and springs up spontaneously. In any case it is not an artificial thing or a product of pressure from without. Such teachers still exist in India. (It should not be necessary to sound the warning that I am not speaking here of spiritual teachers who have the power to lead the aspirants to liberation.) Such teachers have no use for flattery. Respect for them must be natural and so is the love of the teacher for his pupil. That being so, the teacher is ever ready to give, and the pupil equally ready to receive. *(Navajivan, 3 July 1928)*

Some Related Questions

Having written the previous three articles about primary education, it is now somewhat easy to answer the following questions:

> *You once wrote that if the burden of English were lightened it will save a few precious years in the life of the students which are now wasted. What is your estimate of this wastage in terms of years and of the loss it means to society?*

Let me first explain what I mean by lightening the burden of English. I do not mean that the students should stop learning English altogether. We may learn it and use it but only as a Frenchman knows and uses English; that is, we should learn and know it as one does a foreign language. If we try to limit our learning of English to this extend, we would not be required to think in English and speak it correctly with the right pronunciation and to write it with the mastery of an Englishman. I am inclined to think that every student wastes at least five years of his life in this useless endeavour. Not only that, this forced labour over a thing for which he feels no genuine attraction cripples his power of original thinking. His body weakens and he becomes almost a blotting-paper—a blind imitator of superfluities. How much more a man can acquire if he spends five years in acquiring knowledge through his mother tongue? How much time and energy would he save? He will easily get to know the best thought through his own language and yet be saved from the great trouble in mastering the difficult pronunciation of a foreign language.

Child education at one end and college education at the other are both very expensive. Are both these to be included in national education? Have you a scheme to provide both and an equally high type of education at a cheaper cost?

I have tried to show in the three previous articles how the education of the children can be made cheaper; even, almost self-supporting. If we could bring the same approach to bear on college education, it too could be made cheaper, and the students well enabled to acquire such knowledge which will strengthen the nation. If by the expression—'an equally high type of education' the correspondent means an education resembling that to be found in Government institution, the question does not arise, because I do not consider Government type of education to be desirable at all. The education offered in national colleges or national schools is different from the former and often original in many ways. Therefore, it is good in its own way.

Do you think that teachers have the right to impart religious instruction to the boys in their charge in whatever way they like?

Teachers have to conform to the policy or policies laid down by the organisation to which they belong; they cannot, therefore, claim the right to give religious education in the way they would like to do it. As in other subject so also in the matter of religious instruction the teacher must carry out the policy decided upon by those in charge of the organisation. Of course, the teacher should be free to choose his method of teaching, but what he teaches will have to be in conformity with the ideals accepted by the organisation in the matter of religion. It is true that while one may teach other subjects by reading a few selected books on those subjects, this is not possible in the case of religious education. In fact, it cannot be imparted through books at all. While instruction in other subjects is mostly through the intellect, in religious education it has to be from the heart to the heart. Therefore, a teacher should not undertake to teach religion unless he is himself deeply religious.

It is also necessary to exercise a certain discrimination. For example, nothing that is likely to promote violence should be taught in a school which accepts nonviolence as the highest form of religion. Similarly, there should be no room for any propaganda against any of the other religions in a school which has adopted for itself the ideal of love, charity and tolerance in regard to all religions. In short, if a school accepts the need for providing religious education, it must also clearly define the content of such education, and not leave it to the whims of the teachers concerned as this would result in chaos.

If it is considered necessary for every student to know at least three to four languages don't you think it is equally necessary to introduce students to the basic tenets, rites, dogmas and superstitions of all the existing religions?

If we want to create a feeling of respect and love among the students towards every religion—which is religion in the true sense of the word and not an irreligion, we must surely provide them a knowledge of its main tenets. I do not think it is necessary to know the superstitions which have crept in into different religions and the special rites pertaining to each of them. In a country like India everyone who keeps his eyes and ears open can easily see for himself what these rites and superstitions are.

If we would become seekers of good—wherever we find it, as we must, we should not want to know the rites and superstitions of every religion. They are quite unnecessary. It should be enough to know the rites and superstitions of our own religion and to impress upon the boys the need to reform them wherever necessary. That would itself take up enough of their time.

Since you believe in the *varna*, *i.e.*, the four-fold division of society, do you accept, or not accept, that education provided to students should differ according to the *varna*?

I do not think that education should differ according to *varna*. There is much that is common between the different *varnas* and the education provided to them should be the same. The chief aim of education is to make of the students decent men and women. And he who would become a decent man would easily learn the laws of conduct governing human society—the laws which add to the glory of men. My conception of *varna* is that since the *varna* division rests on the difference in vocations, and every *varna* has to earn its livelihood through its appointed vocation, it would be found that men belonging to a particular *varna* generally inherit the characteristics of their class. I do not mean that a particular *varna* does not or cannot have the characteristics of the other three *varnas*.

A Brahman would not earn his bread by working for others on hire-purchase basis, but if he does not know the art of service or is ashamed of it, he is not a *Brahman* at all. In the same way, though a *Shudra* may not teach the *Vedas*, etc. and has to live on alms voluntarily given, he would surely have been given a sufficient grounding in the *Vedas*, etc. in a well-organized society. Is it true that training in useful crafts automatically includes all other education and that intellectual education is no more than a superficial decoration? If it is true, why do you approve and support the education given by the Mahavidyalaya?

This view is as true as it is false. Where people have idolized intellectual education I say that training in crafts includes all other education, for there is no insurmountable barrier between what is called intellectual education and the crafts. They are not like two watertight compartments without any relation with each other. On the contrary, training in arts and crafts offers full scope for the development of the intellect. And I venture to claim that without it the development of intellect is impossible. If a mason knows just enough to earn his bread, he cannot be said to have had any education. The education of a mason should therefore include: the place of this craft in social life, the science of bricklaying, the need of housing, the requisites of a good house, and the close relation between civilization and houses for human habitation. To think that intellectual education means no more than a knowledge of certain facts is a gross misapprehension. Development of intellect is fully possible without any such knowledge. A teacher who turns the mind of students into a cupboard for storing all manner of facts has himself not learnt even the first lesson in teaching.

The reader must, by now, have gathered from the above why I have called the view stated by the correspondent both true and false. It is false if my view about the training in crafts and intellectual training is accepted. But it is true if the question has been framed keeping in view the misunderstanding which springs from regarding intellectual education and training in useful crafts as two different things. It should be easy to see now why, and on what conditions, I approve and support the Mahvidyalaya and the education provided by it. In the institution of my conception the mason, the carpenter and the weaver will be intelligent social workers and not mere bread-earners who know only as much of their job as may be sufficient for the purpose. I hope for Kabir, Bhoja Bhagat, Akha and Guru Govind springing up respectively from the weavers, cobblers, goldsmiths and peasants studying at the Mahavidyalaya. Who would say that Kabir, Bhoja Bhagat, Akha and Guru Govind were not men with an intellectual education?

If training in crafts be the essence of education why shouldn't you entrust the Vidyapith to a committee composed of carpenters, blacksmiths and weavers? Let them then engage the services of teachers having to do with intellectual education if they so choose.

I think the answer to this question is already covered before. If I had weavers like Kabir I would certainly place the direction of the Vidyapith in their charge, and I am sure 'the teachers having to do with intellectual education' would consider it an honour to work as servants under them. That we did not consider arts and crafts fit to be included in the content of education is the reason why our craftsmen are relegated today to an inferior status in society and we cannot get any help from them in our endeavour to serve society.

It is mentioned in the statement of the aims and objects of Vidyapith that the progress of the country depends on the villages and not on the cities. If it is so, why do you spoil our city boys? Give village education to the village boys, if you must. But the city boys desire to live a city life. Why not arrange to give them an education which would suit them? And don't you get all the money for the Vidyapith from the cities? Of course, we will have nothing to say if you would transfer the Vidyapith to some ideal village and collect the necessary money, grain and cotton locally from the village itself.

Fortunately, this question does not arise in the mind of many city people or city students. How can the city people who have expressed their readiness to atone for the wrong done to the villages ask for the village education to be given to the village boys at their own expense? The Vidyapith has come into existence as a result of the city people's attention being drawn to the villages.

It is the city people who decided to start the Vidyapith after they had their eyes opened. How could the villagers be called upon to pay its bill if it aims specially at the uplift of the villages? It is up to the city people to provide the wherewithal for the education even in the villages for the time being at least. The villagers can bring against us the same charge as we do against the Government. They may well say: "You city people have exploited us and are still exploiting us. Please stop it now. We will forget the past. Some of us realized the reality of the situation and woke up to our duty. We saw the wrong we have done to the villagers and resolved to make amends for it. The first part of this process was to non-co-operate with the Government under whose protection and with whose help we could and still can drain out the sap of life from them.

The next was that as we learnt the deeper implications of noncooperation, we also learnt to reject the illegitimate gains of that cooperation. If, after launching out on noncooperation, we had simply sat quietly, it could justly be said against us that we had not grasped the meaning of noncooperation. Supposing somebody started plundering our house, then it would not be enough not to help him. We must also step in to stop him from his nefarious business as also desist from sharing the spoils.

Then only can it be called true noncooperation with the plunderer. This noncooperation can either be violent or nonviolent, riotous or peaceful, based on brute-force or on soul-force. We have chosen to practise nonviolent and peaceful noncooperation based on soul-force.

And we have come to realize in the process that as an expiation for the exploitation of the wealth of the villages which many city people indulge in, we should render some service at least to the villagers. The Vidyapith had its birth as a result of this realisation on our part. And as some of us are wakeful and persistent in our efforts to know the truth, we are realizing the secret of noncooperation more clearly every day, and to that extent trying to give a truer shape to the Vidyapith. This is sufficient reason why a major portion of the money donated by the city people should be spent on bringing education to the villagers. And the education for time being should be carried to them only through the students from the cities trained by the Vidyapith?

I am of the opinion that any other use of the money received by the Vidyapith will be a betrayal of the assurance given to the people. The donors have given the money in the belief that it will be used in providing education which will be of a different kind from the present one and conform to my conception of it.

The Vidyapith has consistently followed a policy of the removal of untouchability for the past eight years. How many *vinitas* and *snatakas* from among the untouchables has it turned out during this period?

The question appears strange, and suggests ignorance to me. The removal of untouchability does not and should not mean that we are to make the so-called "untouchable" boys *vinitas* and *snatakas*. It is quite possible that in the course of time some of them may become *vinitas* and *snatakas*. And that would be welcome. It is also right that the Vidyapith should be ready to help such boys. But to turn out *snatakas* from among the untouchables is in no way a part of the campaign for the removal of untouchability. The Vidyapith has demonstrated its love for the cause of the removal of untouchability by refusing thousands, if not lakhs, of rupees offered to it, by staking its very existence and by foregoing the valuable help of quite a few who were otherwise very able men in organizing its work.

We see quite clearly that in the absence of *Brahmacharya* the nation has become both physically and mentally weak and its capacity for adventure, enterprise and perseverance has gone down. How is it then that you have not included *Brahmacharya* in the last article of the constitution dealing with its aims and objects?

It is a good question. It cannot be proved that the physical and mental weakness afflicting the nation and the slackening of its capacity for adventure and enterprise are all due directly to the absence of *Brahmacharya.* Nor can it be proved that *Brahmacharya* will always result in physical strength. It is not therefore proper to connect *Brahmacharya* with physical strength or weakness—which is after all an ephemeral good—and thus to detract from the importance of that celestial virtue. The people of the West are not *brahmacharis,* but they are not physically or mentally weak. Their capacity for sustained work and enterprise are excellent and exemplary.

It may be said that the Gurkhas, Pathans, Sikhs, Dogras, and the English among the soldiers are not *brahmacharis,* but they have strongly built bodies. They will easily beat the student of our *vyayamshala* in a physical contest. It can thus be proved that it is not quite correct to maintain that physical strength, even a kind of mental energy, capacity for persistent effort and enterprise are impossible to achieve except through *Brahmacharya.* The *Brahmacharya* of my conception—the *Brahmacharya* which leads one to the realisation of *Brahma* is beyond physical and mental fitness. It is itself both the end and the means. I will, therefore, be willing to sacrifice the body to be able to observe it and achieve it. He who is attached to the body can hardly observe unbroken *Brahmacharya.* Examples of its observance by Bhishma and others are likely to misdirect us in this case. Literal acceptance of things mentioned in the *Mahabharata* and *Ramayana* will lead us astray. What is required is to grasp their inner meaning which we should then put into practice. If we do that in the spirit of true inquiry and experimentation we would surely march forward.

The body is not a thing to be carelessly thrown away. It has to be preserved. The body, if it is at times the abode of Ravana, is also the Ayodhya of Rama. If it is *Kurukshetra*—the field of action, it is also *dharmakshetra*—the field of duty. Hence, it cannot be ignored. It has to be kept fit and strong. Physical exercise is therefore necessary. But this is as far as we can go to praise physical exercise and this should be enough to popularize it among the students. We cannot insist on an unbreakable relation between physical exercise and *Brahmacharya*. It will not only be an exaggeration; there is in it the further danger of a person abandoning *Brahmacharya* when he finds himself lagging behind in physical strength in the erroneous belief that the reason for his failure lies in his practice of *Brahmacharya*.

Brahmacharya does not need the support of physical strength. Its importance and need lie elsewhere. The West may have physical strength and mental energy, but they do not have soul-force. How can we entertain any feeling of envy for their physical strength and mental energy when we see that they succumb to inferior passions at every moment, cannot put up with the least opposition to their will, and spend all their energy, industry and enterprise in plundering and destroying other races? How can we think of copying them? Their strength and energy, shows lack of *Brahmacharya;* this is why it has proved disastrous to the real progress of the world, and that is why I have called it satanic. I am not condemning the West, nor belittling it.

There are many in the West who are votaries of truth and other moral principles. There are also many *brahmacharis* there. They understand these undesirable features of Western life I am referring to here. And so we can, in spite of our love and respect for the West, speak of all the sad results its furious endeavours have led to. If the civilization of the West had been raised on the secure foundations of the *Brahmacharya* ideal, the world today would have been a different place. It would not then be the sorry mess it is, but a happy and beautiful habitation of noble men and women. Knowing thus the evil consequences of the non-observance of *Brahmacharya,* we should put forward the ideal of *Brahmacharya* before the people.

Full development of the soul is impossible without it. A man may behave like an unbridled wild horse without *Brahmacharya,* but he cannot achieve refinement and purity which is the mark of culture. There can be no *sattwik, i.e.,* pure and enlightened endeavour and enterprise without *Brahmacharya.* One may seem to have a strong and energetic mind even without *Brahmacharya,* but then it will be a prey to a thousand passions and lures. Similarly, one may have a well-built and strong body even without *Brahmacharya,* but it will not be a truly healthy body. It is not necessary for health to strengthen the muscles and put on fat. A body which, though lean and thin like a chip of wood, can bear cold and sun and rain and yet remain healthy—such a healthy body is impossible to have without *Brahmacharya.* This is not a belief which I have come to hold today; it is an old belief and is moreover based on experience. I can give you numerous examples from my life and from the life of my friends and co-workers as to how every single impure thought wastes man's energy and destroys his soul. I will say, therefore, that those who seek self-realization should preserve their *Brahmacharya* even though the body may decline.

The reason for the weakness of the body and the mind to be found in our students lies elsewhere. The reasons are: child-marriage, the burden of the family, the lack of good food due to poverty, etc. Let not the readers make the mistake of regarding child-marriage as just non-*Brahmacharya*. Great and persistent efforts are necessary in order to eradicate these evil habits. The harmful customs prevailing in society have to be reformed, and the burden of the present artificial type of education should be lightened. This is however a different subject; I will therefore not dwell on it here. I will merely state that our students cannot have a strong and healthy body merely by taking physical exercise. Efforts will have to be made in all directions; only then may we hope to achieve the results we desire.

Ever since you made your entry into the public life of this country, there has been a tendency to approach you and get your view of a problem whenever a person or persons have been in doubt and have thus failed to reach a clear-cut conclusion. People are eager to know from you whether a certain thing on a certain occasion is right or not. I am only describing the situation as it really is. It shows that all your activity is basically of a religious nature. Would it be right that when you are no more, these decisions be delivered by a body of persons by a majority vote if necessary? If not, is it not necessary to create what may prove to be continuous line of knowledgeable men, versed in the precepts of *dharma*?

I do not deem it worthy that people should approach me and ask me to pronounce judgment on disputable points. It is true that all my activities, whatever their outer form, are fundamentally religious. But the fact that I am asked to pronounce judgments on every disputed matter shows that people have either not understood the principles which I follow in shaping my conduct, or they have doubts about them. And because I am known as the Mahatma or respected as a good man, our people are credulous and not given to thinking for themselves, they continue to put all forms of questions to me. This may gratify my sense of pride or even help me up to a point in doing my work, but it does not appear to me if it helps in any appreciable way either the people or questioners. Indeed, I have often felt how nice it would be if I stopped making any pronouncements and did whatever suggested itself to me silently. But in that case I must first stop this weekly that I am now conducting, as also severely cut down much of my present correspondence. That, however, would need a courage which I do not feel within myself. But, there is the great friend of man, the Lord of Death, who can extend his invitation to me at any time and put a stop to all this chatter on my part whether I agree or not.

I do not see any wrong in bodies or associations of men following my principles and giving their opinions on disputed questions by a majority vote when I am no more, or even now whilst I am alive. But as in the case of individuals so also in that of groups they must be inspired by the ideal of *dharma*.

The education in the Vidyapith is divided into three distinct stages: the primary, the secondary and the higher. How far would it be right to name these respectively as the education for the village, education for the city, and the education for those who would take up social service work?

I do not like the meanings suggested here by the correspondent to the primary, the secondary and the higher education respectively. Why should we want village people to be satisfied merely with primary education? They too have a right to receive secondary and higher education—those of them at least who want it. And the boys in the cities cannot do without primary education. The object of all the three should be the prosperity of the villages.

Why do you always attach so much importance to music?

It is said that the study of music is generally neglected in our country today. Without it, the entire educational system seems to me to be incomplete. Music brings sweetness to the individual and to the social life of the people. Even as *pranayam* is necessary for the regulation of breath, so is music for disciplining the voice. A dissemination of the knowledge of music among the people will greatly help in controlling and stopping the noise which is an usual feature of public meetings in this country. Music pacifies anger and its judicious use is highly helpful in leading a man to the vision of God. It does not mean shouting and shrieking a tune anyhow like a rigmarole, nor does it mean the singing of film songs. I have already referred to its ordinary meaning above, but its deeper meaning is that our whole life should be sweet and musical like a song. It goes without saying that life cannot be made like that without the practice of virtues such as truth, honesty, etc. To make life musical means to make it one with God, to merge it into Him. He who has not rid himself of *raga* and *dwesha*, *i.e.*, likes and dislike, who has not tasted of the joy of service, cannot have any understanding of celestial music. A study of music, which does not take account of this deeper aspect of this divine art, has little or no value for me.

The art of painting means an expression of the emotions of the artist through line and colour. If this definition of painting were to be accepted, would you include painting as an essential part of the scheme of national education which should be universally taught to all?

Some people are of the view that such subjects as grammar, compound interest, higher geometry, etc., which the learners are apt to forget in after years should not be included in the courses to be framed for purposes of national education. Do you agree to this? If you do, why should not Urdu also be put in the same category? When Hindus and Muslims feel the urge to come into close contact with each other and to understand each other's cultures, then only will the knowledge of Sanskrit and Urdu prove useful and lasting. Knowledge of Urdu will be put to active use and hence increase only when there is respect for and a desire to learn the culture of which Urdu is the vehicle. Until then it is bound to remain no more than a religious rite like the worship of Ganesha—a formal affair without any practical value.

I do not understand why grammar, compound interest and higher geometry have all been classed together. I have always believed that grammar is absolutely necessary for the mastery of a language, and that grammar and higher geometry are highly interesting subjects. Both provide innocent intellectual entertainment. Besides, grammar is indispensable for the study of philology. I will, therefore, accord a place to both these subjects in the courses of study for national education. In the same way, he who wants to be good at accounts cannot do so without learning compound interest. Therefore, all the three things mentioned by the correspondent in the question will have their due place in the syllabus for national education.

The point is that there are things which are common to all schemes of education. Today, we have to differentiate between Government education and National education because the former is detrimental to national development. But there are many things in Government schools which will and must also be in our schools. Thus, though there are points of similarity between the two, the atmosphere in Government schools strengthens the bonds of slavery and is used at critical moments to suppress us.

Therefore, such schools are to be renounced. Besides, as we have already seen, a portion, at least, of the education imparted there is wholly unnecessary; it is just a burden and nothing more. But I am moving away from the subject under discussion. I have thought it fit to offer this clarification under the impression that I might not have grasped the point behind this question.

Urdu stands apart from the above-mentioned subjects: the question of its study must be considered separately. Hindus and Muslims will ultimately unite but in our national schools we must continue to strive unremittingly to bring them closer together. For this, we must acquaint ourselves with each other's religion. If the students forget whatever little of Urdu they learn, evidently they are not serious about its study and must be learning it only because they must. But this can also be said about Hindi. Only God knows how interest in Hindi or Urdu can be created among the students, but there is no doubt in my mind that its knowledge is necessary for the progress of the nation.

Students should have full freedom; there should be nothing which will obstruct their free growth; to achieve this objective the teachers should have no prejudices for or against anything; while they teach they should so conduct themselves as though they have no partiality for any particular rule or habit or principle: This ideal for a teacher is coming to be accepted in many places. Do you accept it?

What has been said above can be supported as well as opposed. If it does not help in preserving the real essence, is should be opposed, and if it does help, the students may well be allowed full freedom and the teachers remain as detached and neutral as they like. They may do what they wish with a view to securing the independence of the students, the only condition being that they must mix with the students to the extent of being one of them. In the language of Akha, I will say to them:

> *"Live in the world as you like, but keep constantly before your mind the aim of attaining to God at any cost."*

An ideal teacher never had nor should he ever have any other aim before him. *(Navajivan, 3 June–1 July 1928 (The Problem of Education, pp. 154–69))*

National University

The National University stands today as a protest against British injustice, and as a vindication of national honour. But it has come to stay. It draws its inspiration from the national ideals of a united India. It stands for a religion which is the Dharma of the Hindus and Islam of Mohammedans. It wants to rescue the Indian vernaculars from unmerited oblivion and make them the fountains of national regeneration and Indian culture. It holds that a systematic study of Asiatic cultures is no less essential than the study of Western sciences for a complete education for life. The vast treasures of Sanskrit and Arabic, Persian and Pali, and Magadhi have to be ransacked in order to discover wherein lies the source of strength for the nation.

It does not propose merely to feed on, or repeat, the ancient cultures. It rather hopes to build a new culture based on the traditions of the past, enriched by the experience of later times. It stands for the synthesis of the different cultures that have come to stay in India, that have influenced Indian life and that in their turn, have themselves been influenced by the spirit of the soil. This synthesis will naturally be of the Swadeshi type where each culture is assured its legitimate place, and not of American pattern, where one dominant culture absorbs the rest, and where the aim is not towards harmony, but towards an artificial and forced unity. That is why the University has desired a study of all the Indian religions by its students.

The Hindus may thus have an opportunity of studying the Koran and the Muslims of knowing what the Hindus Shastras contain. If the University has excluded anything, it is the spirit of exclusion that regards any section of humanity as permanently untouchable. The study of Hindustani, which is a national blend of Sanskrit, Hindi and Persianized Urdu, has been made compulsory. The spirit of independence will be fostered not only through Religion, Politics and History but through vocational training also, which alone can give the youths of the country economic independence and a backbone that comes out of a sense of self-respect.

The University hopes to organize higher schools throughout the mofussil towns, so that education may be spread broadcast and filtered down to the masses as early as possible. The use of Gujarati as the medium of education will facilitate this process and, ere long, the suicidal cleavage between the educated and the non-educated will be bridged. And as an effect of industrial education to the genteel folks, and literary education for the industrial classes, the unequal distribution of wealth and the consequent social discontent will be considerably checked.

The greatest defect of the Government Universities has been their alien control and the false values they have created as regards 'careers'. The Gujarat Universities by non-co-operating with the Government has automatically eradicated both these evils from its own system. If the founders and promoters stick to this resolve till the Government becomes nationalized, it will help them to cultivate a clear perception of national ideals and national needs. *(Tagore, pp. 455–57; 17 November 1920 (CW 18, p. 481))*

College Education

I would revolutionize college education and relate it to national necessities. There would be degrees for mechanical and other engineers. They would be attached to the different industries which should pay for the training of the graduates they need. Thus the Tatas would be expected to run a college for training engineers under the supervision of the State, the mill associations would run among them a college for training graduates whom they need.

Similarly for the other industries that may be named. Commerce will have its college. There remain arts, medicine and agriculture. Several private arts colleges are today self-supporting. The State would, therefore, cease to run its own. Medical colleges would be attached to certified hospitals. As they are popular among moneyed men they may be expected by voluntary contributions to support medical colleges.

And agricultural colleges to be worthy of the name must be self-supporting. I have a painful experience of some agricultural graduates. Their knowledge is superficial. They lack practical experience. But if they had their apprenticeship on farms which are self-sustained and answer the requirements of the country, they would not have to gain experience after getting their degrees and at the expense of their employers. *(Harijan, 31 July 1937 (CW 65, p. 451))*

State Universities

Higher education should be left to private enterprise and for meeting national requirements whether in the various industries, technical arts, belles-letters or fine arts.

The State Universities should be purely examining bodies, self-supporting through the fees charged for examinations.

Universities will look after the whole of the field of education and will prepare and approve courses of studies in the various departments of education. No private school should be run without the previous sanction of the respective Universities. University charters should be given liberally to any body of persons of proved worth and integrity, it being always understood that the Universities will not cost the State anything except that it will bear the cost of running a Central Education Department.

The foregoing scheme does not absolve the State from running such seminaries as may be required for supplying State needs. *(Harijan, 2 October 1937)*

Higher Education

1. I am not opposed to education even of the highest type attainable in the world.
2. The State must pay for it wherever it has definite use for it.
3. I am opposed to all higher education being paid for from the general revenue.
4. It is my firm conviction that the vast amount of the so-called education in arts, given in our colleges, is sheer waste and has resulted in unemployment among the educated classes. What is more, it has destroyed the health, both mental and physical, of the boys and girls who have the misfortune to go through the grind in our colleges.
5. The medium of a foreign language through which higher education has been imparted in India has caused incalculable intellectual and moral injury to the nation. We are too near our own times to judge the enormity of the damage done. And we who have received such

education have both to be victims and judges—an almost impossible feat.

Thus I claim that I am not an enemy of Higher Education. But I am an enemy of Higher Education as it is given in this country. Under my scheme there will be more and better libraries, more and better laboratories, more and better research institutes. Under it we should have an army of chemists, engineers and other experts who will be real servants of the nation, and answer the varied and growing requirements of a people who are becoming increasingly conscious of their rights and wants. And all these experts will speak, not a foreign language, but the language of the people. The knowledge gained by them will be the common property of the people. There will be truly original work instead of mere imitation. And the cost will be evenly and justly distributed. *(Harijan, 9 July 1938 (CW 67, p. 158))*

Self-Supporting Universities

Your third conclusion about general revenue and claims of Higher Education and its corollary, *viz.* that Universities should be self-supporting, has left me unconvinced. I believe that every country to be a progressive country must have sufficient facilities for the pursuit of *all* branches of knowledge—not merely chemistry, medicine and engineering, but every kind of knowledge, literature, philosophy, history, sociology, both abstract and applied. All higher pursuits require many facilities which cannot be had without State support. A country depending *only* on voluntary effort for such pursuits is sure to fall behind and suffer.

It can never hope to be free and be able to maintain that freedom. The State must be jealously watchful over the position of higher education in *all* fields. Voluntary effort must be there and we must have our Nuffields and Rockfellers. But the State cannot and must not be allowed to remain a silent spectator. It must actively come forward to organize, help and direct. I wish you to clarify this aspect of the question.

You say at the end of your article: 'Under my scheme there will be more and better libraries.' I do not find *The Scheme* you speak of in your article, nor am I able to make out how 'more and better libraries and laboratories' will come into being thereunder. I am of opinion that such libraries and laboratories must be maintained, and so long as donors and voluntary agencies are not coming forward in sufficient numbers, the State cannot divest itself of this responsibility.

My article is clear enough if the expression 'definite use' mentioned in it is given its extensive meaning. I have not pictured a poverty-stricken India containing ignorant millions. I have pictured to myself an India continually progressing along the lines best suited to her genius. I do not, however, picture it as a third class or even a first class copy of the dying civilization of the West. If my dream is fulfilled and every one of the seven lakhs of villages becomes a well-living republic in which there are no illiterates, in which no one is idle for want of work, in which everyone is usefully occupied and has nourishing food, well-ventilated dwellings, and sufficient Khadi for covering the body, and in which all the villagers know and observe the laws of hygiene and sanitation, such a State must have varied and increasing needs, which it must supply unless it would stagnate. I can therefore well imagine the State financing all the education my correspondent mentions and much more that I could add. And if the State has such requirements, surely it will have corresponding libraries.

What, however, according to my view the State will not have is an army of B.A.'s and M.A.'s with their brains sapped with too much cramming and minds almost paralyzed by the impossible attempt to speak and write English like Englishmen. The majority of these have no work, no employment. And when they have the latter, it is usually clerkships at which most of the knowledge gained during their twelve years of High Schools and Colleges is of no use whatsoever to them.

University training becomes self-supporting when it is utilized by the State. It is criminal to pay for a training which benefits neither the nation nor the individual. In my opinion there is no such thing as individual benefit which cannot be proved to be also national benefit. And since most of my critics seem to be agreed that the existing Higher Education, and for that matter both Primary and Secondary, are not connected with realities, it cannot be of benefit to the State. When it is directly based on realities and is wholly given through the mother tongue, I shall perhaps have nothing to say against it. To be based on realities is to be based on national, *i.e.*, State, requirements. And the State will pay for it. Even when that happy time comes, we shall find that many institutions will be conducted by voluntary contributions. They may or may not benefit the State. Much of what passes for education today in India belongs to that category and would therefore not be paid for from the general revenue, if I had the way. *(Harijan, 30 July 1938 (CW 67, pp. 210–12))*

Reorientation of University Education

Gandhiji remarked at the Conference of Education Ministers in Poona that what he had said about adult education applied to University education. It must be originally related to the Indian scene. It must therefore be an extension and continuation of the Basic Education course. That was the central point. If they did not see eye to eye with him on that point, he was afraid they would have little use for his advice. If, on the other hand, they agreed with him that the present University education did not fit them for independence but only enslaved them, they would be as impatient as he was to completely overhaul and scrap that system and remodel it on new lines consonant with the national requirement.

Today the youth educated in our universities either ran after the Government jobs or fell into devious ways and sought outlet for their frustration by fomenting unrest. They were not even ashamed to beg or sponge upon others. Such was their sad plight. The aim of University education should be to turn out true servants of the people, who would live and die for the country's freedom. He was therefore of opinion that University education should be coordinated and brought into line with Basic Education, by taking in teachers from the Talimi Sangh. *(Harijan, 25 August 1946)*

New Universities

There seems to be a mania for establishing new universities in the provinces. Gujarat wants one for Gujarati, Maharashtra for Marathi, Karnatic for Kannad, Orissa for Uriya, Assam for

Assami and what not. I do believe that there should be such universities if these rich provincial languages and the people who speak them are to attain their full height.

At the same time I fear that we betray ourselves into undue haste in accomplishing the object. The first step should be linguistic political redistribution of provinces. Their separate administration will naturally lead to the establishment of universities where there are none. The province of Bombay absorbs three languages: Gujarati, Marathi and Kannad and, therefore, stunts their growth. Madras absorbs four: Tamil, Telugu, Malayalam and Kannad. Thus there is overlapping also. That Andradesh has an Andhra University is true. In my opinion it does not occupy the place it would, if Andhra was a separate administrative unit, free from foreign control. India attained that freedom only two months ago. The same thing can be said of the Annamalai University. Who can say that Tamil has come to its own in that University?

There should be a proper background for new universities. They should have feeders in the shape of schools and colleges which will impart instruction through the medium of their respective provincial languages. Then only can there be a proper milieu. University is at the top. A majestic top can only be sustained if there is a sound foundation.

Though we are politically free, we are hardly free from the subtle domination of the West. I have nothing to say to that school of politicians who believe that knowledge can only come from the West. Nor do I subscribe to the belief that nothing good can come out of the West. I do fear, however, that we are unable as yet to come to a correct decision in the matter. It is to be hoped that no one contends that because we seem to be politically free from foreign domination the mere fact gives us freedom from the more subtle influence of the foreign language and foreign thought.

Is it not wisdom, does not duty to the country dictate, that before we embark on new universities we should stop and fill our own lungs first with the ozone of our newly got freedom? A university never needs a pile of majestic buildings and treasures of gold and silver. What it does need most of all is the intelligent backing of public opinion. It should have a large reservoir of teachers to draw upon. Its founders should be farseeing.

In my opinion it is not for a democratic State to find money for founding universities. If the people want them they will supply the funds. Universities so founded will adorn the country which they represent. Where administration is in foreign hands, whatever comes to the people comes from the top and thus they become more and more dependent. Where it is broad-based on popular will, everything goes from bottom upward and hence it lasts.

Infant Education

We should try to draw all the children towards us. We should admit that it is our fault if some do not come to us. They should all want to come to us.

We should treat those children who come to us as our own children. If their body and mind become sound and they acquire normal discipline, we should be satisfied that our purpose has been served.

I have taught many boys. I never allowed them to indulge in mischief. If they were under my care, I would educate them in such a way that they would learn from their very childhood that the desire to destroy was a very bad thing. Whatever they do, they should create something, produce something. There is an art in making anything and whatever they make should be artistic.

I do not believe that children are either good or bad from their very birth. Some tendency is there, but we have to mould them. This means that an infant starts learning right from the time of conception. At that time I would teach the mother. That would be a part of adult education. The training of the infant begins from that stage. We have to train the future generation on these lines. Till the child is separated from the mother, I would teach the mother. The infant is ever moving its hands and feet and is able to do something. If we are able to take under our care children of two or two and a half years of age and if they learn to move their hands and feet according to our method, I cannot set any limits to their progress.

If the child is put under our care, he will not destroy anything. He will feel hurt in doing so.

Whatever education we give to the children, it should be constructive and creative but never destructive.

When the child starts speaking, he starts learning a language. First you should teach him to distinguish different colours. Begin teaching him the letters of the alphabet only with the help of the pictures. Don't you have charts showing 1-2, A-B and so on? Reading, writing and arithmetic will come in due course of time and the child will not be overstrained. His education should be a form of play.

Whatever thing he makes should be useful. In this way his mind and hands and feet develop in coordination.

There are no distinctions between work and play in basic education. For a child everything is play. I would go so far as to say that thus his whole life becomes a kind of game. I have been doing this for many years now. I never feel that it is time for play and I should go and play. For me even writing is a game. Under basic education of my conception children will learn while playing.

5

MAHATMA'S EDUCATION AIMS

Introduction

In my humble opinion, knowledge should never be used for acquiring wealth. Business should be the only means of doing so. The means of livelihood should be labour, *i.e.*, weaving, carpentry, tailoring and such other occupations essential for maintaining human life. I believe that one of the chief reasons for our moral fall is that doctors, lawyers, teachers and others acquire their knowledge mainly for getting money and, in fact, use it for that purpose. What I have set out is, of course, an ideal, which we cannot attain. I have no doubt, however, that the nearer we get to it, the better for us. *(Navajivan, 1 July 1924 (CW 24, p. 174))*

Making a True Student

The education that you are receiving is intended for swaraj. I have taken up the responsibilities of a chancellor in Gujarat. That too I have done in my capacity as a fighter for freedom and with the intention of training students to be fighters for freedom. I landed in England on 4th of August, 1914. What did I see there? As the War spread, the Inns of Courts went on closing. Many faculties in Oxford and Cambridge were also closed. During the War, they allotted a minor role to education. And why should they not? The outcome of education is that the student becomes an ideal citizen, an ideal patriot and an ornament to his family, his community and his nation. *(Convocation address at Tilak Mahavidyalaya, Poona, 4 September 1924 (CW 25, p. 89))*

Service of Humanity

In asking them to study the lives of lawyers like Ghose, Mahatma Gandhi asked them not merely to be satisfied with the heritage those great lawyers had left for them, but wished the present generation to do better. They should become the poor man's friend in every sense and then alone would they be able to justify the legal profession. Their end was not to get more than a decent livelihood or how to shine in life, but to serve humanity in order to serve the motherland. They ought not to become lawyers in order to increase cases.

The education they received ought not to be prostituted to the base use of earning a livelihood, it ought to be used to promote moral growth to enable them to realize themselves, to understand that there was the Maker who saw everything and registered all thoughts, pure and impure, and the learning they derived should be dedicated to a vigorous self-analysis and not prostituted. *(Speech at Law College, Trivandrum, 14 March 1925 (CW 26, p. 307))*

Fearlessness

The little boys of the school had all been waiting in the sun with the handsome purse they had collected and they had the lesson of fearlessness from Gandhiji's lips:

> *Fearlessness is the foundation of all education, the beginning and not the end. If you do not build on that foundation, the edifice of all your education will topple over.*

And to send the lesson home to them he told them the story of Prahalda and exhorted them to declare the truth courteously and bravely without regard for the consequences as the twelve-year-old Prahalda did. *(Speech at Boys' Meeting, Kolhapur, Young India, 31 March 1927 (CW 33, p. 192))*

Purity of Personal Life

Purity of personal life is the one indispensable condition for building a sound education. And my meetings with thousands of students and the correspondence which I continuously have with the students in which they pour out their innermost feelings and take me into their confidence show me quite clearly that there is much left to be desired. I am sure that all of you understand thoroughly what I mean. In our languages, there is a beautiful word, equivalent for the word student, that is, *Brahmachari*. *Vidyarthi* is a coined word and a poor equivalent for *Brahmachari*. And I hope you know what the word *Brahmachari* means. It means searcher after God, one who conducts himself so as to bring himself nearest to God in the least possible time. And all the great religions of the world, however much they may differ, are absolutely one on this fundamental thing that no man or woman with an impure heart can possibly appear before the Great White Throne. All our learning or recitation of the Vedas, correct knowledge of Sanskrit, Latin, Greek and what not will avail us nothing if they do not enable us to cultivate absolute purity of heart. The end of all knowledge must be building of character. *(Speech at Voorhee's College, Vellore, 30 August 1927 (CW 34, pp. 422–23))*

Freedom from Bondage

You have asked for my blessings. Them you certainly have. But you have them on the condition that you impart lustre to this Vidyalaya and its name. The Patidars also should benefit by it and should disgrace neither the Vallabh Vidyalaya nor my name. I do not care for the sort of Vidyalaya which may prove a millstone round my neck and be a burden to me. Education liberates us, frees us from bondage, helps us to shine, adds to the country's wealth, enriches character: our boys and girls become smart and intelligent thereby. This Vidyalaya has been established with this end in view. May this end be realized. *(Speech at Vallabh Vidyalaya Bochasan, 10 May 1931 (CW 46, p. 101))*

Quest for Truth

True education is that which helps us to know the *atman*, our true self, God and Truth. To acquire this knowledge, some persons may feel the need for a study of literature, some for a study of physical sciences and some others for art. But every branch of knowledge should have as its goal, knowledge of the self. That is so in the Ashram. We carry on numerous activities with that aim in view. All of them are, in my sense of the term, true education. Those activities can also be carried on without any reference to the goal of knowledge of the self. When they are so carried on, they may serve as a means of livelihood or of something else, but they are not education.

In an activity carried on as education, a proper understanding of its meaning, devotion to duty and the spirit of service are necessary. The first necessarily brings about development of the intellect. In doing any piece of work, however small, we should be inspired by a holy aim and, while doing it, we should try to understand the purpose which it will serve and the scientific method of doing it. There is a science of every type of work—whether it be cooking, sanitation, carpentry or spinning. Everybody who does his work with the attitude of a student knows its science or discovers it. *(From a microfilm of the Gujarati: M.M.U./II, 10 July 1932 (CW 50, p. 182))*

Sparing the Rod

Our aim is not just to impart education to children or teach them discipline, but to build character in them. Education, discipline, etc., are means to that end. If the result of building character in them is that education and discipline are neglected, let that be so. I understand your arguments, though. I also see that there is no ill will behind your use of the rod. But there are certainly anger and impatience behind them. May I make a suggestion? Call a meeting of the children. If any of them, say, "You may punish us, and in this manner, if we play mischief or disobey you", you may punish them in the manner which they suggest. *(Letter to Premabehn Kantak, 14 December 1930 (CW 44, p. 380))*

Selfless Service

Studies should be undertaken only with the aim of equipping oneself for service. Since, however, service of others gives one the highest joy, one may say that studies are for joy. I have not heard of anyone, however, who found unbroken joy in life through literary pursuits alone without devoting himself to service. *(Letter to Premabehn Kantak, 3 August 1932 (CW 50, p. 326))*

National Character

What is your goal in education when India obtains self-rule?

Character-building. I would try to develop courage, strength, virtue, the ability to forget oneself in working towards great aims. This is more important than literacy, academic learning is only a means to this greater end. That is why India's great lack of literacy, deplorable as it is, does not appeal to me nor make me feel that India is unfit for self-rule.

Would you try to bring about any specific kind of social organisation through education.

I would feel that if we succeed in building the character of the individual, society will take care of itself. I would be quite willing to trust the organisation of society to individuals so developed.

In developing the new national spirit in India would you like to make patriotic feelings so strong that duty to one's country would be a higher good than obeying one's personal conscience?

I hope that will never be. One's own inner convictions come first always. But in a nation where character is developed in all individuals, there can be no conflict between the dictates of one's own conscience and those of the State. *(Remakers of Mankind, 1932, pp. 104–05)*

Self Control

The true aim of education is spiritual development. One should, therefore, go in for such kind of education as will bring it about. It need not be of one fixed type. Hence it is not necessary to say anything on that subject. One should lead a life of self-control. *(Letter to Bhogilal, 20 February 1933 (CW 53, p. 366))*

Humility

With this introduction I would like to tell the students, boys and girls, that humility is the primary thing to be acquired. One who is not humble cannot put one's learning to proper use. What does it matter if he has obtained double first class or has stood first? One does not achieve everything by just passing an examination. It is possible that it may help in securing a good job or a good marriage alliance. But, if learning is to be put to proper use, if it is to be used only for the sake of service, one should acquire more and more humility every day. No service is possible without it. *(Speech at Dayaram Jethamal College, Karachi, 10 July 1934 (CW 58, p. 164))*

Developing Independent Thinking

At present, the minds of the students become dull there. They can only imitate. Instead of this, they must acquire the power of independent thinking. We are born into this world not for indulging in sensuous activities but for sacrifice, for restraint. The purpose of education is that we know God and progress towards the ideal, and get closer to Him. It is the strict law of God that anyone who desires to be close to Him should renounce the world and yet be in it. This is what the first *mantra* of the *Ishopanishad* exhorts us to do. This thing is difficult and yet easy at the same time. It is easy if we believe that we have to live for service. We acquire learning not for sensuous pleasures and for earning but for *mukti.* Education is considered necessary to save ourselves from darkness, sensuous pleasures and capricious behaviour. *(Speech at students' meeting, Lahore, 13 July 1934 (CW 58, p. 183))*

Wholesome Educational Environment

That boy will grow into a courageous, healthy and service-minded boy, provided he gets a wholesome, environment. His body as well as his mind will develop in right proportion. He will be free of any fraud or immorality. Staying in the village he will serve the villagers and will be content to live on the subsistence provided by the villagers. Through his service and the knowledge acquired by him he will provide proper guidance to the people around him and thus train more young men. I expect that a student trained under the Nayee Taleem would develop on these lines.

Education is just a means. If it is not accompanied by truthfulness, firmness, patience and other virtues, it remains sterile, and sometimes does harm instead of good. The object of education is not to be able to earn money, but to improve oneself and to serve the country. If this object is not realized, it must be taken that the money spent on education has been wasted.

Public Good

The Indian community has a moral to learn from this case. Without the right kind of education, the community will not only remain backward, but become increasingly so. Education in England, the study of English, world history and of the sciences—all these are essential in the world of today. Without them one is crippled. It is also necessary to learn how to put the knowledge thus acquired to proper use. In itself knowledge is only a means. It can be employed for good, for making money, and in the service of public causes. Knowledge is justified only when it is put to good use and employed in the public cause. Otherwise, as we pointed out once earlier and as everyone will readily admit, it is like poison

Cardinal Virtues

If you practise the three virtues if they become part of your life so far as I am concerned, you will have completed your education—your training. Armed with them, believe me, you will earn your bread in any part of the world and you will have paved the way to acquire a true knowledge of the soul, yourself and God. This does not mean that you should not receive instruction in letters. That you should and you are doing. But it is a thing over which you need not fret yourself. You have plenty of time for it and after all you are to receive such instruction in order that your training may be of use to the others. *(Letter to Manilal Gandhi, 25 March 1909 (CW 9, p. 205))*

Not Mere Employment

You—the students of Madras as well as students all over India—are you receiving an education which will make you worthy to realise that ideal and which will draw the best out of you, or is it an education which has become a factory for making Government employees or clerks in commercial offices?

Is the goal of the education that you are receiving that of mere employment whether in the Government departments or other departments? If that be the goal of your education, if that is the goal that you have set before yourselves, I feel and I fear that the vision which the poet pictured for himself is far from being realised. *(Speech at Y.M.C.A., Madras, 27 April 1915 (CW 13, p. 65))*

National Service

Pupils are to receive education which will incline them to do nothing but national service when their studies are over. If, on growing up, they leave the Ashram, the education will have failed to that extent. Should any occasion of the kind arise, the student will be free [to follow his inclination]. It is not the aim, however, that the students should return to their parents and get lost in the sea of practical affairs. *(Letter to Ranchhodlal Patwari, 10 June 1915 (CW 13, p. 105))*

Thinking and Becoming

But I am afraid that most of the students do not pay any regard to the real aim of education. They go to school merely because it is the custom to do so. Some go to be able to obtain employment later on. In my opinion, to think of education as a means of earning a living betrays an unworthy disposition of mind. The body is the means of earning a living while the school is the place for building character. To regard the latter as the means of fulfilling one's bodily needs is like killing a buffalo for a small piece of hide. The body should be maintained through doing physical work. How can the *atma*, the spirit, be employed for this purpose? You earn your bread by the sweat of your brow—this is one of the most significant sayings of Christ. The Gita also seems to say the same.

Students who attend school without taking thought as to the true aim of education, should first make sure what it should be. Such a student may resolve this very day that, henceforth, he will regard school as a place for building character. I am sure that he will effect a change for the better in his character in the course of a month and that his companions will also bear witness to his having done so. The shastras assert that we become what we think. *(Speech at Bihar Students' Conference, Bhagalpur, 19 July 1917—(CW 14, pp. 134–35))*

Knowing the Self

As I have earlier pointed out, most of the students look listless and devoid of energy. Many have asked me what they should do to overcome lethargy and serve the country? What should they do to earn their living? I have the impression that they are anxious about this matter. Before answering these questions it is necessary to find out the aim of education. Huxley has said that the aim of education is the building up of character. Our seers aver that, if in spite of his knowledge of the Vedas and shastras, a man fails to know himself and acquire the power to liberate himself from all bonds, his knowledge is useless. They have also said: "He who has known the Self knows all." Knowledge of the Self is possible without any literary education. Prophet Mohammed was an illiterate man. Christ too did not attend school. But it would be impudent to deny that these great men had acquired knowledge of the Self. Though they did not pass any examination, yet we hold them in high esteem and worship them. They were in possession of all the fruits of learning. They were *mahatmas*—men of great spiritual attainment. *(Speech at Bihar Students' Conference, Bhagalpur, 19 July 1917 (CW 14, p. 133))*

Building Character

All education must aim at building character. I cannot see how this can be done except through religion. We are yet to realize that gradually we are being reduced to a state in which we shall have lost our own without having acquired the new. I cannot go more into this, but I have met hundreds of teachers and they sighed in pain as they told me of their experiences... If pupils in schools lose their character, everything will have been lost. *(Speech at Gujarat Educational Conference, Broach, 20 October 1917 (CW 14, p. 29))*

Manliness and Self-Respect

If education is to be bought at the price of manliness and self-respect, the price is too heavy. "Man does not live by bread alone." Self-respect and character are above means of livelihood or a career. I am sorry that so many students have taken their expulsion so much to heart. The parents as well as students must revise their ideas about education. Education is treated merely as a means of earning a livelihood and acquiring a status in society. These are not unworthy ambitions. But they are not everything in life. There are many other honourable means of acquiring wealth and status.

There are many independent activities in life which one may undertake without having to contemplate loss of self-respect. And there is no better or cleaner passport to status in society than honesty and selfless service of fellow-beings. If, therefore, after due effort, the college door remains banged in the students' faces, they should not lose heart but seek other means of livelihood. And if the other students will empty the recalcitrant colleges as a matter of respectful protest, they and India will not be losers, but both will be considerable gainers. *(Young India, 1 October 1919 (CW 16, pp. 175–76))*

Kindness to All

He said the essence of all education was kindness—kindness to all, friends, foes, men and beasts. The chief object of education was the building of character which could be done by strict observance of *Brahmacharya*. Mr. Gandhi then explained to the students the necessity of learning Hindi and spinning and said that if the whole younger generation was educated in the manner in which they were trained in national schools then there would not have been any difficulty in getting swaraj. *(Speech at National College, Bombay—The Bombay Chronicle, 17 March 1921 (CW 14, p. 441))*

Knowledge to Character

That is certainly what we mean. Even imparting knowledge should aim at character-building. Knowledge is the means and character-building is the end.

6

GANDHI'S CONCEPTUALIZATION OF POLITICAL LIFE

Introduction

Gandhi's conceptualization of political life and redefinitions of such central concepts as liberty *(Swaraj)*, equality *(samata)*, citizenship *(nagarikata)*, rights *(adhikar)*, obligation *(dharma)* and tolerance *(sahisnuta)* also contain important insights and deserve close study. We shall take the first three by way of illustration.

Like many Hindu philosophers Gandhi took little interest in the concept of human nature, largely because he took a radically individualistic view of man. Each individual was unique, followed his own path of moral and spiritual evolution, and had a distinct *swabhava*, that is, a distinct and firm but relatively open and within limits malleable constitution or nature. It was true that all men shared certain *gunas* or qualities in common. However these were too general and indeterminate to account for the unique constitution of each individual. The qualities were also largely passive, capable of neither mechanical nor teleological casualty, and unable to explain human conduct. Since the concept of human nature had no explanatory power, it had neither theoretical nor practical significance for Gandhi.

For Gandhi the individual's *swabhava* had two sources. First, he was endowed at birth with a specific physical and mental constitution, temperament, tendencies and dispositions. Gandhi thought this a legacy of his previous life, but we need not accept such an explanation. Second, each individual was a member of a specific community which deeply shaped his habits, character, memories, ideals and values, and gave his personality a distinct tone and colour. The two together shaped his psychological and moral constitution *(swabhava),* which was thus a unique blend of his socially transcendental and socially acquired characteristics. It held him together, persisted over time, and formed the basis of his personal identity. Since it was the basis of his being and made him the person he was, it constituted his ontological foundation or truth *(satya).* The Sanskrit word *satya,* meaning truth, is derived from *sat* meaning reality or that which endures over time. The opposite of *sat* is *maya,* meaning illusory, ephemeral, transient or only relatively real.

The *satya* or the truth of an individual limited and guided but did not predetermine his choices and decisions. As a rational being endowed with such capacities as introspection, critical self-reflection and choice, he was able to uncover and take a critical view of some of the constitutive elements of his identity and to reconstitute it in a desired manner. Many aspects of his constitution, however, were too deep to be excavated by even the most rigorous self-examination, and remained beyond his control. And some of those aspects of which he did become aware were often too deeply entrenched and tenacious to be changed without superhuman courage.

Human beings were therefore neither absolutely free nor totally determined, but free within limits. The depth and extent of the limits were not and could not be the same for all. They depended on such factors as their capacity for self-analysis, moral honesty, willpower, and the kind of society in which they lived. A cooperative and relaxed society, whose members freely commented on each other's conduct and contributed to their self-knowledge, was more conducive to their self-transformation and freedom than one in which they scrupulously kept their distance.

Not how to be absolutely:free or fully autonomous but how to change in harmony with one's truth was the central moral problem for Gandhi, as for most Hindu thinkers. Faced with a ceaselessly changing world, the self must change or risk disintegration. And critical self-reflection constantly exposed failings and limitations which a moral being should try to overcome. The art of living consisted in how to change and yet 'remain true to oneself, how to grow without losing one's being without losing a sense of balance and coherence. A wise man resisted attractive but impossible ideals, knew and lived in harmony with his constitution, and strove for goals that accorded with his 'truth'.

Unlike the traditional liberal conception of individuality which stresses differences:from others and is necessarily comparative, integration or wholeness in Gandhi's sense referred to the individual's relation to himself rather than to others and to his manner of ontologically carrying himself in the world. An integrated individual had integrity and was always 'true' or 'honest' to himself. In being true to himself and changing at his own pace, he retained his uniqueness or individuality, which was thus a by-product of self-integration and not a form of eccentricity or an abstract desire to be different from others. Individuality presupposed inner coherence, and the latter in turn required critical self-reflection. An unreflective person, one not in the habit of reflecting on and reconstituting her being, was constantly in danger of becoming an eclectic collection of borrowed and discordant properties. Critical self-reflection was the source of self-knowledge, and a necessary condition of wholeness and individuality.

As an uniquely constituted and situated being, each individual necessarily saw and experienced the world differently and formed his own beliefs and opinions. To force him to act against his sincerely held beliefs was to violate his truth, to ask him to be untrue to 'himself, to plant a lie at the very heart of his being. He might be mistaken, but he must discover that for himself. Others might, indeed they had a duty to, argue with him and to show him why he was mistaken. If he remained unpersuaded, they should leave him alone. For Gandhi respect for an individual's integrity or wholeness requited that his views should grow out of *his* way of looking at the world and reflect *his* truth. That was why persuasion was qualitatively different from coercion. Unlike the latter, it respected and reinforced the other's wholeness, and ensured that the new way of looking at the world took roots in and grew out of his changed being. To seek to persuade someone was to cooperate in reconstituting his being. Gandhi thought that an individual could be legitimately compelled only when his conduct had grave social consequences and when he could not be deterred in any other way. And even then no euphemism or verbal sophistry should be allowed to obscure the fact that compulsion violated his truth or integrity and was a regrettable necessity.

For Gandhi freedom consisted in being true to oneself, in living by 'one's own light' and growing at 'one's own pace'. It was form of wholeness or integrity. It involved knowing and accepting oneself as one was, recognizing one's limits and possibilities, and making choices on the basis of that knowledge. It my way of life suited me and if I was content with it, I did not cease to be free simply because I had not chosen it. Or if I realised on reflection that a specific desire did not harmonize with my being and decided not to gratify it, I could not be said to be unfree simply because I had to restrain my desire. Freedom did not consist in choice *per se* as some liberals argue, nor in making choices considered to be *higher* as the idealists argue, but in making choices in harmony with and capable of being integrated into one's being. It had nothing to do with the *number* of alternatives available to the agent either. If they did not include the one she needed, they had no significance for her. And if the one she needed was the only one available to her, the absence of others in no way diminished her freedom.

Like many Indian philosophers, Gandhi subsumed freedom under truth. Only the free man, that is, one able to make his choices and decisions himself was able to discover, develop and live by his unique ontological truth. Freedom was thus the necessary basis and precondition of one's ability to be true to oneself. To deny, a man freedom was to force him to be untrue to himself and to live by someone else's truth. For Gandhi the case for freedom was simple, and the same as that for truthfulness. Respect for truth implied respect for human beings as they were constituted at a given point in time, and for their desire to live by their truth. Love of truth involved love of one's fellow-men as they were constituted, and not as one would like them to be. It could never therefore justify 'forcing them to be free' or sacrificing them at the altar of an abstract and impersonal ideal.

Even as Gandhi radically redefined the concept of freedom, he redefined the concept of equality. In much of the liberal and socialist literature on the subject, equality is defined in comparative, contractual, competitive and individualist terms. As we saw earlier, for Gandhi men were necessarily interdependent, rose and fell together, and were born subject to non-repayable debts. He located the idea of equality in this context. Relations between human beings were mediated by their membership of the social whole, and thus non-atomic and noncontractual in nature. Human beings grew and fell together, and hence their relations were necessarily noncompetitive and non-conflictual. And since they were uniquely constituted and had different needs and capacities, they were inherently non-comparable and could not be treated according to a uniform standard.

Since society was necessarily a fellowship of unique and interdependent beings, the concept of equality had to be defined in non-comparative, noncompetitive and non-atomic terms. For Gandhi, it basically consisted in each individual enjoying full access to his community's economic, political, moral and cultural resources in order to realise *his* unique potential; that is, not an abstract human potential as determined by a philosophical conception of human nature or by an arbitrary moral standard, but his potential *as an uniquely constituted being*. As a progressive and reflecting being each individual 'grew from truth to truth' and strove to enrich, deepen and reconstitute his being. Equality of human beings consisted in all alike being able to do so. It did not mean that I should get what others get, but rather that I should get what I need for my development as I define it. It was not only in my interest but that of all others that they should treat me equally, for in degrading and demeaning me they degraded and demeaned themselves and deprived themselves of the contribution I would make as a rich human being. Equality thus was not a mechanical concept or a synonym for uniformity. It was at bottom a relationship of mutuality and fellowship.

Gandhi also redefined the concept of citizenship. As a political activist he knew that not consent, nor will, nor fear, but cooperation was the basis of the state. Every state, democratic or otherwise, depended on the cooperation of its citizens, be it silent or vocal, passive or active, willing or unwilling. Since the state was an agency of action, their cooperation consisted in rendering it such specific services as carrying out its orders, paying taxes, and obeying the law. The state did not exist independently of its citizens, and was ultimately nothing more than a system of institutionalized cooperation between them. Since the state was a vast and complex organisation, they did not notice that it was their acts of daily cooperation that sustained it and that they were morally responsible for all it said and did.

Every government was tempted to misuse its power, and the democratic government was in that respect no better than the autocratic. What distinguished the two was the fact that one did and the other did not succumb to the temptation. And that was so because a democratic government knew that if it did, its citizens would refuse to cooperate with it. Notwithstanding all its institutional checks and balances, a democratic government could easily turn evil if its citizens became apathetic, vulnerable to corruption and manipulation, or lost their sense of moral responsibility. For Gandhi the virtues and vices of a government were not inherent in it but derived from those of its people. It was the coward who created the bully, the worm which encouraged others to trample on it, the morally irresponsible citizen who created a tyrant.

As a moral being the citizen had a duty to decide whom to give his loyalty and support and under what conditions. His self-respect and dignity required that his loyalty should not be unconditional or taken for granted. When a law was just, he had a 'sacred duty' to give it his 'willing and spontaneous obedience'. The duty had a dual basis. As a moral being he had a general duty to do or support the good. And as a citizen he had a specific moral duty to the community into which he was born and rooted, by which he was profoundly shaped, whose benefits he had enjoyed, and to whose members he was bound by the ties of loyalty and mutual expectation. If a law was unjust or morally unacceptable, he had a duty to protest against and even to disobey it. To obey an unjust law was to 'participate in evil' and to incur moral responsibility for its immoral consequences. In Gandhi's view it was a 'mere superstition' and an attitude worthy of a 'slave' to believe that a citizen should uncritically obey all laws. To be a citizen was to be co-responsible for the activities of the government. And to obey a law was necessarily to support the government. Citizenship was not an autonomous and discrete role, but a mode of expressing and realizing one's wholeness and humanity through the medium of the state. No human being could extend uncritical and absolute support to the state without forfeiting his humanity.

I have so far concentrated on Gandhi's thought, and that is only a small and ultimately perhaps not the most important part of his remarkable life. Unlike men of thought whose ideas can be detached from and examined in isolation from their lives, Gandhi's thought, like that of Jesus and the Buddha, is deeply embedded in and of a piece with his way of life. His ideas grew out of his reflections on his experiences, even as his life represented a determined attempt to live out the ideals he espoused. The two formed a unity such that his ideas are best articulated not in the books and articles he wrote but in the kind of life he lived. His life was his greatest book and provides the most reliable clue to his writings.

For the first thirty odd years of his life, Gandhi was a *Grihasthi* who, in dutiful obedience to the conventions of his society, married, raised children, and discharged his social obligations. After that he felt free to disregard the social conventions and to write the script of his life as he thought proper. His central moral passion from now onwards was to attain *moksha*" a Hindu concept which had exercised him greatly for the past few years and which he radically redefined in the light of his understanding of his own religious tradition as well as Christianity and Judaism. In this redefinition *moksha* meant three things: first, total mastery of all 'the senses including sexuality; second, a mind freed of fear, jealousy, pettiness, meanness, vanity, and so on; and third, total dissolution of the sense of selfhood and the consequent identification-with all living beings in a spirit of universal love and dedication to the cause of 'wiping away every tear from every eye'.

The first two primarily related to the personal, and the third to the social and political areas of life. Gandhi carried on an intense struggle at all three levels and sought to forge a pure and beautiful soul. The struggle was fierce and uncompromising and marked by moments of doubts and despair, but the overall result was a life of rare moral and spiritual grandeur.

A few random incidents of his remarkable life tell the story. During one of his many periods of incarceration, a black warder was bitten by a scorpion. When Gandhi heard his screams, he rushed to the spot, called for a doctor, and in the meantime started sucking out the poisoned blood, without the slightest thought for his life and in utter disregard of his own bleeding teeth. He went on spitting out the sucked blood until the victim felt relief, and quietly left the place as if nothing had happened.

Indulal Yajnik, his one-time close colleague, turned against him and wrote a vicious attack on him. He regretted this later and went to Gandhi to apolozise. It was Gandhi's day of silence. He saw Yajnik among his visitors and, before the latter could say anything greeted him with a reassuring smile and sent him a hastily scribbled note complementing him for changing sides only once whereas he, Gandhi, had done so more often. The poor Yajnik was in tears.

Maulana Azad, the Congress President, had without Gandhi's knowledge and against his wishes sent Stafford Cripps, the visiting British minister, a confidential note saying that he and the Congress had an open mind on the partition of India. When Cripps called on Gandhi, he was surprised to find that Gandhi knew nothing about the note and left it with him to mull over. When Azad went to see Gandhi the next day, the latter asked him if there was any communication between him and Cripps. Azad lied. Although his note to Cripps was lying on Gandhi's desk, Gandhi kept quiet. After Maulana's departure Gandhi's secretary suggested that the note should be copied and kept for a future occasion. Gandhi rebuked him, asked him to return the original to Cripps, and blamed himself for being unworthy of Azad's trust.

At one of his prayer meetings in 1947, a bomb exploded. As the frightened crowd began to scatter, Gandhi rebuked it for being frightened of a 'mere bomb', and continued to pray unperturbed. When the Government of India insisted that he should henceforth curtail his activities or at least accept protection, he rejoined that both courses of action compromised his commitment to nonviolence and were unacceptable to him. When Indian independence was drawing near, there was extensive inter-communal violence. Gandhi was deeply distressed and thought his entire life a failure. Not given to despair and defeat, he decided to fight the wave of violence single-handed.

Disregarding their physical safety, he and his followers fanned out into remote trouble spots and strove to create inter-communal peace. Believing, wrongly in my view, that he would be able to end the violence only if he eliminated all traces of violence and aggressiveness in himself, he embarked upon the daredevil experiments of sleeping naked with his female associates to achieve total purity Although attacked and shunned by his colleagues, he stuck to his guns. Just because they had made him a Mahatma, he was not prepared to confirm to their expectations of him.

His life was his and it had to be based on *his* truth. If that meant losing his Mahatmahood, he was only too happy to shed the burden, and if it involved public criticism, he was prepared to brave it so long as he was convinced after deepest reflection that his action was right. Such an uncompromising spirit of moral independence is rare in any society; in a largely conventional India, it stood out as an enduring public symbol of dissent and defiance.

It is difficult to say whether or not and which of Gandhi's ideas would prove of lasting value. However there is little doubt that his life had a rare grandeur about it. His uncompromising commitments to truth and justice, his courage to write the script of his life himself, his relentless search for coherence and wholeness, his total lack of fear, his constant experiments with the possibilities of human existence, and so on are lasting sources of inspiration. As Gandhi said in 1937, 'My writings should be cremated with my body. What I have done will endure, not what I have said or written'. His life is surely his greatest legacy. And since it was a carefully crafted text, his thought too shares in its permanence.

Contribution of Gandhi's Nonviolence to World Civilization

All over the world, in different ways and in different fields, several developments are taking place that indicate a growing interest in a non-materialistic, nonviolent alternative to present modes of thinking. Whether or not those involved in these developments use or are even aware of Mahatma Gandhi's name and message, they are nevertheless promoting the values and principles he stood for.

I will discuss this with reference to different types of movements some small, some big, but each of them sharing the new directions to peace and freedom for one's country and the world. The only way if we are to even survive another 100 years. I shall dwell in detail on events in South Africa, prior to the Sharpeville incident.

Terrorism and political violence, which stalks us in Kashmir today, made their first newspaper headlines as a result of Palestinian activities. It was the Palestinian guerrillas who master-minded the world's first plane hijack outside of the Cuban area. It is since then that hijacking and other forms of terrorism have spread to various comers of the world, including our own country and Sri Lanka.

Each Palestinian liberation group had attempted to outdo the other in rhetoric and violence, so much so, that the Israel-Arab feud was seen as an inherently bloody standoff. Therefore, it came as a very pleasant surprise to note among all those fighting for Palestinian liberation there was one courageous individual who swore by nonviolence and treated Mahatma Gandhi as his ideal. Today we see a great change in the 'official' Palestinian movement of Yasser Arafat, which is negotiating a settlement with the Israeli government.

This is, in a way, the result of Awad and his group of non-violent followers. Awad was born in 1943, but soon after lost his father in the terrible battles that preceded the creation of the state of Israel. He was therefore raised in an orphanage, and must have experienced the same loneliness and bewilderment that the other young Palestinians did. But unlike his friends, who became active in the various terrorist groups,

Awad felt love and compassion, rather than resentment and bitterness. Not that he felt injustice had not been done to Palestine, but he was convinced that the route to redressal did not lie through hatred and vengeance. He became deeply influenced by Mahatma Gandhi and decided to follow the same tactic of civil disobedience against the Israelies as Gandhi had done against the British. His civil disobedience campaign picked up considerable steam during his tenure as a teacher in a Mennonite school in Beit Jallah, near Bethlehem. Finally, the Israeli authorities would stand it no more, and in 1969 expelled him to the United States.

He returned to Jerusalem, his birth place, in 1983 in order to found the Palestine Centre for Nonviolence. In a short span of five years, his activities had become so very embarrassing to the Israeli authorities that they decided to expel him once again. But the very order of expulsion turned him into a hero, getting him support from many unexpected quarters. Even the Reagan administration, no great champion of nonviolence, protested, insisting that "you need more Awads in Jerusalem" to promote nonviolence.

Mubarak Awad was proud to be a trouble maker. Strite returning to his native East Jerusalem in 1983, the 44-year old naturalized American citizen agitated for nonviolent resistance to the Israeli occupation of the West Bank and Gaza Strip. A self-proclaimed disciple of Mahatma Gandhi, Awad urged a program of disruption and civil disobedience, including tax resistance, boycott and "the deliberate commission of (other) illegal acts".

But the other implication of the accusation that A wad was a "troublemaker" was not quite fair. While it was true that the Israeli authorities look upon him that way, especially because they were at a loss to know how to deal with him, the fact of the matter was that A wad wanted to end and not make trouble. Gandhi too was called a 'troublemaker' by the British authorities, but they were able to come to terms at the end of the colonial era with much less trouble, and much more dignity, than any of the other Imperial powers, because of Gandhi. The fact that British nationals like Attenborough and Marjorie Sykes were among Gandhi's greatest admirers was no coincidence. Similar to Gandhi is the impact that A wad created among the Israelies. To the authorities, he was a 'troublemaker', but among the citizens, many looked upon him as the hope of the future. The reason is simple. A wad was planting the seeds of nonviolence among the Palestinians.

The work of Mubarak A wad was proof that the Gandhian ideal was being kept alive even in the unlikeliest of places by a new generation of dedicated, idealistic workers.

On 14 May 1987, the Fiji government was ousted by a military coup led by lieutenant Colonel Sitiveni Rabuka. The response to Rabuka's regime both within Fiji and overseas provided a useful test of the theory and the practice of nonviolent action.

Fiji was taken over by the British as a colony in the 1870s. The native peoples are ethnically Malanesian. The British brought indentured workers from India to work on the sugar plantations. Today, the Indo-Fijians-born and bred in Fiji with ancestors from India make up half the population of 7,00,000. Malanesians make up 45% and Europeans, part-Europeans and others the remainder.

From independence until 1987, the Alliance Party held power under Prime Minister Ratu Sir Kamisease Nara. The Alliance was built and supported by Malenesians, Fijians. The opposition National Federation Party (NPP), which was built around and supported by Indo-Fijians, was riven by splits. The 'general electors', associated with the small European population, supported the Alliance. In effect, ethnic divisions were exploited by the chiefs, using the vehicle of the Alliance Party, to mobilize support for a feudal-style hierarchy which put them in a privileged position.

In 1985 the multi-racial Fiji Labour Party was formed. It was an attempt to promote class-based, rather than race-based, politics. The Labour Party criticized both other parties for serving the rich, and promoted the claims of workers, the unemployed and the poor.

The Labour Party rapidly gained strength and several NPP politicians defected to its ranks. In the 1987 election, the Labour Party joined with the NPP as a coalition and together they won control of parliament. It was this government that only six weeks later was toppled by a military coup.

The Fiji coup is being discussed from the point of view of opposing coups with nonviolent action within and without the country concerned. I would like to discuss possible actions that could have been taken against the coups, especially by people of other countries, the pressure of international public opinion and governments. The Australian Government, which had cut off aid to Fiji, decided to resume part of the aid, keeping in suspense a major part of it, till a democratic political system was restored in Fiji. This showed both the weakness and strength of outside forces. Australia, should have continued a total ban to pressurize Rabuka fully-nevertheless it was still a potentially strong method, one which needed to be boosted and strengthened.

Nonviolent action is a form of political action which encompasses methods such as demonstrations, boycotts, strikes, sit-ins, parallel governments and a host of other techniques. Social defence can be defined as the use of nonviolent action to serve as an alternative to military defence. As a proposed alternative to military force, social defence can be used in two basic ways. First as a defence against a foreign invasion. Here the best example is the spontaneous Czechoslovak resistance to the Soviet invasion in 1968. Another example is the German resistance in 1923 to the French occupation of the Ruhr. Nonviolent resistance within Fiji had taken a variety of forms.

At the most basic level, numerous people had spoken out against Rabuka's regime, criticizing its illegality and violations of human rights. Members of the Labour Party tried to build grassroots support, travelling to villages and explaining how the 1970 constitution guaranteed the right of Malenesian Fijians. There were demonstrations and strikes in cities, and many shopkeepers closed their shops in protest. Even more powerfully, workers in the cane fields stopped work; the threat of failure of the sugar crop, Fiji's major export earner, was a serious one. Of long-term significance, many Fijians emigrated to escape the repressive political system and those who left were mostly the educated and highly skilled.

The resistance to the Fiji military regime had been explicitly and consistently nonviolent.

The coup in Fiji, on the other hand, also succeeded with a minimum of force. There were relatively few soldiers involved. If there had been a concerted non-resistance from the outset, possibly the initial coup could have been thwarted. But the reality was quite different from this hypothetical resistance. A large number of Malenesian Fijians supported the first coup, while the Indo-Fijians failed to put up a show of support for the government. The mass rallies during the election campaign in support of the Labour Party failed to materialize in opposition to the coup.

The initial coup succeeded because it drew upon the ethnic divisions in Fiji, mobilizing Malenesian Fijians and demoralizing Indo-Fijians. The use of ethnic divisions for political purpose has a long history in Fiji. The Labour Party itself represented a challenge to this political use of ethnicity, and the coup represented a reversion to the status quo.

Also involved in the early support for and acquiescence to the coup was the lack of vehement opposition by figures of powerful symbolic importance.

The dilemma was not the implementation of nonviolent action, but rather the difficulty of mobilizing people to take action. Without strong support from key symbolic figures, in the face of long-standing ethnic and other divisions, and lacking leadership, preparation and training in nonviolent action and strategy, a unified response was not made. This negative assessment should not obscure the considerable and powerful resistance that did occur and had forced Rabuka to form some sort of 'popular' Government. The point here is that nonviolent action theory devotes much more attention to the consequences of actions that are actually taken, than to the structural and ideological obstacles to taking action in the first place.

Another neglected area in the theory of nonviolent action is the role of groups outside what seems to be the immediate area of struggle. In the case of Fiji, a large number of people in other countries were startled and disturbed by the coup. Outside Fiji, the stated reasons for the coup sounded hollow;

and the ethnic divisions which helped sustain the new regime had little salience. However, outside pressure was not enough to restore democracy in Fiji. There are various methods whereby people and countries from outside could have used nonviolent methods to help overthrow oppressive regimes.

The following methods can be used vigorously for effective results: (1) attacks from various types of media; (2) The stoppage of all economic and military aid; (3) The holding of public meetings to support peoples resistance within the affected country; (4) Action by foreign Governments against the illegal regimes by not recognizing such regimes; (5) The public lobbying their own Government for this; (6) Action through international trade union movements to stop the flow of goods and services to and from the illegal regime; (7) In places like Fiji instant stoppage of tourist traffic to Fiji would have greatly affected the Fiji Government.

If all these actions had been strongly and continuously carried out it is quite possible that Fiji would have been able to overthrow the dictator Rabuka. However the response was not strong enough in these areas and Rabuka continued for long. Non violent action needs to be strengthened and developed internationally so that it can be successfully implemented.

To counteract military attacks and large scale destructions in the world, Gandhi had started a movement to use nonviolence to oppose wars. His teachings on this have led to developments in the world of the concepts of a "Living Wall" and "Peace Army". When the Mahatma was in London in 1932, he met with activists such as Dr. Maude Royden to organize such activities and this started the idea of a Peace Army to counteract the Sino/Japanese War. As a result the Peace Army group issued a letter which became very famous all over the world.

The letter urged that' 'men and women who believed it to be their duty should volunteer to place themselves between the combatants... We have written to the League of Nations offering ourselves for service in such a Peace Army". The Army, wider Sheppard's leadership, was to act as a human barrier between the combatant parties and thus end the fighting. Royden explained that what they wanted was" an army of pacifists who would offer themselves to the League of Nations as the 'shock troops' of peace."

The operation of such an army could only come into being when 'the circumstances were correct, and in this case the proposers believed that they were.

The idea was to put the peace army between the Chinese and Japanese armies along the sea coast of Shanghai to stop the Japanese Navy from unloading its army. Unfortunately, the Peace Army could gather only about 1000 people and therefore could not get the necessary League of Nations or British Government help. Nevertheless it was decided that "a permanent Peace Army should be built up for future emergencies, and for Constructive peace work", The country was divided into districts and subdivided into groups where there were to be active units. The "Anny" was organized into two sections: one composed of the interposing "shock troops" and the other of war resisters who would be willing' 'to render constructive peace service wherever it may be required, or if not able to go themselves, to help in sending others". Contact was attempted with people in a number of different countries, and it was hoped that Peace Annies would eventually be established all over the world.

The tasks of interposition had been too great for the Peace Anny and so emphasis shifted to its second aim of peace making (working to bring about negotiations and mediating) and peace building. Members journeyed to Palestine to undertake reconciliation work. However, the 1938 effort ended in tragedy when one of the two team members, Hugh Bingham, was shot and fatally wounded. From preventing or stopping wars by the interposition of a peaceful buffer force, the focus of pacifist activities in Britain became the Peace Pledge Union organised in 1934 by Canon Sheppard. The Union was sponsored by the likes of Royden and Bertrand Russell and its first secretary was the Christian mystic Max Plowman. At its height in 1937, close to 150,000 Union members had signed the pledge that stated: "We renounce war and never again will we support or sanction another."

The idea was rekindled when British MP Henry Osborne wrote to the *Manchester Guardian,* in 1956, urging that the

United Nations should recruit a volunteer corps of 10,000 unarmed people to patrol and hold a two kilometre-wide demilitarized zone close to the Egyptian!`Israeli border and when former British MP, Sir Richard Acland proposed a similar scheme two years later. While Maude Royden's Peace Anny may not have seen action, the attempt continued to provide inspiration to those who sought peaceful ways of solving international conflict.

Following in her footsteps and reiterating Gandhi's call for a "living wall", another impetus for unarmed peace keeping, found embodiment in a more limited way in the 'World Peace Brigade' and later the "Peace Brigades International" which was re-established in 1960. In that year Spanish writer, pacifist, former League of Nations champion, and political critic, Salvador de Madariaga, and Jayaprakash Narayana, wrote to UN Secretary General Dag Hammarskj old proposing the setting up of a "World Guard".

Hopefully the tradition will continue until the world has finally solved the problem of major bloody international conflicts and the only armies will be the unarmed forces of a world government engaged in peace making and peace building projects, and on the rare occasions where it may become necessary, in peace keeping. Today in face of the Bosnian and Chechniyan conflicts, these moves are all the more needed. Another part of the World in which Gandhi's philosophy of Nonviolence has been accepted as a method to combat injustice and oppression is in Africa, where Gandhi first experimented with peaceful civil disobedience.

Gandhiji had not a shadow of doubt that only through non-violent organisation could the emancipation of the coloured races come and the tragedy of a global clash of colour averted. And so, when Jomo Kenyatta saw him in London during the Second Round Table Conference and asked for a message. Gandhiji scribbled on a leaf of his table diary, "Truth and Nonviolence can deliver any nation from bondage." By then, as he had anticipated, the impact of the Indian struggle had begun to be felt' in South Africa and a number of Africans had begun to apply the moral of the Indian struggle to their own case. They were particularly concerned about three questions:

1. To what quarter should they look for deliverance?
2. Now could they apply the lesson of the Indian struggle to their own case?
3. What help could India render them in their struggle?

In the last years of his life, from the signs of the times and the shape of things to come, Gandhiji had begun to have a very lively apprehension that the clash of colour that was developing in South Africa might one day imperil world peace and even white civilization itself. A wave of awakening had come over the African population and coloured people in other parts of the world also had developed a consciousness of their rights and the injustice they were suffering. Many African freedom movements have been successfully based on the Gandhian methods of nonviolence.

Of the African leaders, Dr. K warne Nkrumah, it is pointed out, had learned about Gandhiji's use of nonviolence when he studied at Lincoln University in the United States. He used it in his country's struggle against British political control. As is well known, that struggle was successful. He was eager to have the idea used by many other African people to help them to win their freedom. In his autobiography, Ghana, Dr. Nkrumah wrote "I began to see that, when backed by strong political organization, it (the Gandhian philosophy of nonviolence) could be the solution of the Colonial problem. Again, many years later,: "We repudiate war and violence". "Our battles shall be against the old ideas that men keep trammelled in their own greed; against the crass stupidities that breed hatred, fear and inhumanity".

Jayaprakash Narayana, in June 1962 had meetings with Mr. Kenneth Kaunda and Mr. Julius Nyerere. According to an interview he gave on his return home, "his discussions with the two leaders had convinced him that the freedom struggle was based on the Gandhian principle of nonviolence. Mr. Kaunda bad told him that he had been deeply impressed by some booklets on the works of Gandhi published in his mother tongue by an Indian many years ago. Mr. Kaunda also told the Indian leader that his people in their tribal life were essentially nonviolent and non-criminal. According to him the crime and violence in their social life was implanted by the Europeans and the Arab slave traders.'

In an interview to M. V. Karnath of The Times of India, Mr. Patrice Lumumba had observed, "We have wrought our freedom by applying the principle of nonviolent action in our fight against Colonialism. This we owe to Mahatma Gandhi.'

Even in South Africa, the political leaders, particularly those of the A N C (African National Congress) used nonviolent peaceful means against the Apartheid Regime, till they were forced to resort to violent protests, at times, after 1961. Their motto was 'by' nonviolence if we can, by violence only if we must". One of the best examples of a nonviolent struggle was that conducted by black women in South Africa against 'passes' in 1956.

The extension of the hated pass system to African women was the subject of more impassioned and widespread protests during 1956 than any other source of grievance. African women in the Orange Free State had resisted the issuance of "passes" to them as early as 1913, and soon afterwards the provincial requirements ceased to be enforced. In 1952, the Natives (Abolition of Passes and Coordination of Documents) Act nominally abolished passes but provided for "reference books" that were to be carried by African youths over sixteen and African women.

The Act applied also to Africans who had formerly been exempt because of their profession, *e.g.* teachers or clerics, they were to carry reference books of a different colour. Government spokesmen argued that the books were protective in nature and essentially the same as the identity-cards required under the Population Registration Act. The Reference book, however, contained work contracts, tax receipts, and other documents essential to the enforcement of' 'influx controls", curfews, and other restrictions. Africans who had formerly been exempt continued to be exempt from curfew regulations, but became subject to influx control.

If an African failed to produce the reference book on demand, he or she was subject to criminal penalties. He was liable to a fine of £ 10 or one month's imprisonment, which meant serving under harsh and degrading conditions as a farm labourer. By 1956, when the government began systematically issuing reference books to all African women, opposition leaders had no difficulty in convincing them that 'passes' were badges of subordinate status, symbols of humiliation and harassment, and instruments for the control and supply of cheap labour. Much of the initiative in organizing demonstrations by women was taken by the Federation of South African Women, a nonracial organization which became an adjunct of the Congress alliance.

The ANC's Women's League worked closely with it but was not formally affiliated with it. Lilian Nagoyi, one of the first Vice-Presidents of the Federation, was elected national president at its conference of August 11-12, 1956, when she was also national President of the ANC Women's League.

Late in 1955 and during 1956, the ANC Women's League and the Federation stimulated a remarkable series of spirited demonstrations by African women, usually outside the offices of Native Commissioners throughout the country. Luthuli, paying tribute to the strength of women in the anti-apartheid movement said in August 1956, "when the women begin to take an active part in the struggle as they are doing now, no power on earth can stop us from achieving Freedom in our Lifetime". An early instance of illegal protest by women occurred on April 9, 1956, in the small town of Win burg in the Orange Free State, where the government had chosen to begin issuing reference books. Several hundred women who had accepted books claimed that they had been "tricked", returned to the site of the magistrate's court, and burned their books. A series of arrests and prosecutions followed.

The most widely publicized demonstrations were multiracial processions through the streets of Pretoria and the gardens of the Union Buildings. The first took place on October 27, 1955, when petitions were left at the door of the minister of native affairs, and the second on August 9, 1956, when petitions were left for the prime minister. The women's leaders also left a statement (Document 15) describing passes for African women as an "insult to all women.' The first demonstration attracted an estimated 1,000 to 2,000 women from the Transvaal. The second attracted a vast and colourful crowd of up to 20,000 women, including about 200 from other provinces, notably Mrs. Luthuli and a group from Stanger, Natal.

Some women members of the Liberal Party joined the demonstration; the women of the Black Sash, originally organized to protest the packing of the Senate, expressed sympathy, but explained that their constitution forbade joining with other bodies. On both occasions, authorities sought to impede the mobilization with tactics similar to those that preceded the Congress of the People. The women also found it necessary to circumvent bans on walking in procession and holding meetings. As 1956 was coming to a close, the government was still moving slowly, issuing reference books only in small, out-of-the-way centres. "The present struggle against the passes for women", said a report of the national consultative committee late in the year, "can well prove to be the decisive turning point of the whole long drawn out war". On December 2, 1956, a regional conference of the Federation in the Transvaal resolved "to organize a final mass protest at the Union Buildings in the event of legislation being introduced to prohibit such demonstrations". Three days later, leading members of the ANC's Women's League and the Federation were among the nineteen women arrested in the treason raids, Because reference books were issued slowly, it was not until December 1960 that all African women expected to possess a reference book and were liable to arrest if they did not.

A series of events early in 1960 appeared to shake the government in some respects, and put it on the defensive. Momentum had begun to gather internationally for a boycott of South African goods. The British prime minister, Harold Macmillan, in a speech before Parliament in Cape Town on February 3, 1960, goaded the Nationalist Party by criticizing apartheid and pro-claiming that' 'winds of change" were sweeping through Africa. The Pan African Congress (PAC) now began to take the lead. The first targets in its unfolding program were abolition of the pass laws and the achievement of a guaranteed minimum wage of £35 ($98) a month for all Africans. African men were to prepare themselves, they said, to receive the call from national headquarters. When the call came, all were to leave their passes at home and surrender for arrest at their, local police stations; no one was to resort to violence or to let himself be provoked by police or agents provocateurs.

The people were to be instructed to observe the rules of strict nonviolence; no one was to resort to violence and emotionalism in the belief that the PAC was trying to engage in "revolutionary warfare". In a somewhat different vein, a party flyer issued at about the same time declared that the pass laws had to be "blown to oblivion this year, now and for ever."

PAC circulars announcing the launching date were already in the streets. "I have appealed to the African people", Sobukwe told the press, "to make sure that this campaign is conducted in a spirit of absolute nonviolence, and I am quite certain they will heed my call... If the other side so desires", he went on, sounding a prophetic note, "we will provide them with an opportunity to demonstrate to the world how brutal they can be. We are ready to die for our cause..." Thirty-five miles south of Johannesburg however, in the industrial complex around Vereeniging, PAC militants had organised well, with little or no competition from the ANC, which had never been strong in that area.

Several hundred men presented themselves for arrest without passes, but the police refused to imprison them on the grounds that jail facilities were inadequate. Military aircraft were sent to swoop low over the assembled crowds in the morning; by night-fall no violent incidents had occurred. At Venderbijl park, a large industrial town about 12 miles from Evaton, several thousand protesters who were gathered at the police station refused to disperse either when the aircraft dived at them or when police threw tear gas. Police fired at protesters who were throwing stones, and two men were killed. A police baton charge eventually scattered the crowd, and by midday police reinforcements began shifting from Venderbijl park to Sharpeville a few miles away, where the demonstration appeared to be getting out of control.

Witnesses sympathetic towards demonstrators testified, both at the official commission of inquiry and at the trial of the Sharpeville PAC leaders, that the crowd was unarmed, amiable, well-mannered, and unaggressive. They estimated that at the time the shooting occurred in the early afternoon, the size of the crowd was between 3,000 and 10,000. Police witnesses testified that the number of people was much larger (official reports placed it at 20,000), that many were armed with sticks and other weapons, and that the crowd's mood was hostile, aggressive and volatile. Tear gas had failed to stop demonstrators marching through the town earlier in the day, and some witnesses estimated that diving aircrafts had only attracted more people to the site of the demonstration. Moreover, apparently unknown to the police, a rumour had spread in the township that a high ranking official was coming to address the crowd at the police station.

The size of the crowd, the insults and threats (including cries of "Cato Manor") shouted by individuals in the throng, combined with the natural anxiety of white men surrounded and outnumbered by people whom they regarded as the "enemy", brought police nerves after several hours to a snapping point. No order was given to shoot, and no warning shots were fired to frighten the crowd back from the fence surrounding the station. In a moment of panic, a line of white police opened fire on the crowd and continued to fire from 10 to 30 seconds, (according to the findings of the commission of inquiry) as the demonstrators fled. Sixty-seven Africans were shot dead, the great majority hit in the back as they ran; 186 others were wounded, including 40 women and 8 children. All this is very reminiscent of the Jallianwalah Bagh tragedy.

At a series of large meetings on Sunday, March 20, PAC speakers had exhorted Africans to avoid violence of any kind, and at two meetings, one in Langa and one in Nyanga, Philip Kgosana, the PAC regional secretary for the western Cape, had delivered a "launching address" (Document 50) quoting Sobukwe's final instructions for the campaign.

At dawn on Monday morning, a large throng marched from Nyanga to Philippi police station, and about 1,500 men gave themselves up for arrest. After their names were taken, they were told to go home and appear in court on a later date. At Langa, large crowds which had gathered in the early morning were ordered by police to disperse. PAC organizers told people to assemble again in the late afternoon, and despite a government order banning further meetings, a crowd estimated at about 10,000 people had gathered at Langa by 5.30 P.M. As at Sharpeville, rumours had spread at Langa that a high official would make an announcement, and the crowd became confused and angry when police arrived in force and instead of making the anticipated announcement, launched a baton charge.

When some people resisted this attempt to disperse the crowd, the police used fire-arms and two demonstrators were killed. As the people scattered, full-scale rioting erupted, lasting several hours. Whites on the scene were attacked, public buildings were set afire, African policemen stoned and assaulted, and a coloured driver employed by the Cape Times was killed. By late evening the rioting had subsided, but for the city of Cape Town it was only the beginning of three tense weeks of violence and confrontation.

With this incident the stage of nonviolence had weakened but was not totally given up. African movements, like those all-over, needed to be supported by help and pressure on their governments from outside, a possibility which appeared to be strengthening, with the increasing international move to boycott South Africa.

The incidents I have cited show how far, and in most unexpected places and ways, the Gandhian concept and practice of nonviolence has spread in the world. That it has not succeeded fully in each case, does not invalidate the method, but only points to the need of such movements to persist in the face of violence as Gandhi did, and calls for a much more committed and lasting support for such movements from both people Of their own and through governments. That such movements can succeed is proved by two events such as the anti-Marcos movement in the Philippines and the S. Korean movement displacing the dictators. The strength of nonviolence should not be underestimated but strengthened by all possible means, especially today when violence seems to be on an increase. A ray of light appears with Aung San Suu Kyi's release. Does it not show the power of nonviolent protest exhibited by her and kept alive through her silently in the hearts of millions of Burmese people. This is a powerful pressure, which will have to be reckoned with.

Patriotic Songs in Gujarat (1920-1947): The Gandhian Inspiration

The freedom struggle against British rule, amongst other things, led to the creation of a vast body of patriotic literature in the various languages of India. The Gandhian era, in particular witnessed a tremendous proliferation of patriotic songs which were enthusiastically song all over the country. They were sung collectively at political gatherings and in protest processions, expressing as they did political sentiments of the masses. Utilizing many different folk forms such as-*raasdas, garba, bhajan, akhyan* and *pawda,* riddles, regional popillar lyrics, these songs established a whole new genre, which helped stir the patriotic fervour of the awakened Indian. The folk and popillar literary forms in their turn, acquired new vigour from the patriotic content which infused these songs. Using traditional symbols, popular metaphors and idioms, these songs achieved their aim-to effectively disseminate patriotic and nationalistic messages to the people and to reach their heart.

What was unusual about such songs, was that they were not always written by well-known poets, but were often composed by anonymous patriots, literate and illiterate, who were inspired by the times they lived in and the intense patriotic fervour which pervaded the very air of those times. Because these songs are a reflection of the sentiments of the masses, they give us significant insights into their sociocultural sensibilities, thus providing an important source of study of the history of the freedom struggle from below.

This paper examines popular patriotic songs composed during the Gandhian period in Gujarat, in a historical context, and discusses in particular, songs composed by women who actively involved themselves in the freedom struggle under Gandhiji's guidance.

Gujarat had a variegated pattern of political culture in the pre-Gandhian period, different regions and cities responding differently to British rule. While commercial Ahmedabad was moderate in its politics, Surat remained a centre of agitational politics. Its citizens reacted sharply against unjust British laws in 1844, 1848, 1860 and again in 1878. Its press was both militant and vociferous and the district a stronghold of extremist politics, under the Patidars and Anavil Brahmins. Though, revolutionary politics did not take root in Gujarat, the regions of Baroda and Kheda did witness revolutionary activities under the influence of the Arya Samaj and the presence of revolutionaries such as Aurobindo Ghosh and others in the State of Baroda. The Swadeshi movement, that had developed in Gujarat much before the Partition of Bengal contributed greatly to promoting partriotism and politicizing the urban masses of Gujarat. However, large masses of rural and tribal areas were untouched by political movements.

During the pre-Gandhian period, Gujarati literature dealt some-what sporadically with the themes of patriotism and nationalism. Dalpatram (1820-1898) though an admirer of British rule, was the first poet who in his long poem 'Hunnar Khan ni Chadhai' written in 1851, revealed the spirit of economic nationalism. He pointed out the importance of Swadeshi, explaining how the country was being drained of its wealth by the influx of *Vilayati* or foreign goods. He appealed to start industries. His contemporary, Narmad (1833-1886), in his poems 'Virsinha', 'Sahu Chalo Jeetva Jang', 'Jai Jai Garvi Gujarat', demonstrated a fiery patriotic zeal. The first patriotic novel *Hind ane Britannia,* written in 1885 by Ichharam Suryaram Desai (1853-1912) boldly criticized British policies in strong, telling phrases which evinced intense patriotic fervour.

B. M. Malabari (1853-1912) (a well known social reformer) and Khabardar (1881-1853), two Parsee poets composed many poems reflecting patriotism. Another noteworthy poet of this period was Harilal Harshadrai Dhruv (1856-1896), whose poems showed his intense devotion for the country and his anti-British sentiments. His collection of songs, *Kunj Vihar,* published in 1895, has a section of poems on *Swadesh Bhakti,* that is, devotion to one's country.

During this period, many amateur poets, inspired by patriotism, wrote patriotic songs and poems that were incorporated later in the collection of popular national songs of the Gandhian period. Vasant Vinodi (Chandulal Desai) a doctor, Maganbhai Patel (1905-1970) and Jivabhai Patel, lawyers, were such poets.

The Gujarat Sahitya Sabha compiled the first collection of patriotic poems entitled '*Deshbhakti Na Kavyo* I in 1905. But it was *Swadeshi Kirtan* which formed the first collection of popular patriotic songs composed to be sung collectively. It was compiled by the Swadeshi Mitra Mandal of Ahmedabad in 1909, priced at only half an anna, in order to invoke *bhakti* or devotion to Hind devi, the new object of worship. The Swadeshi Mitra Mandal was established in 1906 in the wake of the fervour generated during the Bengal Partition Movement.

It organized Swadeshi Kirtan Programmes in order to propagate the idea of *Swadeshi* at the grassroots level. A picture of Hind devi, a new icon, was worshipped at such programmes and popular songs from this collection were sung as *bhajans* or *kirtans*. Thus, a patriotic song was elevated to the status of *bhajan or kirtan*. This was the first successful experiment to utilize a traditional popular literary form for the purpose of infusing patriotism among the masses. This collection contained poems and songs of Narmad; H. Dhruv, Vasant Vinodi, Jivabhai Patel, Maganbhai Patel, Khabardar, etc.

Gandhiji's arrival in Ahmedabad in 1915 soon transformed the political culture of Gujarat. He infused radical ideas and a new life in the political life of Gujarat. He electrified Gujarat. His striking genius is seen in his politically mobilizing all sections and communities of society-Hindus, Muslims, Parsees, mill-owners, traders, workers, peasants, students, women, children, the western-educated middle class, etc. As a result, the freedom struggle assumed the character of a mass movement. Gandhiji's influence was not only confined to political activities but it pervaded the field of education, literature and the social reform movement.

The entire nation breathed in the Gandhian ethos. During this Gandhian period, patriotic songs became the effective carriers of Gandhiji's message to illiterate people of the rural urban and tribal regions. They were written in a simple language and captured the spirit of the age. Through these songs, Gandhian ideas filtered down to the very grassroots. They stirred feelings of patriotism among the masses and inspired them to fight against an unjust, alien rule. They also shaped public opinion. Themes such as Kham, the spinning wheel, temperance, Hindu-Muslim unity, the removal of untouchability, nonviolence, formed the repertoire of these songs. Some songs also had woven into them, stories of national events such as Jallianwalah Bagh tragedy, the Dandi March, etc. These songs not only became an integral part of mass participation in the national movement but were also written to be sung on various occasions such as weddings, festivals, etc.

This period witnessed a great spurt in the writing and composing of patriotic songs. The popular poets of this period were not always intellectuals. Many of them were patriots and were inspired by the love for their country. Many unknown and anonymous poets also composed some famous patriotic songs. Some prolific poets were, the blind poet Hansraj, Vasant Vinodi, Maganbhai C. Patel, Dr. Hariprasad, Lalit, Khabardar, Jyotsnaben Shukla, Keshavdas G. Shah, Gijubhai, Tribhovan Vyas, Kunvarji Mehta, Jugatram Dave, etc. During this period innumerable collections of national and patriotic songs were published. Their price ranged from one paisa to eight annas.

Not always containing great literary merit, these songs were nevertheless important because they echoed the patriotic sentiments of the people, and more significantly, helped to maintain the momentum of the freedom struggle. Their popularity can be evinced from the rapid sale of these booklets. Eight thousand copies of *Sangram Geeto,* published in 1930 by the Satyagraha Chhavni, Ananda were sold out in just four days. Five thousand copies of *Vanarsenana Geeto* written by Gijubhai, published-in 1930, of *Ranshingu,* published in 1930 from Bombay were sold out in two days.

The spinning wheel or *Rentio* became the national symbol of *Swaraj. Khadi* hand spun and hand woven cloth and *Rentio* became the subject matter of many popular songs. In 1922, Maganlal Bapuji (Godhrawala) composed a song in the folk form of *garba* which was addressed to women. It became very famous and popular. Here, the poet appealed to women to give up foreign cloth, pomp, show, fashions and adopt Khadi however coarse it may be. He adds: "by doing so, Oh, my sister, we shall easily win Swaraj."

Another popular song was entitled: 'Balak ni Mangani' (A child's demand) written in simple language, by an anonymous poet.

In 1930, a collection of songs was published by C. P. Chudgar entitled Khadi ane Lagan na Geeto from Wadhwan. Poets were inspired by various events of the freedom struggle and skilfully wove these events into folk and literary forms. Tribhuvan Vyas, teacher and a leading poet from Saurashtra wrote a narrative garba-Ratanbano Garbo-in which the episode of Jallianwalah Bagh was vividly described. This katha or a narrative garba written in verse was set to music while being narrated to the masses. It was an adaptation of the akhyan form or Manbhattas katha form to suit the new context. An anonymous poet composed a popular song Danko Vagyo.. that was sung throughout the Gandhian period. It is in the form of a battle cry.

"There is a battle cry, oh brave soldiers: awake; those who are cowards will flee."

Another notable prolific poet was a blind poet, Hansraj. He hailed from Amreli. His songs reflected intense patriotism in which he expressed his strong anti-British feelings. His long poem "Topiwalana tola Uttarya' became very famous.

The song was published in 1922 and immediately became very popular. The British Government found it seditious and wanted to arrest him, but did not do so because Hansraj was a blind man. Another famous song he wrote was sung by the masses through out the struggle in India, and published on the front page of Navjivan dated 4th June, 1922. It was written in Gujarati-Hindi.

This poem expresses the poet's anger against the oppressive government. Here he most emphatically demands that such an autocratic government should be done away with. The song refers to the massacre of thousands of unarmed people at Jallianwalah Bagh by the oppressive British Government and also the imprisonment of Lala Lajpat Rai after the incident. Swami Ananda wrote in 1922 that whenever this song was sung during the Congress meetings at Ananda, people used to be greatly moved. In 1923, Keshawdas G. Shah published collection of some militant songs entitled Hamara Hakko, from Broach. It was priced at one paisa. He was the manager of the Gujarat Sahitya Mandir of Broach. These songs became popular. Later he restarted his Paisa series from Bhavnagar in 1930 entitled Deshi Geeto ane Swaraj Bansi, Yuddha Geeto ane Swaraj Kirtan, Desh Darpan ane Swaraj Murli, Desh Darshan ane Swaraj Veena, etc.

Quite often, Gandhi, the fountain head of the patriotic movement, was himself the subject of many raasdas and garbas.

During the Bardoli Satyagraha Movement of peasants in 1928, short and simple songs that kept up the spirit and morale of the people were sung in villages. When the rural folk gathered in Sabhas, they sang and danced national garbas and raasdas. Religious songs or bhajans composed by Meera, Narasinha Mehta, Kabir, Brahmanand were also sung at these meetings.

The following songs of Fulchand Shah became popular during the Bardoli Satyagraha.

This song says: "The oppressive rule is tottering because my Bapu's battle cry is heard everywhere."

The Civil Disobedience Movement inspired many poets. The stirring Dandi March became the theme of many popular songs and kathas. A song entitled 'Mohan Mithu Pakave' became popular.

This song describes Gandhiji with his 104 volunteers extracting salt on the shores of Dandi. It also tells how, without any weapon, Gandhiji and his soldiers fought against the oppressive government.

From the 1930s onwards, a number of songs were written on the national flag, or Jhanda. Collections of children's songs and Prabhat Pheris or morning processions, were published in large numbers. All these collections usually repeated older popular songs but added some new songs.

Here it is interesting to note that some collections contained militant songs that overtly criticized the British Government and showed intense hatred of British rule. A series of such collections were published by Shivdas Kesaria (probably a pen-name) in 1930, from Bombay, entitled Sarkarna Uthamnu

(Funeral of the Government), Nar Yagna (Human Sacrifice), Dagmagti Satta (Tottering Power), etc. These collections were priced at one, two to three paise and were sold in great numbers. Militancy in tone as well as in content increased during the Quit India Movement, leading to the confiscation by the government of many such collections of aggressive songs. One such confiscated collection entitled Ranchandi, is discussed in detail in the next section.

A popular representative militant song is cited here:

> *The song says, "Oh Government: it is not too late for you to be cautious. The tolling of your death knell can be heard, and your power is being uprooted, Your boat is drowning, it has become heavy with your past sins. Your bones are melting in the heat of the curse of thirty crores of people."*

Though it is not in the purview of the theme of this paper, a mention may be made of some elitist poets, who inspired by Gandhiji's ideals, wrote patriotic poems. Nahnalal Kavi, Umashankar Joshi, Sundaram, Jhaverchand Meghani, Sneherashmi were some such poets, Meghani's songs gained great popularity among the masses because of its style of folk lore.

A significant feature of the Gandhian period was the wide participation of women in the national movement. Thousands of them left the seclusion of their homes in order to participate in the freedom struggle, They picked shops selling foreign cloth or liquor. They propagated 'Khadi', a symbol of Swaraj. They marched shoulder to shoulder with men in processions and sang patriotic songs. The song became their weapon in the nonviolent struggle. Prabhat Pheri (morning procession), was an important activity, when women went in procession in the early morning, singing national songs. These songs infused the atmosphere with the spirit of patriotism. Gandhiji had advised women to sing appropriate songs and bhajans during the picketing of shops. As a result many songs were specially composed for women, while some women even composed their own songs.

These songs also carried the message of Khadi, Swadeshi, temperance, etc. to women. This was significant as more than

95 per cent of women in India at that time, were illiterate. Nationalistic songs were composed for women to be sung on occasions of wedding, Gorov and Navratra festivals. Folk literary forms such as garbas, kirtan, garbi, katha, traditionally nurtured in Gujarat, were utilized creatively and meaningfully in order to mobilize women politically. These songs used traditional symbols and metaphors in a new context.

Shardaben Mehta, a prominent woman leader reminisces in her book that garbas based on themes of nationalism and women's emancipation were sung by women during the Navratra Festival in the Maha Vidhyalaya of Ahmedabad.6 Many Rashtriya Garbavalis or collections of national garbas were composed during the Gandhian phase.

During the Bardoli Satyagraha many peasant women actively participated in the passive resistance against British rule. Some middle class women leaders such as Sharadaben Mehta, Mithuben Petit, Jyotsnaben Shukla, Bhaktiba, actively encouraged these peasant women in the Satyagraha. Special songs garbas, raasdas were composed to keep up their spirits and morale. Interestingly many women such as Jyotsnaben Shukla, Vadangauri, Pushpaben Vyas, and an anonymous rural lady from Valod, composed national songs.

The last mentioned poetess was a peasant woman and her song 'Dhanya Bardoli' became very famous. The style and language of the song were distinctly rural. The most out-standing among them was Jyotsnaben Shukla who became the leading poet of the Gandhian period and her poems found a permanent place in most of the important collections of national songs. She was not a professional poet but was inspired by patriotism and nationalism.

Jyotsnaben was born in a Brahmin family in Surat in 1892. She studied in the Sanatana Dhanna Kanyashala. In 1904, she was married to Bahusukhram Shukla, a teacher in a Baroda School. Baroda at that time was a centre of revolutionary activities and Mr. Shukla was influenced by revolutionary ideas and their home soon became a meeting place of revolutionaries. Jyotsnaben too was greatly influenced by them and was infused with feelings of patriotism and hatred against British rule. Her natal family, too, was nationalistic in outlook and had adopted the ideal of Swadeshi.

Her husband died in 1914 and she moved to Surat where she became the secretary of the Stree Samaj, a woman's organization. She became an honorary teacher in a girls' school but wrote for journals and newspapers. She had great respect for Gandhiji but did not join the Indian National Congress. However, in 1928 she plunged into the Bardoli Satyagraha and thereafter remained very active in the national movement She became one of the most outstanding women leaders of Gujarat and went to jail many times. The following song written by her became popular during the Bardoli Satyagraha.

This poem praises steadfastness of peasants of Bardoli. It says, "Their brave women inspired them to face death boldly."

Other topical songs were 'Satta Bale Chhe', 'Bardolino Rang', 'Veer Poojan', etc. During the Civil Disobedience Movement of 1930 she wrote 'Swarajnu Mangulsutra' a famous song. Later she also prepared a collection of songs for young girls to be sung during the festival of Gorav. She wrote:

> *"Gonna's husband, Kesaria with spindle and cotton in his hands, is spinning his way to Swaraj."*

Her collection of poems entitled Bapu was published in 1948. It contained poems and songs on Gandhiji composed on different occasions from 1928 to 1948.

In 1930, Rukshmani Ranchhoddas Parekh published a collection of her own poems from Bombay, entitled Swarajya Strotaswini. It had poems on the nationalist themes such as Rentio, Ahimsa, National Flag, Swadeshi, etc.

In the same year, Indumati Chimanlal Sheth and Mrudulaben Sarabhai, eminent women leaders of Ahmedabad and Secretaries of the Videshi Kapad Bhahishkar Samiti, published a collection of national songs entitled Geeto containing songs on Khadi and Swadeshi.'

One of them was important which made a fervent appeal to women to wake up and abandon foreign goods. This collection advertised the use of Khadi.

In Ahmedabad, in 1930, another collection was published consisting of popular songs to be sung for the Prabhat Pheris.

It was compiled and published by Lilavati Harilal Desai, the Secretary of the Picketing Committee, in Ratanpol, Ahmedabad. It was priced at one anna and contained songs for each day of the week.

In 1930, an interesting collection of songs published from Wadhwar, was lagnna gee to, songs to be sung on the occasion of weddings by C. Chudgar. Here again, while the structure and style were of the traditional wedding songs, the content was strongly Gandhian and patriotic. The songs in this collection emphasized the importance of Khadi and Swadeshi. A representative song is cited below:

> *The song welcome guests from the bride's in-law's family and expresses happiness at their wearing Khadi clothes. It congratulates them on obeying Gandhiji's wishes, and on giving up foreign goods for by doing this they are adding to the prosperity of the country.*

In 1942, during the Quit India Movement, songs became more militant and aggressive. Gandhiji had provided the people with an inspiring slogan of 'Do Or Die'. People fought against the British rulers with great determination. As many national leaders were in jail, the angry masses became violent. Poets too became militant and expressed their fury in songs. Many poets wrote garba ongs, invoking fierce goddesses-Chandika, Kali, Durga, Bahuchari, Ambika-to destroy the British empire in India. These garbas were sung and performed at the Navratra festival by urban and rural men and women. The Navratra Festival is dedicated to the goddess Shakti, the universal energy, the almighty and powerful deity who destroys evil.

In Indian mythology she is Mahishasuramardini, the destroyer of the demon Mahishasur. She is invoked by devotees to protect them from evil and demonic powers. Women dance around the Garbo or perforated pot with a lighted lamp inside, a symbol of the goddess herself. Poets of Gujarat, keeping these religious aspects in mind, utilised the 'garbo' for, to express their acute hatred against British rule. They invoked the goddess in order to destroy the oppressive rule of the British. Thus, they added a political dimension to garba. These political garbas were meant to incite people against British rule. Poets retained the garba's traditional lyrical structure and style. In these new political garbas the British were represented as demonic and evil while Indians were represented as benevolent and good. Churchill and other British leaders were depicted as Satanic and wicked, while Gandhiji, Jawaharlal, Vallabhbhai, Subhashchandra were shown as good and heroic.

Ranchandi, a collection of similar defiant garbas was published in 1942 from Bombay by one Kunvarji Shah, the owner of a printing press in Kalbadevi. He edited and published them in the name of Mohanlal Desai, Vasantram Vakil and Munshi Maheshwari. These garbas were ascribed to the poet Chandidas. The collection was nominally priced at one anna. In order to popularize these garbas, the publishers stated that their pennission was not required for reprinting them. This collection of fiery garbas was confiscated by the Government, and Kunvariji Shah, the publisher was arrested and jailed.

Excerpts from three representative garbas cited below, show the intensity of patriotic fervour in these songs. Here the poet expresses his fury against the British. Chandika, the fierce goddess is invoked to burn Britain. It says, "for two centuries, the British have exploited and harassed us, now Chandika, in her rage of fury will destroy them." The poet also exhorts the people of India to be vigilant as the British have not left India in spite of being warned by the 'Quit India' movement. Finally, he feels sure that Britain will definitely be defeated by India as it has already been badly trounced by Japan and Hitler.

This garba in scathing language expresses wrath against the British. The garba is addressed to Britannia (who in the poem is given a male identity) who is asked to pack his bags and leave the country which he has oppressed. Britannia is warned that he faces sure death. Though his empire is in flames, he still does not take care. He is condemned as a shameless, cunning traitor and a liar. The poet adds: "Other invaders in the past looted India but none was as bad as you." He says angrily at the end, "get out Britannia, shame on you! Your power will soon be uprooted."

Here, Bharatmata is shown as sending a letter to the goddess Kali (a fierce goddess) inviting her to come soon and kill the "Topiwallas" (British) with her sharp dagger and to make herself a necklace of their skulls.

All these political and nationalistic garbas had a fiery tone and a patriotic content. These songs sung enthusiastically by the masses reflected the patriotic ethos of the country during the Gandhian period. They formed a significant part of the popular culture of those times. They referred to contemporary events and situations, and were meant to incite people against British rule in a situation which was already volatile, and were greatly successful in their aim.

What is Prayer?

June 10, 1926

A medical graduate asks:

> *What is the best form of prayer? How much time should be spent at it? In my opinion to do justice is the best form of prayer and one who is sincere about doing justice to all does not need to do any more praying. Some people spend a long time over sandhya and 95% of them do not understand the meaning of what they say. In my opinion prayer should be said in one's mother tongue. It alone can affect the soul best. I should say that a sincere prayer for one minute is enough. It should suffice to promise God not to sin.*

Prayer means asking God for something in a reverent attitude. But the word is used also to denote any devotional act. Worship is a better term to use for what the correspondent has in mind. But definition apart, what is it that millions of Hindus, Mussulmans, Christians and Jews and others do every day during the time set apart for the adoration of the Maker? It seems to me that it is a yearning of the heart to be one with the Maker, an invocation for His blessing. It is in this case the attitude that matters, not words uttered or muttered. And often the association of words that have been handed down from ancient times has an effect which in their rendering into one's mother tongue they will lose altogether.

Thus the Gayatri translated and recited in, say, Gujarati, will not have the same effect as the original. The utterance of the word "Rama" will'. instantaneously affect millions of Hindus, when the word "God", although they may understand the meaning, will leave them untouched. Words after all acquire a power by long usage and sacredness associated with their use. There is much therefore to be said for the retention of the old Sanskrit formulae for the most prevalent mantra; or verses. That the meaning of them should be properly understood goes without saying.

There can be no fixed rule laid down as to the time these devotional acts should take. It depends upon individual temperament. These are precious moments in one's daily life. The exercises are intended to sober and humble us and enable us to realize that nothing happens without His will and that we are but "clay in the hands of the Potter". These are moments when one reviews one's immediate past, confesses one's weakness, asks for forgiveness and strength to be and do better. One minute may be enough for some, twenty-four hours may be too little for others. For those who are filled with the presence of God in them, to labour is to pray. Their life is one continuous prayer or act of worship.

For those others who act only to sin, to indulge themselves, and live for self, no time is too much. If they had patience and faith and the will to be pure, they would pray till they feel the definite purifying presence of God within them. For us ordinary mortals there-must be a middle path between these two extremes. We are not so exalted as to be able to say that all our acts are a dedication nor perhaps are we so far gone as to be living purely for self. Hence have all religions set apart times for general devotion. Unfortunately these have nowadays become merely mechanical and formal, where they are not hypocritical. What is necessary therefore is the correct attitude to accompany these devotions.

For definite personal prayer in' the sense of asking God for something, it should certainly be own tongue. Nothing can be grander than to to make us act justly towards everything that lives.

Young India, 10-6-1926

New or Basic Education

This is a new subject. But the members of the Working Committee felt so much interested in it that they gave a charter to the organisers of the Hindustani Talimi Sangh which has been functioning since the Haripura session. This is a big field of work for many Congressmen. This education is meant to transform village children into model villagers. It is principally designed for them. The inspiration for it has come from the villages. Congressmen who want to build up the' structure of Swaraj from its very foundation dare not neglect the children. Foreign rule has unconsciously, though none the less surely, begun with the children in the field of education. Primary education is a farce designed without regard to the wants of the India of the villages and for that Ipatter even of the cities.

Basic education links the children, whether of the cities or the villages, to all that is best and lasting in India. It develops both the body and the mind, and keeps the child rooted to the soil with a glorious vision of the future in the realization.of which he or she begins to take his or her share from the very commencement of his or her career in school. Congressmen would find it of absorbing interest benefiting themselves equally with the children with whom they come in contact: Let those who wish, put themselves in touch with the Secretary of the Sangh at Sevagram.

Adult Education

This has been woefully neglected by Congressmen. Where they have not neglected it, they have been satisfied with teaching illiterates to read and write. If I had charge of adult education, I should begin with opening the minds of the adult pupils to the greatness and vastness of their country. The villager's India is contained in his village. If he goes to another village, he talks of his own village as his home. Hindustan is for him a geographical term. We have no notion I of the ignorance prevailing in the villages. The villagers know nothing of foreign rule and its evils. What little knowledge they have picked up fills them with the awe the foreigner inspires. The result is the dread and hatred of the foreigner and his rule. They do not know how to get rid of it.

They do not know that the foreigner's presence is due to their own weaknesses and their ignorance of the power they possess to rid themselves of the foreign rule. My adult education means, therefore, first, true political education of the adult by word of mouth. Seeing that this will be mapped out, it can be given without fear. I imagine that it is too late in the day for authority to interfere with this type of education; but if there is interference, there must be a fight for this elementary right without which there can be no Swaraj.

Of course, in all I have written, openness has been assumed. Nonviolence abhors fear and, therefore, secrecy. Side by side with the education by the mouth will be the literary education. This is itself a specialty. Many methods are being tried in order to shorten the period of education. A temporary or permanent board of experts may be appointed by the Working Committee to give shape to the idea here adumbrat'd and guide the workers. I admit that what I have said in this paragraph only points the way but does not tell the average Congressman how to go about it. Nor is every Congressman fitted for this highly special work. But Congressmen who are teachers should find no difficulty in laying down a course in keeping with the suggestions made herein.

Women

I have included service of women in the constructive programme, for though Satyagraha has automatically brought India's women out from their darkness, as nothing else could have in such an incredibly short space of time, Congressmen have not felt the call to see that women became equal partners in the fight for Swaraj. They have not realized that woman must be the true helpmate of man in the mission of service. Woman has been suppressed under custom and law for which man was responsible and in the shaping of which she had no hand. In a plan of life based on nonviolence, woman has as much right to shape her own destiny as man has to shape his.

But as every right in a nonviolent society proceeds from the previous performance of a duty, it follows that rules of social conduct must be framed by mutual cooperation and consultation. They can never be imposed from outside. Men have not realized this truth in its fullness in their behaviour towards women. They have considered themselves to be lords and masters of women instead of considering them as their friends and co-workers. It is the privilege of Congressmen to give the women of India a lifting hand. Women are in the position somewhat of the slave of old who did not know that he could or ever had to be free. And when freedom came, for the moment he felt helpless. Women have been taught to regard themselves as slaves of men. It is up to Congressmen to see that they enable them to realize their full status and play their part as equals of men.

This revolution is easy, if the mind is made up. Let Congressmen begin with their own homes. Wives should not be dolls and objects of indulgence, but should be treated as honoured comrades in common service. To this end those who have not received a liberal education should receive such instruction as is possible from their husbands. The same observation applies, with the necessary changes, to mothers and daughters.

It is hardly necessary to point out that I have given a one-sided picture of the helpless state of India's women. I am quite conscious of the fact that in the villages generally they hold their own with their men folk and in some respects even rule them. But to the impartial outsider the legal and customary status of woman is bad enough throughout and demands radical alteration.

Education in Health and Hygiene

Having given a place to village sanitation, the question may be asked why give a separate place to education in health and hygiene? It might have been bracketed with sanitation, but I did not wish to interfere with the items. Mention of mere sanitation is not enough to include health and hygiene. The art of keeping one's health and the knowledge of hygiene is by itself a separate subject of study and corresponding practice. In a well-ordered society the citizens know and observe the laws of health and hygiene.

It is established beyond doubt that ignorance and neglect of the laws of health and hygiene are responsible for the majority of diseases to which mankind is heir. The very high death rate among us is no doubt due largely to our gnawing poverty, but it could be mitigated if the people were properly educated about health and hygiene.

Mens sana in corpore sana is perhaps the first law for humanity. A healthy mind in a healthy body is self-evident truth. There is an inevitable connection between mind and body. If we were in possession of healthy minds, we would shed all violence and, naturally obeying the laws of health, we would have healthy bodies without an effort. I hope, therefore, that no Congressman will disregard this item of the constructive programme. The fundamental laws of health and hygiene are simple and easily learnt. The difficulty is about their observance. Here are some:

Think the purest thoughts and banish all idle and impure thoughts.

Breathe the freshest air day and night.

Establish a balance between bodily and mental work.

Stand erect, sit erect, and be neat and clean in everyone of your acts, and let these be an expression of your inner condition.

Eat to live for service of fellow-men. Do not live for indulging yourselves. Hence your food must be just enough to keep your mind and body in good order. Man becomes what he eats.

Your water, food and air must be clean, and you will not be satisfied with mere personal cleanliness, but you will infect your surroundings with the same threefold cleanliness that you will desire for yourselves.

National Language

And then for all-India intercourse we need, from among the Indian stock, a language which the largest number of people already know and understand and which the others can easily pick up. This language is indisputably Hindi. It is spoken and understood by both Hindus and Muslims of the North. It is called Urdu when it is written in the Urdu character. The Congress, in its famous resolution passed at the Cawnpore session in 1925, called this all-India speech Hindustani. And since that time, in theory at least, Hindustani has been the Rashtra Bhasha. I say 'in theory' because even Congressmen have not practised it as they should have.

In 1920 a/ deliberate attempt was begun to recognize the importance of Indian languages for the political education of the masses, as also of an all India common speech which politically-minded India could easily speak and which Congressmen from the different provinces could under-stand at all-India gatherings of the Congress. Such National language should enable one to understand and speak both forms of speech and write in both the scripts.

I am sorry to have to say that many Congressmen have failed to carry out that resolution. And so we have, in my opinion, the shameful spectacle of Congressmen insisting on speaking in English and compelling others to do likewise for their sakes. The spell that English has cast on us is not yet broken. Being under it, we are impeding the progress of India towards her goal. Our love of the masses must be skin-deep, if we will not take the trouble of spending over learning Hindustani" as many months as the years we spend over learning English.

Students

I have reserved students to the last. I have always cultivated close contact with them. They know me and I know them. They have given me service. Many ex-collegians are my esteemed co-workers, I know that they are the hope of the future. In the heyday of noncooperation they were invited to leave their schools and colleges. Some professors and students who responded to the congress call have remained steadfast and gained much for the country and themselves. The call has not been repeated for there is not the atmosphere for it.

But experience has shown that the lure of the current education, though it is false and unnatural, is too much for the youth of the country. College education provides a career. It is a passport for entrance to the charmed circle. Pardonable hunger for knowledge cannot be satisfied otherwise than by going through the usual rut. They do not mind the waste of precious years in acquiring knowledge of an utterly foreign language which takes the place of the mother tongue. The sin of it is never felt. They and their teachers have made up their minds that the indigenous languages are useless for gaining access to modern thought and the modern sciences. I wonder how the Japanese-are faring. For, their education, I understand, is all given in Japanese. The Chinese Generalissimo knows very little, if anything, of English.

But such as the students are, it is from these young men and women that the future leaders of the nation are to rise. Unfortunately they are acted upon, by every variety of influence Nonviolence offers them little attraction. A blow for a blow or two Of one is an easily understandable proposition. It seems to yield immediate result though momentary.

It is a never-ending trial of brute strength as we see in time of war among brutes or among human beings. Appreciation of nonviolence means patient research and still more patient and difficult practice. I have not entered the list of competitors for the students' hand, for the reasons that have dictated my course about Kisans and Labour. But I am myself a fellow-student, using the word in its broader sense. My university is different from theirs. They have a standing invitation from me to come to my university and join me in my search. Here are the terms:

1. Students must not take part in party politics. They are students, searchers; not politicians.
2. They may not resort to political strikes. They must have their heroes, but their devotion to them is to be shown by copying the best in their heroes, not by going on strikes, if the heroes are imprisoned or die or are even sent to the gallows. If their grief is unbearable and if all the students feel equally, schools or colleges may be closed on such occasions, with the consent of their principals. If the principals will not listen, it is open to the students to leave their institutions in becoming manner till the managers repent and recall them. On no account may they use coercion against dissentients or against the authorities. They must have the confidence that, if they are united and dignified in their conduct, they are sure to win.
3. They must all do sacrificial spinning m a scientific manner. Their tools shall be always neat, clean, and in good order and condition. If possible, they will learn to

make them themselves. Their yarn will naturally be of the highest quality. They will study the literature about spinning with all Its economic, social, moral and political implications.

4. They will be khadi-users all through and use village products to the exclusion of all analogous things, foreign or machine-made.
5. They may not Impose Vande Mataram or the National Flag on others. "they may wear National Flag buttons on their own persons but not force others to do the same.
6. They can enforce the message of the tricolour nag in their own persons and harbour neither communalism nor untouchability in their hearts. They will cultivate real friend-ship with students of other faiths and with Harijans as if they were their own kith and kin.'
7. They will make it a point to give first aid to their injured neighbours and do scavenging and cleaning in the neighbouring villages and instruct village children and adults.
8. They will learn the national language, Hindustani, its present double dress, two forms of speech and two scripts, so that they may feel at home whether Hindi,Urdu is spoken and nagari or Urdu script is written.
9. They will translate into their own mother tongue every thing new they may learn, and transmit it in their weekly rounds to the surrounding villages.'
10. They will do nothing in secret, they will be above board in all their dealings, they will lead a pure life of self-restraint shed an fear and be always ready to protect their weak fellow-students, and ready to quell riots by nonviolent conduct at the risk of their lives. And when the final heat of the struggle comes they will leave their institutions and, if need be sacrifice themselves for the freedom of their country.
11. They will be scrupulously correct and chivalrous in their behaviour towards their girl fellow-students.

For working out the programme I have sketched for them the students must find time. I know that they waste a great deal of time in idleness. By strict economy, they can save many hours. But I do not want to put an undue strain upon any student. I would, therefore, advise patriotic students to lose one year, not at a stretch but spread it over their whole study. They will find that one year so given will not be a waste of time. The effort will add to their equipment, mental, moral and physical, and they will have made even during their studies it substantial contribution to the freedom movement.

I am most grateful to the staff of the Centre of South Asian Studies of the School of Oriental and African Studies for doing me the honour of inviting me to deliver the Annual Lecture. Since the lecture is part of the conference on Gandhi's Legacy, I thought it proper to devote it to that theme. Both the conference and the lecture mark the 125th anniversary of Gandhi's birth. The anniversary is particularly important and even poignant because Gandhi had repeatedly declared that he wished to live until that age. Believing in the power of the spirit over the body, he saw no reason why a spiritually and, physically disciplined life should remain confined to the conventional maximum of a hundred years.

Even nearly four decades after Gandhi's death, opinions about his achievements remain deeply divided. For some he was too implacably hostile to modem civilization to offer an adequate understanding of its nature, let alone provide answers to its malaise. For them he was basically a man of action whose major or even. sole contribution consisted in leading his country's struggle for independence. Some of his critics regard even this as a mixed legacy.

They argue that his basically conservative, puritanical, pro-bourgeois and pacifist thought hindered the development of radical political movements, did much long-term harm to the cause of the *Dalits,* burdened the Indian psyche with a paralyzing sense of guilt about economic development, hampered the emergence of a strong and powerful state, created a national schizophrenia about the need to acquire and exercise political power, and perpetuated unrealistic and confused ideas about human sexuality.

Gandhi's admirers take a radically different view. For them he was a man of both thought and action, a rare combination. As a man of thought he saw through the malaise and madness of modernity, and offered an alternative vision that combined the best insights of both the pre-modem and modem world-views while avoiding the confusions and contradictions of the currently fashionable post-modernism. Indeed, argue his admirers, if Indians were to be asked to mention their greatest twentieth-century thinker, most would unhesitatingly refer to Gandhi and would feel hard pressed to mention another. Gandhi was also a man of action, and was unique in acting at both political and personal levels.

He led the greatest anti-colonial struggle in history, organised his deeply divided countrymen, gave them a sense of collective pride, forged tools of collective action that continue to stand India in good stead, and developed a unique method of struggle that combined the energy and effectiveness of violence with the peacefulness and humility of nonviolence. At the personal or moral level, he restlessly strove to create a beautiful soul free of all that was petty, mean, coarse and vulgar, successfully embarked upon a most heroic struggle to conquer all his senses including sexuality, and offered a rare example of how to lead a political life without compromising one's integrity.

Some of Gandhi's admirers go even further and argue that we should not be surprised if one day he were to prove as influential, and be placed on the same footing, as Jesus of Nazareth and the Buddha. Einstein set the tone for such a view when he remarked in a tribute to Gandhi on his seventieth birthday: 'Generations to come, it may be, will scarce believe that such a one as this in flesh and blood walked upon this earth' Ralph Boultjens echoed Einstein's view in 1984:

> *Thirty-five years after the crucifixion of Jesus Christ there was no indication that Christianity would emerge as one of the great spiritual forces of history. Around 450 B.C., three decades after the death of Confucius, nobody could have predicted how influential his ideas eventually became. And around 1915, thirty years after Karl Marx, the Communist movement seemed doomed to be an*

inconsequential political aberration. Perhaps, then we are too near Gandhi to evaluate his impact on history.

In my view Gandhi's detractors underestimate the originality of some of his ideas, the depth of his political and moral influence on India and on the rest of the world, and the sheer grandeur and moral beauty of his life. By contrast his worshippers make the opposite mistake of ignoring his confusions and ambiguities as well as the dark underside of some of his ideas and actions.

Since this is not the occasion to undertake a detailed critical assessment of Gandhi and to arbitrate between his detractors and worshippers, I have decided to concentrate on what I take to be of lasting value in his life and thought. Accordingly I shall take three areas for close examination. I have selected these three because they relate to issues that agonise us today and about which Gandhi has something extremely important and original to say. These are first, the nature of fundamentalism and religious identity; second the sources of human suffering and an adequate theory of social change; and third, Gandhi's redefinition of fundamental liberal values and his attempt to give them a much-needed moral and ontological depth.

Religious fundamentalism has been a considerable source of violence and suffering in recent years in almost every part of the world, including such developed countries as the U.S.A. and such developing countries as Iran, Pakistan, and India. Fundamentalism is a frightened religion's response to the crisis of identity and integrity, and consists in seeking to recapture and uncompromisingly assert what it takes to be its fundamental beliefs and practices.

Fundamentalism cannot be countered by abstractly condemning either the religious consciousness itself or its perversions in a spirit of secularist fundamentalism. The best way to deal with it is to understand and criticize it from within, and to show how the fundamentalist approach to religion, although understandable in a specific historical context, profoundly corrupts and ultimately destroys the integrity of the religious consciousness itself. I can think of few who-Understood the nature of religious consciousness and undermined fundamentalism from within the religious perspective itself as sensitively and effectively as Gandhi did.

For Gandhi every major religion articulated a unique vision of God and emphasized different features of the human condition. The idea of God as loving Father was most fully developed in Christianity, and the emphasis on love and suffering was also unique to it. As he put it: 'I cannot say that it is singular, or that it is not to be found in other religions. But the presentation is unique'. Austere and rigorous mono-theism and the spirit of equality were 'most beautifully' articulated in Islam. The distinction between the Impersonal, and conceptions of God, the principle of the unity of all life and the doctrine of *ahimsa* (nonviolence) were distinctive to Hinduism. For Gandhi every religion had a distinct moral and spiritual ethos and represented a wonderful and irreplaceable 'spiritual composition'. To a truly religious person all religions should be 'equally dear'.

Gandhi argued that since God was infinite and since the limited human mind could grasp only a 'fragment' of Him and that too inadequately, every religion was necessarily limited and partial. Even the religions claiming to be directly revealed by God were revealed to men with their fair share of inescapable human limitations and were communicated in the necessarily inadequate human languages.

For Gandhi, every man was born into a particular religion. Since no religion was wholly false, he should be able to work out his destiny in and through it. And if he felt attracted to some aspects of another religion, he should be at liberty to borrow them. When Madeleine Slade wished to become a Hindu, Gandhi advised her against it. She should, he insisted, live by her own Christian faith and absorb into it whatever-she liked in Hinduism. Merely changing over to a new religion would not improve her conduct or way of life, the only thing that ultimately mattered. When they were overwhelmed with doubts, Gandhi encouraged his Christian mends to draw new inspiration and strength from their own religion. An American missionary, Stanley Jones, spoke for many of them when he said that Gandhi had reconverted him to Christianity. In a different context he told his Jewish mend, Mrs. Polak, that she need not 'become' a Christian in order to 'be' one. She could draw inspiration from Jesus's life and teachings and live *like* a Christian without ceasing to be a Jew.

Religions are commonly thought of as closed worlds, almost like sovereign states zealously guarding their territorial boundaries. No one is allowed to belong to more than one religion, or to borrow the ideas and practices of another, without feeling guilty or threatened at the dilution of his or her religious identity. Interfaith dialogue is therefore expected to occur within and to do nothing to weaken the religious boundaries. Gandhi took a very different view. For him a religion was not a monolithic structure of ideas and practices, but a *resource* from which one freely borrowed whatever one found attractive and persuasive. As such, it was a collective property and a common human heritage. Every man was born into and deeply shaped by a specific religious tradition which as it were constituted his original family. He also enjoyed varying degrees of membership of other cultural and religious families, to whose achievements he enjoyed an unrestricted right of access.

Gandhi said that as a Hindu he was an heir to its rich and ancient heritage. As an Indian he was a privileged inheritor of its diverse religious and cultural traditions. As a human being the great achievements of mankind constituted a collective human capital to which he had as much right as their native claimants. While remaining firmly rooted in his own tradition, he therefore felt free to draw upon the moral and spiritual resources of the others. To express the two central ideas of rootedness and openness, he often used the metaphor of living in a house with its windows wide open to allow cultural winds from all directions to blow into it and to enable him to breathe fresh air at his own pace and in his own way. *Ano Bhadra ritavo yantu vishvatah* (May noble thoughts from all-over the world come to us) was one of his favourite classical maxims.

Gandhi took full advantage of his self-proclaimed intellectual freedom. He abstracted what he took to be the central vales of Hinduism and set up a critical dialogue, even a confrontation, between them and those derived from other religious traditions. Thus he took over the Hindu concept of *ahimsa* (nonviolence), in his view one of its central moral principles. He found it negative and passive and reinterpreted it in the light of the activist and socially-oriented Christian concept of *caritas*. However, he felt that the latter was too emotive, led to worldly attachments and compromised the agent's self-sufficiency, and so he redefined it in the light of the Hindu concept of *anasakti* (non-attachment). His double conversion, his Christianization of a Hindu category after he had suitably Hinduized the Christian concept, yielded the novel idea of an active and positive but detached and non-emotive love.

Again, he took over the traditional Hindu practice of fasting as a protest, combined it with the Judaic concept of representative leadership, and the Christian concepts of vicarious atonement and suffering love, interpreted and reinterpreted each in the light of the others, and developed the amazing notion of a 'voluntary crucifixion of the flesh'. It involved fasting undertaken by the acknowledged leader of a community to atone for the evil deeds of his followers, to awaken their senses of shame and guilt, and to mobilize their moral and spiritual energies for redemptive purposes.

For Gandhi a religion was not a sovereign system of authoritative beliefs and practices which its adherents may violate only on pain of punishment, but a great cultural resource which, like great works of art and literature, belonged to all mankind. One did not have to *be* a Christian in order to feel entitled to adopt Christian beliefs and practices. And a Hindu or a Muslim who did so did not *become* a Christian. Indeed, the very terms Christian, Hindu and Muslim were mistaken and a source of much mischief. They reified respective religions, set up rigid boundaries between them, sanctioned false proprietary claims, and created a psychological and moral pressure towards conformity. In the ultimate analysis, argued Gandhi, there were neither Christians nor Hindus, only whole and unfragmented human beings who freely helped themselves with the moral and spiritual resources of these and other great religious traditions.

One could admire Jesus and even accept him as the son of God, but one could also hold the Buddha, Moses, Mahavira, Zarathustra and others in equally high regard Men and women who did so belonged to their specific religions but also to several others. They were Christians or Muslims or Buddhists in the sense that these religious traditions were their native homes or points of spiritual orientation, and satisfied them the most. However they also cherished and freely drew upon other religious traditions, and carried parts of these into their religion. Whatever one may think of Gandhi's views, he offers the clearest antithesis to fundamentalism and shows that the religious identity, like other kinds of identity, is both rooted and open, both firm and flexible, and is constantly reconstituted in the light of the agent's constantly changing self-understanding. As Gandhi rightly stressed, cultural and religious identities are neither primordial and unalterable as the fundamentalist imagines, nor volitionalist projects to be undertaken and executed at will as the secular rationalist maintains, but products of periodic self-reconstitution based on the inherited resources of one's tradition as interpreted and enriched in the light of changing needs and knowledge of other traditions.

Gandhi saw more clearly than most other writers both the interdependence of human beings and the ways in which systems of domination were built up and sustained. He argued that all systems of domination rested on a profound misunderstanding of human nature, and wrongly assumed that it was possible for one man or group of men to harm another without also harming themselves. Human beings were necessarily interdependent and formed an organic whole. An individual owed his existence to his parents without whose countless sacrifices he would neither survive nor grow into a sane human being. He grew and realised his potential in a stable and peaceful society, made possible by the efforts and sacrifices of thousands of anonymous men and women. He became a rational, reflective and moral human being only within a rich civilization created by scores of sages, saints, savants and scientists.

In short, every human being owned his humanity to others, and benefited from a world to the creation of which he contributed nothing. As Gandhi put it, every man was 'born a debtor', a beneficiary of others' gifts, and his inherited debts were too vast to be repaid. Even a whole lifetime was not enough to pay back what a man owned to his parents, let alone all others. Furthermore the creditors were by their very nature unspecifiable. Most of them were dead or remained anonymous, and those alive were so numerous and their contributions so varied and complex that it was impossible to decide what one owed to whom. To talk about repaying the debts did not therefore make sense except as a clumsy and metaphorical way of describing one's response to unsolicited but indispensable gifts.

Since the debts could never be 'repaid' and the favours 'returned', all a man could do was to 'recognise the conditions of his existence' and to continue the ongoing universal *yajna* or system of sacrifices by accepting his full share of collective responsibility. The only adequate response to the fact that he was born in and constantly sustained by *yajna* was to look upon his own life as *yajna,* an offering at the universal altar, and to find profound joy in contributing to the maintenance and enrichment of both the human world and the cosmos. As Gandhi put it, '*Yajna* having come to us with our birth we are debtors all our lives, and thus for ever bound to serve the universe'. Not rights but obligations were the basis of moral life, and one's rights were embedded in and grew out of others' discharge of their duties.

Since humankind constituted an organic whole and since human beings were necessarily interdependent, every human action was both self-and other-regarding. Directly or indirectly, visibly or invisibly, it affected the collective ethos and shaped the quality of the prevailing pattern of human relationship. 'We cannot see this, near-sighted as we are', but it remained an inescapable feature of the necessarily interdependent world. 'Rot in one part must inevitably poison the whole system.' When human beings developed themselves they awakened others to their potentialities, and inspired, encouraged and raised them as well. And when they acted inhumanely, both they and others suffered. Even a trivial crime was enough to create a general sense of insecurity, to heighten mutual suspicions, and to lower the moral tone of the entire community. 'I believe that if one man gains spiritually the whole world gains with him, and if one man falls the world falls to that extent'.

For Gandhi humanity was indivisible, in the sense that no man could degrade or brutalize another without also degrading or brutalizing himself, or inflict psychic and moral damage on others without inflicting it on himself as well. This was so in at least three ways. First, to degrade others was to imply that a human being may be so treated, and thus to lower the expected level of the moral minimum due to every human being from which all alike suffered. "To slight a single human being is... to harm not only that human being but with him the whole world.' Second, to degrade and dehumanize others was to damage their pride, self-respect and potential for good, and thus both to deny oneself and the world the benefits of their possible contributions and to add to the collective moral, psychological and financial cost of repairing the damage they were likely to do to themselves and to others.

Third, as beings capable of morality and critical self-reflection, human beings could not degrade or maltreat others without hardening themselves against the latter's suffering and cries for help, building up distorted systems of self-justification, coarsening their moral sensibilities, and lowering their own and the collective level of humanity. As Gandhi put it, no man 'takes another down a pit without descending into it himself and sinning in the bargain.' Since humanity was indivisible and since basic human interests were harmonious, every man was responsible to and for others and should be deeply concerned about how they lived.

Gandhi's concept of indivisible humanity formed the basis of his critique of systems of oppression and exploitation. Such dominant groups as the whites in South Africa, the colonial governments in India and elsewhere, and the rich and the powerful in every society, naively imagined that their exploitation and degradation of their respective victims did not in any way damage them as well. In fact they suffered as much as their victims and sometimes even more. The white South Africans could not deprive the blacks of their livelihood and dignity without suppressing their inner doubts and tender feelings, damaging their capacities for critical self-reflection and impartial self-assessment, and falling victim to moral conceit, morbid fears, and irrational obsessions.

In brutalizing the blacks they also brutalized themselves, and were only prevented by their arrogance from noticing how sad, empty and pitiable their lives had become. They did enjoy more material comforts, but they were neither happier nor better human beings. The colonial rulers met the same fate. They could not dismiss the natives as 'effeminate' and 'childlike' without thinking of themselves as tough, hypermasculine and unemotional adults, a self-image to which they could not conform without distorting and impoverishing their potential. In misrepresenting the natives, they misrepresented themselves and fell into their own traps. They also took home the attitudes, habits and styles of government acquired abroad, and corrupted their own society. Colonialism did promote their material interests, but only at the expense of their larger and infinitely more important moral and spiritual interests. For Gandhi material interests had only an ins1nnnental significance, and were positively harmful when they hampered moral and spiritual development.

On the, basis of his concept of human unity Gandhi arrived at a novel theory of social change. He readily agreed that no dominant group ever gave up power without a struggle. However he was convinced that such a struggle could not be adequately conceptualized in terms of, and conducted by means advocated by, the fundamentally flawed traditional theory of revolution. In his view the fact that almost every revolution so far had led to terror, devoured its children, and failed to create a better society was a proof of this. These failures were not accidental but sprang from the Manichean view of the world lying at the basis of the traditional theory of revolution. The theory neatly separated good and evil, and saw human existence as a mortal struggle between them. Since no cause could be nobler than the elimination of evil, everything done to eliminate evil including the use of massive violence was considered justified. The misguided belief that evil had no rights lay at the basis of revolutionary morality. Those identified as evil were deemed to have forfeited their humanity, and the concomitant claims on their fellow-men's understanding and charity.

Gandhi argued that far from being mutually exclusive, good and evil were conceptually and existentially inseparable. Nothing was good except in a specific context and within a specific pattern of human relationship; what was good in one context was not so in another; good turned into evil when pressed beyond a certain point; and what was good for one man might not be so for another. Given the scarcity of time, money, energy and emotional resources, a moral agent had to make choices, and sometimes had to sacrifice or forego good in order to achieve what in his view was better. Every moral deed had a price and good was necessarily shadowed by evil. Furthermore in a world full of evil, good could not exist let alone be effective without participating in evil, and no evil could last a day without some basis of goodness to give it strength and organisation.

Since good and evil were inseparable and at times indistinguishable, they could not be socially separated and ascribed to different classes or groups. Groups were composed of men, each a bearer of good and evil properties. Even the apparently innocent victims of an unjust social order actively or passively, wittingly or unwittingly, collaborated in their oppression and bore some responsibility for their predicament. Mankind therefore could not be divided into two neat classes, one so fallen or corrupt that it forfeited its claim to humanity, the other so privileged that it had a right to punish the rest. This did not mean that some men or groups might not behave in an evil manner and deserve to be restrained, but rather that this reflected only one aspect of their personality and did not foreclose the possibility of their future regeneration.

In Gandhi's view the traditional theory of revolution did not fully appreciate the subtle ways in which good suffered corruption in its struggle against evil. The theory located good in the ends of an action, judging the allegedly amoral means in exclusively instrumental forms. Since the so-called ends were in turn means to some other allegedly higher ends, everything ultimately got reduced to a mere means. Violence, mendacity, cunning, duplicity, manipulation of the opponent, and so on were all considered legitimate if used in the pursuit of good ends. By resorting to such means. good subtly became transformed into evil and its victory was really its defeat. Gandhi argued that we needed a new theory of revolution that was free from the defects of the old and structurally protected against degeneration into terror.

Such a theory had to be grounded in the three central principles of the unity of man, the indivisibility of means and ends. and a non-Manichean view of the world. It should stand up not just for the interests of the oppressed but for the shared interests of all including the oppressors and aim at a society in which *all* alike led richer and more humane lives. For Gandhi imperialism damaged *both* the British and the Indians and needed to be ended in the interests of *both*. Untouchability inflicted a grave moral and emotional damage not just on the untouchables but also on the caste Hindus and its abolition promoted the interests of *both*. A revolution was justified only if the society it sought to establish did not replace one set of masters by another and put an end to all forms of class rule.

Like Marx. Gandhi argued that revolutionary consciousness sprang from an intense sensitivity to human suffering and had a special affinity with the oppressed its natural constituency and object of concern. Unlike Marx, however, he insisted that the oppressed were never wholly innocent and free from their share of human failings nor the oppressors wholly evil and devoid of their share of human virtues. Both alike were caught up in a self-reproducing system which debilitated and brutalized them all and from which they needed to be liberated. Being more de-harmonized and brutalized than the rest the oppressed were more acutely aware of the need for liberation and had to initiate the emancipatory process.

However, even as no oppressive system could last without the cooperation of its morally implicated victims it could not be conclusively ended without the cooperation, however grudging of its erstwhile masters. The latter had to be assured that the revolution did not intend to physically eliminate them, that it was concerned with their well-being as well, and that it recognized them as human beings entitled to decency and respect.

For Gandhi the means-end dichotomy lying at the heart of the traditional revolutionary theory was fundamentally false. In human life the so-caned means consisted not of implements and inanimate tools but of human actions, and by definition these could not fall outside the jurisdiction of morality. Furthermore the method of fighting for an objective was not external to but an integral part of it. Every step towards a desired goal shaped its character, and utmost care had to be taken to ensure that the steps taken to realize it did not distort or damage the goal. The goal did not exist *at the end* of a series of actions designed to achieve it; it shadowed them from the very beginning. The so-called means were really ends in an embryonic form, the seeds of which the so-called ends were a natural flowering. Since this was so, the fight for a just society could not be conducted by unjust means.

Gandhi's theory of *Satyagraha,* the 'surgery of the soul' as he called it, was his alternative to the traditional theory of revolution. It was not so much a nonviolent *method* of achieving revolutionary ends as a novel way of *defining* the very idea of revolution. Like Trotsky's permanent revolution, it was a form of gentle but sustained social pressure designed to break down emotional, ideological and moral barriers that different groups built around themselves, to unfreeze the flow of social sympathy, and to enrich and deepen their consciousness of independence. Even as every community required a widespread sense of justice to hold it together, it presupposed a deeper sense of shared humanity to give meaning and energy to its sense of justice.

The sense of humanity consisted in the recognition of the fundamental ontological fact that humanity was indivisible, that human beings grew and fell together, and that in degrading and brutalizing others, they degraded and brutalized themselves. It constituted a community's vital moral capital without which it had no defense, and no resources to fight against the forces of injustice, exploitation and oppression. The slow and painful task of cultivating and consolidating the sense of humanity, and thereby laying the foundations of a truly moral community, was an essential collective responsibility, which the *Satyagrahi* took upon himself to discharge. He assumed the burden of the common evil, sought to liberate both himself and his opponent from its tyrannical automatism, and helped reduce the prevailing level of inhumanity. He overcame his opponent by refusing to see him as one, and by appealing instead to his sense of decency and their common humanity. As Gandhi put it, the old sages 'returned good for evil and killed it'. The *Satyagrahi* took his stand on this 'fundamental moral truth'.

For Gandhi a *Satyagrahi* relied on the power of suffering love. Confronted with untruth he sought a dialogue with his opponent. When this was denied or reduced to an insincere exercise in public relations, he took a stand and accepted whatever punishment was meted out to him. Since his sole concern was to evoke a moral response in his opponent, he did everything necessary to put him at ease and nothing to harass, embarrass, anger or frighten him. In the meantime he suffered the punishment without hatred or ill-will in the hope of triggering off in him a slow, intensely personal, and highly complex process of self-examination. The moment his opponent showed willingness to talk in a spirit of genuine good will, he suspended the struggle and gave reason a chance to work in a more hospitable climate.

With all its limitations which I cannot here explore, Gandhi's theory of *Satyagraha* offered important insights into the nature of political *praxis.* Like the rationalists, he stressed the importance of rational discussion; unlike them, however, he realised that what passed as rational discussion was often little more than alternative monologues or a public relations exercise, and that sticking to it under such circumstances was an act of irrationality. Even as Gandhi was aware of the limits of rationality, he was acutely conscious of the dangers of violence. He knew that narrow rationalism and violence tended to feed off each other, and that the failure of rationality rendered violence morally respectable.

Accordingly he sought to break through the narrow straitjacket of the reason-violence dichotomy lying at the basis of traditional rationalism. He imaginatively explored the uncharted terrain between reason and violence and arrived at novel forms of political *praxis.* His *Satyagraha* was basically a new form of dialogue, a new conception of discussion, embedded in a richer and more realistic theory of rationality. Although not rational in the narrow sense of the term, it was not irrational either. It was a way of enabling human beings to realize their potential for rationality and goodness, and to reach and act on the basis of an inherently tentative and constantly deepening perception of consensual truth.

7

RELIGIOUS EDUCATION AND INSTRUCTIONS

Introduction

The other day, in the course of a conversation, a missionary friend asked me, if India was really a spiritually advanced country, why it was that he found only a few students having any knowledge of their own religion, even of the *Bhagavad Gita*. In support of the statement, the friend who is himself an educationist told me that he had made it a point to ask the students he met whether they had any knowledge of their religion or of the *Bhagavad Gita*. A vast majority of them were found to be innocent of any such knowledge.

I do not propose to take up at the present moment the inference that because certain students had no knowledge of their own religion, India was not a spiritually advanced country, beyond saying that the ignorance on the part of the students of religious books did not necessarily mean absence of all religious life or want of spirituality among the people to which the students belonged. But there is no doubt that the vast majority of students who pass through the Government educational institutions are devoid of any religious instruction. The remark of the missionary had reference to the Mysore students, and I was somewhat pained to observe that even the students of Mysore had no religious instruction in the State schools. I know that there is a school of thought which believes in only secular instruction being given in public schools. I know also that in a country like India, where there are most religions of the world represented and where there are so many denominations in the same religion, there must be difficulty about making provision for religious instruction.

Addressing the Collegiate High School students at Shimoga, I found upon enquiry at the meeting that out of a hundred or more Hindu boys, there were hardly eight who had read the *Bhagavad Gita*. None raised his hand in answer to the question, whether of the few who had read the *Gita* there was any who understood it. Out of five or six Musalman boys all raised their hands as having read the Koran. But only one could say that he knew its meaning. The *Gita* is, in my opinion, a very easy book to understand. It does present some fundamental problems which are no doubt difficult of solution. But the general trend of the *Gita* is in my opinion unmistakable. It is accepted by all Hindu sects as authoritative. It is free from any form of dogma.

In a short compass it gives a complete reasoned moral code. It satisfies both the intellect and the heart. It is thus both philosophical and devotional. Its appeal is universal. The language is incredibly simple. But I nevertheless think that there should be an authoritative version in each vernacular, and the translations should be so prepared as to avoid technicalities and in a manner that would make the teaching of the *Gita* intelligible to the average man. The suggestion is not intended in any way to supplement the original. For I reiterate my opinion that every Hindu boy and girl should know Sanskrit. But for a long time to come, there will be millions without any knowledge of Sanskrit. It would be suicidal to keep them deprived of the teachings of the *Bhagavad Gita* because they do not know Sanskrit. *(Young India, 25 August 1927 (CW 34, pp. 394–95))*

Religious versus Fundamental Virtues

To me religion means Truth and *ahimsa* or rather Truth alone, because Truth includes *ahimsa*, *ahimsa* being the necessary and indispensable means for its discovery. Therefore, anything that promotes the practice of these virtues is a means for imparting religious education and the best way to do this, in my opinion, is for the teachers rigorously to practise these virtues in their own person. Their very association with the boys, whether on the playground or in the classroom, will then give the pupils a fine training in these fundamental virtues.

So much for instruction in the universal essentials of religion. A curriculum of religious instruction should include a study of the tenets of faiths other than one's own. For this purpose the students should be trained to cultivate the habit of understanding and appreciating the doctrines of various great religions of the world in a spirit of reverence and broad-minded tolerance. This if properly done would help to give them a spiritual assurance and a better appreciation of their own religion.

There is one rule, however, which should always be kept in mind while studying all great religions and that is that one should study them only through the writings of known votaries of the respective religions. For instance, if one wants to study the *Bhagavata* one should do so not through a translation of it made by a hostile critic but one prepared by a lover of the *Bhagavata.* Similarly to study the Bible one should study it through the commentaries of devoted Christians. This study of other religions besides one's own will give one a grasp of the rock-bottom unity of all religions and afford a glimpse also of that universal and absolute Truth which lies beyond the 'dust of creeds and faiths'.

Let no one even for a moment entertain, the fear that a reverent study of other religions is likely to weaken or shake one's faith in one's own. The Hindu system of philosophy regards all religions as containing the elements of truth in them and enjoins an attitude of respect and reverence towards them all. This of course presupposes regard for one's own religion. Study and appreciation of other religions need not cause a weakening of that regard; it should mean extension of that regard to other religions.

In this respect religion stands on the same footing as culture. Just as preservation of one's own culture does not mean contempt for that of others, but requires assimilation of the best that there may be in all other cultures, even so should be the case with religion. Our present fears and apprehensions are a result of the poisonous atmosphere that has been generated in the country, the atmosphere of mutual hatred, ill-will and distrust. We are constantly labouring under a nightmare of fear lest some one should stealthily undermine our faith or the faith of those who are dear and near to us. But this unnatural state will cease when we have learnt to cultivate respect and tolerance towards other religions and their votaries. *(Young India, 6 December 1928 (True Education, pp. 127-28))*

Religious Instruction Framework

Teachers who teach under a common administrative system have no right to impart religious instruction according to their own viewpoint.

As in the case of other subjects, religious instruction too must be given in accordance with the scheme provided by the administrative authorities. Every teacher will have his own method of teaching within that framework; however, such instruction may be imparted only in accordance with the ideals that have been laid down by the authorities with regard to religion. It is true that instruction in other subjects can be imparted by one who has read certain books on these subjects. That is not the case of religious instruction. It is never given through books. The method of imparting this instruction is quite different from that followed in the case of other subjects. Whereas the latter is communicated through the intellect, the former can proceed from one's heart alone. Hence so long as the teacher is not steeped in religion, he should not impart religious instruction.

Although in this manner the means of imparting religious instruction are different, nevertheless it is necessary to have a certain amount of understanding about the way in which it is to be done. In other words, one cannot impart education which would encourage violence where nonviolence has been accepted as the supreme dharma. Or, instruction antagonistic to other religions cannot be imparted where the ideal of love, tolerance and compassion towards all religions has been accepted as the ideal. In short, there can be no place for a state of anarchy with regard to religious instruction where its necessity has already been accepted. *(Navajivan, 10 June 1928 (CW 36, pp. 383–84) (Translated from Gujarati))*

Satsang

It is true that we lack religious education in the country. Religious instruction can only be imparted through the practice of religion, not by exhibiting mere learning. That's why someone has said: What is there that *Satsang* cannot do for a man? Who does not know the emphasis Tulsidas laid on the importance of *Satsang*? This does not mean that there is no need to read and understand religious books. But the need for books, etc., arises only after a man has had *Satsang* and has purified himself to a certain extent. If one starts studying religious books before this stage then instead of bringing peace this study could hinder the growth.

This means that an intelligent man should put his religion into practice straightaway instead of worrying himself with all manner of questions. Then according to the maxim "as with the individual so with the world", one is bound to influence the other. If each one of us was to take care of one's self, nobody would need to worry about the others. *(Navajivan, 15 August 1929 (CW 41, p. 291) (Translated from Hindi))*

Ethical Teaching in Schools

Should religious instruction form part of the school curriculum as approved by the State? Do you favour separate schools for children belonging to different denominations for facility of religious instruction? Or should religious instruction be left in the hands of private bodies? If so, do you think it is right for the State to subsidize such bodies? I do not believe in State religion even though the whole community has one religion. The State interference would probably always be unwelcome.

Religion is purely a personal matter. There are in reality as many religions as minds. Each mind has a different conception of God from that of the other. I am also opposed to State aid, partly or wholly, to religious bodies. For I know that an institution or group which does not manage to finance its own religious teaching, is a stranger to true religion. This does not mean that the State schools would not give ethical teaching. The fundamental ethics are common to all religions. *(Harijan, 16 March 1947)*

Ethics and Religion

Regarding religious education Dr. Zakir Hussain thought that facilities should be provided for and time apportioned for religious education in our schools so as to enable those, who understood religion, to come and teach. More than that the Government should not undertake, if it wanted to avoid the appearance of undue interference.

Gandhiji said in reply, "You should talk it over with Maulana Saheb. I do not agree that the Government should provide religious education. If there are some people who want to give religious education of the wrong type, you cannot prevent it. If you try to do so, the result can only be bad. Those who want to give religious education may do so on their own, so long as it is not subversive of law and order or morals. The Governments can only teach ethics based on the main principles common to all religions and agreed to by all parties. In fact ours is a secular State." *(Harijan, 9 November 1947 (Basic Education, p. 120))*

Fundamental Ethics

Religious instruction in the sense of denominational religion has been deliberately omitted. Unless there is a State religion it is very difficult, if not impossible, to provide religious instruction as it would mean providing for every denomination. Such instruction is best given at home. The State should allow enough time for every child to receive such instruction at home or otherwise. It is also conceivable that the State should provide facilities for private tuition by those denominations which may wish to instruct their children at school provided that such instruction is paid for by such denominations.

As to the necessity of teaching equal regard for all religions, I personally hold strong views. Till we reach that happy state, I see no prospect of real unity among all the different communities. I regard it as fatal to the growth of a friendly spirit among the children belonging to the different faiths if they are taught either that their religion is superior to every other or that it is the only true religion. If that exclusive spirit is to pervade the nation, the necessary corollary would be that there should be separate schools for every denomination with freedom to each to decry every other, or that the mention of religion must be entirely prohibited.

The result of such a policy is too dreadful to contemplate. Fundamental principles of ethics are common to all religions. These should certainly be taught to the children and that should be regarded as adequate religious instruction so far as the schools under the Wardha scheme are concerned. *(Harijan, 16 July 1938 (CW 67, p. 175))*

Adult Franchise

Considering the minutes of the proposal, I feel that while extending the franchise, it is not at all proper to confine it to literates. It is possible that an educated young man of 21 may not at all be fit to exercise his franchise, whereas an illiterate man of 50, experienced and sensible, may realize the value of his vote and his vote will have its own significance. It has been daily happening that way.

There are many things taken for granted even in the Congress advocacy of adult franchise. I am firmly convinced that the deaf and dumb, known idiots, lunatics, persons indulging in secret crimes and those suffering from incurable diseases cannot enjoy the right to vote even if they have attained the prescribed age.

Moreover, there is no reason to believe that those who have learnt to read and write have achieved something great. I am not prepared to say that those who have not been able so far to get educated are themselves responsible for their ignorance. It is indeed the indifference of the middle-class people that is responsible for the ignorance of the masses. The number of illiterate people in India has remained so large because these people have not discharged their duty.

Hence, in my view it is a double crime to give franchise to those who, by the favour of the Government, have become educated and to deny it to those who, because of the Government's indifference, received no education. It becomes the duty of those in power to arrange for early education of those illiterates who are entitled to exercise their votes. Thus, on the one hand, it would mean atonement for not giving franchise to those who should have had it from the beginning, and, on the other, it would encourage efforts to educate the electorate so that voters can exercise their franchise intelligently. *(Harijanbandhu, 3 October 1937 (CW 66, p. 198) (Translated from Gujarati))*

Mass Illiteracy

In our schemes for adult education should the aim be to promote the spread of literacy or to impart useful knowledge? What about the education of women?

The primary need of those who are come of age and are following an avocation, is to know how to read and write. Mass illiteracy is India's sin and shame and must be liquidated. Of course, the literacy campaign must not begin and end with mere knowledge of the alphabet. It must go hand in hand with the spread of useful knowledge. But municipal bodies should beware of trying to ride two horses at a time, or else they are sure to come a cropper.

As for illiteracy among the women, its cause is not mere laziness and inertia as in the case of men. A more potent cause is the status of inferiority with which an immemorial tradition has unjustly branded her. Man has converted her into a domestic drudge and an instrument of his pleasure, instead of regarding here as his helpmate and 'better half!' The result is a semi-paralysis of our society. Woman has rightly been called the mother of the race. We owe it to her and to ourselves to undo the great wrong that we have done her. *(Harijan, 18 February 1939 (CW 68, p. 341))*

Adult Education

In my opinion what we have reason to deplore and be ashamed of is not so much illiteracy as ignorance. Therefore adult education, too, should have an intensive programme of driving out ignorance through carefully selected teachers with an equally carefully selected syllabus according to which they would educate the adult villagers' mind. This is not to say that I would not give them a knowledge of the alphabet. I value it too much to despise or even belittle its merit as a vehicle of education. I appreciate Prof. Laubach's immense labours in the way of making the alphabet easy and Prof. Bhagwat's great and practical contribution in the same direction. Indeed I have invited the latter to come to Segaon whenever he chooses and try his art on the men, women and even children of Segaon. *(Harijan, 5 June 1937 (CW 65, pp. 234–35))*

Education for Life

As to adult education, Gandhiji observed that it had become clear to him that the scope of basic education had to be extended. It should include the education of everybody at every stage of life.

A basic school teacher must consider himself a universal teacher. As soon as he comes in contact with anybody, man or woman, young or old, he should say to himself: 'Now, what can I give to this person?'

Won't that be supererogation on his part?

No. Supposing I come across an old man who is dirty and ignorant. His village is his universe. It would be my job to teach him cleanliness, to remove his ignorance and widen his mental horizon. I need not tell him that I am to be his teacher. I will try to establish a living contact with his mind and win his confidence. He may reject my advances. I won't accept defeat, but continue my effort till I succeed in making friends with him. Once that is achieved, the rest must follow.

Again, I must have my eye on the children right from their birth. I will go a step further and say that the work of the educationist begins even before that. For instance, if a woman becomes pregnant, Ashadevi will go to her and tell her: 'I am a mother as you will be. I can tell you from my experience what you should do to ensure the health of your unborn baby and your own.' She will tell the husband what his duty towards his wife is and about his share in the care of their expected baby. Thus the basic school teacher will cover the entire span of life. Naturally, his activity will cover adult education.

Some work for adult education is being done in many places. It is mostly concentrated among mill-hands and the like in big cities. No one has really touched the village. Mere three R's and lectures on politics won't satisfy me. Adult education of my conception must make men and women better citizens all round. To work out the syllabus and to organize the work of adult education is a more difficult task than preparation of the seven years' course for children. The common central feature of both will be the imparting of education through village crafts. Agriculture will play an important part in adult education under the basic scheme. Literary instruction must be there. Much information will be given orally. There will be books more for the teachers than the taught. We must teach the majority how to behave towards the minority and vice versa. The right type of adult education should teach good neighbourliness and cut at the very root of untouchability and communal problem.

The particular industry which is to serve as the medium of instruction will be determined by local conditions in each place. For instance, people in a village might tell you that they are interested in agriculture, but they are not interested in the spinning-wheel. In that case, you will choose the former as the medium of instruction. You could make a beginning by taking a census of its cattle. For instance, I find that almost everyone in Sevagram has a bullock and a bullock-cart.

It seems wasteful. The villagers should be taught cooperation. Again, we must inculcate in them the right principles of relationship between men and women. Men get almost double the women's wages for identical work. Sometimes men sit lazily at home and smoke while the women toil the whole day. People should be made to realize that this is doubly wrong and ought to go. If you agree with me that the scope of basic education should be extended, you might have to change your constitution. *(The Hindu, 29 October 1944 (CW 78, pp. 237–38))*

Functional Literacy

The dry knowledge of three R's is not even now, it can never be, permanent part of the villagers' life. They must have knowledge given to them which they must use daily. It must not be thrust upon them. They should have the appetite for it. What they have today is something they neither want nor appreciate. Give the villagers village arithmetic, village geography, village history, and the literacy knowledge that they must use daily, *i.e.*, reading and writing letters, etc. They will treasure such knowledge and pass on to the other stages. They have no use for books which give them nothing of daily use. *(Harijan, 22 June 1940 (CW 72, pp. 180–81))*

Self-supporting Adult Education

It is my firm belief that if Nayee Taleem cannot become self-supporting, then the teachers do not understand what it is. In my view, amongst other characteristics self-reliance is the most important characteristic of Nayee Taleem.

If this is so for the education of boys and girls, then adult education must also be self-supporting. If we believe that it is difficult to convince adults about the value of education, then I have to say that this is nothing but an old illusion. And the teaching of the three R's in adult education is not part of our Nayee Taleem. The meaning of adult education is that we will give them, through their own language, all-round education of a pure and socially useful life. And if they do not easily become self-supporting, in my view there is some serious defect in that education. We should not also forget that complete cooperation should be the basis from the very beginning. Those who know the full meaning of cooperation will raise no doubts about self-reliance. *(Khadi Jagat, November 1945 (CW 82, pp. 143–44))*

Knowledge of Alphabet

In the consideration of public education, knowledge of the alphabet takes subordinate place. It can be said that knowledge of the alphabet has no place at all among the important aspects of life. *Moksha* is for us the final state to be desired. Who will deny that knowledge of the alphabet is not necessary for *moksha* here and hereafter? If we have to wait until crores of people have gained a knowledge of the alphabet in order to win swaraj, attainment of the latter will become almost an impossibility. Moreover, no one has claimed that the great teachers of the world like Jesus Christ had this knowledge.

Knowledge of the alphabet has been given the least important place in this series of articles. It is a means and not an end. It is a well-known fact that as a means it is very useful. However, when considering the type of knowledge that is required for crores of farmers who are engaged in their occupations and have reached a mature age, we find that there is much else that they should be taught before being given a knowledge of the alphabet. *(Navajivan, 15 December 1929 (CW 42, p. 281) (Translated from Gujarati))*

Women's Education

That India is very backward in the education of women is a fact that cannot be denied. But by admitting this, we do not mean to suggest that Indian women fail in their duty. We believe that, as there are in world few men of any class who can compete with the Indians considered from all points of view, so are there few women anywhere in the world who can compare with Indian women. But this position can no longer be kept up in the present squalid, low and helpless state of India. The modern age is such that it does not allow anyone to remain in the same position. Those who do not want to go forward, or do not do so, must fall behind. In so far as this is true, we can see that Indian men have deliberately kept their women backward. Those who pose as reformers as also other well-to-do Indians, whether Hindu or Muslim, Parsi or Christian, either treat their women as if they were playthings or use them as they fancy for self-indulgence, with the result that they themselves become weak and help only to produce weaklings.

And in this way they lead irreligious lives and still say, 'It is God's will that prevails.' If this state of affairs continues, India will remain in its present abominable condition even if she were to secure all her rights from the British Government. In all countries where the people live a decent life, there is no disparity in the condition of men and women. It is easy to see how much the real wealth of India would be attenuated, if one half of her human beings remained ignorant and existed only as playthings of the others. *(Indian Opinion, 19 January 1907 (CW 6, pp. 282–83))*

Yusuf Ali on Women's Education

Mr. Yusuf Ali's book on conditions prevailing in India is widely read. His views on the education of women as expressed therein are worth noting. He says that so long as Indian women do not get proper education, the condition of India is not likely to improve. Woman is known as the better half of man. If a half of one's body ceases to function, we call it paralysis and the person becomes unfit for any activity. Thus, if women in India are not employed as they should be, it can be said that the entire country suffers from paralysis. How is it surprising then that India is not able to keep pace with other countries? All parents should think of this in regard to their daughters, and all Indians should do likewise with regard to the womenfolk of India. We badly need thousands of women who can compare with Mirabai and Rabia Bibi. *(Indian Opinion, 22 June 1907 (CW 7, p. 51) (Translated from Gujarati))*

Equality of Rights for Women

We shall accept equality of rights for women, but I think their education should differ from men's as their nature and functions do. In progressive countries, women receive the very highest education but, after it is over, they do not have to perform the same duties as men and in our country women have never to compete with men for a livelihood. *(Prajabandhu, 27 February 1916 (CW 13, p. 246) (Translated from Gujarati))*

Educated Women's Role

The women whom this message reaches are likely to have had some measure of education. I wish, therefore, to consider one thing. What should educated women do for their illiterate sisters? This is a very important issue. Beyond question, if women choose... they can attain a far greater measure of success in this field than men can ever do. At present, we do not find many women taking to this work. That is, I believe, not their fault but that of their education. The first thing, therefore, which educated women must do is to try and see that their sisters do not fall a victim to it. Modern education fails utterly to prepare women for their distinctive role; this is not questioned by anyone. I do not wish here to examine the shortcomings of modern education or to bother you with the question how they may be overcome. All that I desire is that educated women should make this question their own and that those of them with some experience should dedicate their all to rouse Gujarat over it and focus attention on the right lines [of reform].

Educated women have no contact with those not educated; often, they don't welcome such contacts. This disease must be cured. It is necessary that educated women are made conscious of their most obvious duty. Men also are not free from faults of this kind, but women need not follow in their footsteps. They have the power, denied to men, of creating new ideals and translating them into action. By comparison, man is thoughtless, impatient and given to the pursuit of novelty. *(Gujarati, 2 November 1917 (CW 14, pp. 86–87) (Translated from Gujarati))*

Men versus Women's Education

The education of women is as faulty as that of men. They have not given any thought to the relations obtaining between men and women, or to the place woman occupies in India society.

It may be admitted that for the most part preliminary teaching of both boys and girls would be much the same. Barring that, there is great dissimilarity. There is need for similar distinction between the education of males and females as has been made between them by Mother Nature herself. True, they are equals. But there is a difference in the work they are ordained to do. It is woman's right to rule inside the home. Man is master outside it. Man is the earner of livelihood, woman saves and spends. Woman brings up children. She is their mother. She is responsible for building up their character. She is their educator, and hence the *mother* of the race. Man is not, in that sense, the father of the race. After a certain age a father ceases to influence his son, but not so the mother. The son, even after attaining manhood, behaves like a child in the presence of his mother. He cannot, however, do this with his father.

If this arrangement is considered natural and right a woman should not have to earn her living. A society in which women have to work as telegraph clerks, typists or compositors is, I think, not well-organized. It is a symptom of moral and economic bankruptcy and is an indication that they, *i.e.*, the people belonging to that society, have begun to live on their capital. Hence, just as it is wrong to keep women in ignorance and under suppression on the one hand, it is wrong, on the other hand, to entrust them with the work which is ordinarily done by men; for this is a sign of weakness and is tantamount to oppression.

Therefore, after a certain age, there must be arrangements to provide women with a kind of education different to that of men. Women should be taught the management of the home, the things they should or should not do during pregnancy, and the nursing and care of children. It is difficult to make suitable arrangements for providing such teaching as the idea is a new one. The right course under the circumstances would be to constitute a committee of enlightened and experienced men and women of good character who would then explore the problem, come to the right decision, and produce a suitable plan for the purpose. This committee should find out how best to impart the necessary education to girls after they have completed the period of childhood and enter on that of womanhood. But, unfortunately, there are a large number of girls in our country who get married even while they are in their childhood. Besides, the number goes on increasing. And once they are married, they just disappear from social life. I have expressed my views about them fully in my foreword contributed to the first book of the "Bhagini Pustak-mala" series. I reproduce them here:

> *"We cannot achieve the education of women merely by educating girls. Claimed by the monster of child-marriage, thousands of girls disappear from view at the early age of twelve. From girls they change into house-wives at one stroke. As long as this wicked custom continues, the only alternative is that men must learn to act as teachers to women. A great many of our hopes in regard to the education of women rest on how men discharge their duty in this respect. Women must cease to be our servants and objects of enjoyment as they are at present, and become, instead, our life-companions, equal partners in the battle of life, sharers in our happiness and unhappiness. All our efforts seem utterly futile as long as this is not accomplished. There are some men who regard their women as beasts. For this sad state some of the Sanskrit sayings and the following well-known doha of Tulsidas may be held responsible.*

Tulsidas says at one place in his Ramayana: "The drum, the fool, the Shudra and the woman—all these are fit objects to beat." I hold Tulasidasji in high esteem, but my worship is not blind. Either this couplet is an interpolation, or, if it is his, he must have written it without thought—as reflecting the prevailing views of the then society. As to the saying in Sanskrit, people seem to be labouring under the impression that every shloka written is, as it were, a scriptural precept. We must fight this impression and eradicate from its very root the custom of regarding women as inferior beings. On the other hand, blinded by passion many among us adore women and decorate them with ornaments just as we decorate idols. We must keep away from this evil also. Our ultimate goal, however, will not be achieved until our women become to us what Parvati was to Mahadeva, Sita to Rama, Damayanti to Nala. Then, they will participate in our discussions, argue things with us on an equal basis, understand through their wonderful insight born of sympathy, be partners in our fight for resolving them and become for us, when we need it, the givers of the most soothing peace. This goal cannot be achieved merely by starting girls' schools. As long as we have around our necks the noose of child-marriage, men must be the teachers of their womenfolk. And this education which men will give to women will not be merely literacy; it will be extended to cover social reform and politics. Literacy must be only a preliminary to the teaching of the other subjects mentioned above. These may be taught even without it. A man who undertakes to teach his wife in this manner will have to change his attitude towards her. A man will himself be a student with his wife and will observe complete celibacy in his relation with her until she attains maturity. In no case will he subject a girl of twelve to fifteen years of age to the agony of bearing children to him. One ought to shudder at the very thought of it. If this is done we will not be crushed under the weight of inertia as we are at present.

"Classes are being started for married women and lecturers arranged for them. All this is good as far as it goes. Those who are engaged in this work are sacrificing their time and

energy for a good cause. This is quite creditable. But simultaneously men must also undertake to discharge the duty indicated above, because in its absence all these efforts will not bear much result. On deeper reflection, I am sure that what I have said is self-evident." (Speech at Second Gujarat Educational Conference, 20 October 1917 (CW *14, pp. 31–33))*

Woman, like Man, Needs Education

Though much good and useful work can be done without a knowledge of reading and writing, yet I believe that such knowledge is necessary, for one can hardly do without it these days. Reading of good books develops the intellect and that, in its turn, increases our capacity for service to our people and our country. I do not over-estimate the value of this knowledge, but I should like to give it its due place in the scheme of things. I have pointed out on several occasions that lack of education among women should not be made the reason for men to deprive them of their due human rights.

But proper education is essential in order that they may use those rights well, adorn them and spread them amongst our masses. Without proper education and the knowledge acquired through such education, millions cannot acquire the true knowledge of the Self. Without education, the inexhaustible fund of innocent pleasure which lies in various books is also closed to us. It is no exaggeration but a statement of fact that a man without learning is not far removed from an animal.

Thus, a woman, like man, needs education. Not that a woman should get the same kind of education as given to a man. In the first place, the education that is being given us by the Government is, to a great extent, faulty and harmful. It should therefore be eschewed by both men and women. Even if its defects were removed I would not consider it proper for women. Men and women are equal in status, but they are not the same in physical or mental make-up. They are a unique pair.

They complement each other and are absolutely necessary to each other, so much so that one cannot exist without the other. It follows as a corollary from these facts that anything that will impair the status of either of them will involve the ruin of both, in equal measure.

Those who draw up plans for the education of women must remember this. Man rules the outer circle of the life of a married pair. Therefore he must have the greater knowledge of all those activities of life which constitute his sphere. The woman, on the other hand, is dominant in the inner or domestic circle of their life. She must have special knowledge of the management of the home, care of children, their education, etc. It is not suggested that either men or women should be forbidden from acquiring a knowledge of what belongs specially to the province of the other. But unless courses of instruction are based on a discriminating appreciation of these ideas, both men and women would be deprived of the opportunity of achieving perfection in their respective spheres.

A few words are also necessary about the question as to whether or not women need to know English. I feel that generally speaking, knowledge of English is not necessary either for men or for women. Men might require it for earning their livelihood or for taking part in political work. But I do not believe in women working for a living or undertaking commercial enterprises. Therefore, only a few women would need to learn English. And those who want to may well learn it in the schools for men.

Introducing English in all schools for women will only lead to a prolongation of the period of our helplessness. I have often heard people say that the rich treasures of English literature should be as easily available to women as they are to men. I humbly submit that this is an erroneous view even though the error may not be evident. No one says that the treasures of English literature should be open to men but closed to women. He who loves literature may well explore the literature of the whole world. None will, or can, stop him from doing so, if he has the necessary will. But, since we are concerned with formulating a plan to suit the needs of our people in general, we cannot attend to the special needs of a few lovers of literature.

For them there will have to be—when we are sufficiently advanced and prosperous—separate institutions for learning and research as there are in Europe. When there is a general spread of education, when most of our men and women start getting educated, we may be sure that numerous writers will rise from amongst us who will make available to us the joy of the literatures of other languages. If we continue to derive pleasure only from English literature alone, our language will always remain poor. This means that we as a people will also remain mentally poor. I would even say, if you will forgive me for the simile, that the habit of deriving joy from the literature of another language is like that of a thief who derives joy from stolen property.

The English poet Pope presented to his people, in his beautiful English, whatever joy he tasted in *Iliad*; in the same way, Fitzgerald embodied the joy he derived from the poetry of Omar Khayyam in such attractive English that millions of Englishmen love and treasure his translation of the poetry of Khayyam like their own Bible. Edwin Arnold tasted the nectar of our *Bhagavad Gita*. He did not ask his people to learn Sanskrit to experience the joy that he had experienced in that book.

On the other hand, he made it available to the people in English which is as beautiful as the original Sanskrit and in which besides he has succeeded in pouring out his very soul as it were. Seeing that we are still backward in this respect, we must pay more attention to the work of translating. But it will be possible only when we have made our plan of education along the lines I have indicated and implement it. If we give up being fascinated by English and our distrust of the power of our own language, this will not be difficult to achieve.

It is not necessary for any man or woman to spend his or her time learning English in order to appreciate good literature. I do not say this merely to be a wet blanket. But because I want the pleasure, which the English-educated people derive with great difficulty, made easily available to all of us through translations. The languages of the world are full of many a invaluable gem. And not all the gems of literature are in English. I want all these gems to be brought within the reach of our people. The only way to achieve this end is for those of us who have a flair for languages to learn them and then present the foreign literary classics in our own.

Presidential speech on the occasion of the Second Annual Conference of the Bombay Bhagini Samaj, 1918 (*CW* 14, pp. 207–09)

Higher Education for Women

After primary education, a girl gets another four to five years of secondary education. Expressing his views on the question as to whether in this period she should be taught through English or the mother tongue, Gandhiji said: "I feel that teaching English to them under the circumstances would be like killing them. It will never be possible for hundreds of thousands of women to think or express their thoughts in English; and even if it were possible, it would be undesirable.

> *"If the women for whom we are drawing up this plan are imparted higher education through the mother tongue, they could make their homes as bright and beautiful as gold. Not only that, they could also exert their good influence on their uneducated sisters and thus render valuable service to them as well." (True Education, pp. 157–58)*

Modern Girls' Education

I was really surprised to see the stride that education among girls had taken in the State of Travancore. It was a perfect eye-opener to me. The question has always occurred to me: "What will India do with its modern girls?" I call you modern girls of India. The education that we are receiving in these institutions, in my opinion, does not correspond with the life around us, and, when I say life around us, I do not mean the life around us in the cities but the life around us in the villages. Perhaps some of you girls, if not all of you, know that real India is to be found not here in the very few cities but in the seven hundred thousand villages covering a surface of 1,900 miles long and 1,500 miles broad.

The question is whether you have any message for your sisters in the villages. Men do not need the message perhaps so much as the women, and I have long before come to the conclusion that unless women of India work side by side with men, there is no salvation for India, salvation in more senses than one. I mean political salvation in the broadest sense, and

I mean economic salvation and spiritual salvation also. *(Speech at Women's College, Madras, 24 March 1925 (CW 26, pp. 395–96))*

Curriculum for Girls' Education

Women must learn as part of elementary education at least their own mother tongue, Hindi if it is not their mother tongue, enough Sanskrit to be able to understand the drift of the *Bhagavad Gita*, elementary arithmetic, elementary composition, elementary music and child-care. Along with this, I think they should know well the processes up to the weaving from cotton. When a woman receives this education she should have an environment that will shape her character and enable her to see clearly the evils in society and to avoid them.

I have not mentioned religious education separately as it is acquired by practice and would be covered by general reading. Truly speaking, it is a part of the elevating company of a teacher. This is about girls. The education of a widow or a married woman is of course a different matter. *(Letter to Aanandibai, 22 August 1927 (CW 34, p. 384) (Translated from Gujarati))*

Education to Women

Today we have assembled for the opening of a girls' school. I have made a thorough study of child education. I could say the same thing about girls' education. But how can experts accepts this? Today, even I cannot make that claim. In the prevailing state of affairs it is not easy to talk about girls' education. Everyone may well claim that he is capable of giving education to girls. I will however ask him whether he has imparted true education to his daughter or his wife.

How can he who has not observed his dharma towards his wife, sister, mother or mother-in-law, set out to teach the daughters or sisters of others? They may well become B.As. or M.As. but I shall put them to the same test. I should like to know what kind of husbands and fathers those who write books on girls' education are. *(Speech at Inauguration of Vithal Kanya Vidyalaya, Nadiad, 31 May 1935 (CW 61, p. 118))*

Coeducation

In theory, we are quite in favour of boys and girls receiving education together. But, in practice, it is impossible to ignore deep-rooted habits or prejudices. Experience has shown that Indian parents, as a rule, will not allow their daughters to mingle with boys at a school or elsewhere. And, whenever a forcible mixture takes place, the result is ludicrous in the extreme. Both the boys and girls feel awkward. "Let them", shouts the unthinking reformer. "They will soon be at home, if left alone." But the parents will not wait for the process. They are not reformers and they will not allow experiments to be made at their children's expense. *(Indian Opinion, 19 August 1911 (CW 11, p. 145))*

Coeducation not Compulsory

As for coeducation, the Zakir Hussain Committee has not made it compulsory. Where there is a demand for a separate school for girls, the State will have to make provision. The question of coeducation has been left open. It will regulate itself according to the time-spirit. So far as I am aware the members of the Committee were not all of one mind. Personally I have an open mind. I think that there are just as valid reasons for as against coeducation. And I would not oppose the experiment wherever it is made. *(Harijan, 16 July 1938 (CW 67, p. 175))*

Coeducation in Training Schools

Shri Avinashilingam, the Education Minister of Madras, felt that the coeducation policy of the Talimi Sangh was not suitable to Madras. He had no objection to coeducation among children and among grown-ups, when they knew their own minds. But he was not in favour of coeducation at the impressionable age of 15 or 16 when most of the girls came to training schools. Gandhiji, however, disagreed. "If you keep coeducation in your schools but not in your training-schools, the children will think there is something wrong somewhere. I should allow my children to run the risk. We shall have to rid ourselves one day of this sex mentality. We should not seek for examples from the West. Even in training-schools, if the teachers are intelligent, pure and filled with the spirit of Nayee

Taleem, there is no danger. Supposing if some accidents do take place, we should not be frightened by them. They would take place anywhere. Although I speak thus boldly, I am not unaware of the attendant risks. You, as a responsible Minister, should think for yourself and act accordingly." *(Harijan, 9 November 1947 (CW 89, pp. 332–33))*

Sex Education

May I invite you to discuss in the columns of *Harijanbandhu* a question which you have so far left more or less untouched, I mean the question of imparting sex instruction to young people?

Should sex education be included in the educational curricula of our children? Who should impart it? What would be the necessary qualification for the task? Should this subject be taught in a matter-of-fact manner to all and sundry just like geography or arithmetic? Or is there any limit? And if so, who is to draw the line and where? Again should the aim of sex education be to combat the onset of libido or simply to recognize it as an inevitable fact of nature which has to be accepted and submitted to?

What place has instruction in sexual science in our educational system, or has it any place there at all? Sexual science is of two kinds, that which is used for controlling or overcoming the sexual passion and that which is used to stimulate and feed it. Instruction in the former is as necessary a part of a child's education as the latter is harmful and dangerous and fit therefore only to be shunned. All great religions have rightly regarded 'Kama' as the archenemy of man, anger or hatred coming only in the second place. According to the Gita, the latter is an offspring of the former. The Gita of course uses the word 'Kama' in its wider sense of desire. But the same holds good of the narrow sense in which it is used here.

This, however, still leaves unanswered the question, *i.e.*, whether it is desirable to impart to young pupils a knowledge about the use and function of generative organs. It seems to me that it is necessary to impart such knowledge to a certain extent. At present they are often left to pick up such knowledge anyhow with the result that they are misled into abusive practices. We cannot properly control or conquer the sexual passion by turning a blind eye to it. I am therefore strongly in favour of teaching young boys and girls the significance and right use of their generative organs. And in my own way I have tried to impart this knowledge to young children of both sexes for whose training I was responsible.

But the sex education that I stand for must have for its object the conquest and sublimation of the sex passion. Such education should automatically serve to bring home to children the essential distinction between man and brute, to make them realize that it is man's special privilege and pride to be gifted with the faculties of head and heart both; that he is a thinking no less than a feeling animal, as the very derivation of the word Yktknazk; (man) shows, and to renounce the sovereignty of reason over the blind instincts is therefore to renounce a man's estate. In man reason quickens and guides the feeling, in brute the soul lies ever dormant. To awaken the heart is to awaken the dormant soul, to awaken reason, to inculcate discrimination between good and evil.

Who should teach this true science of sex? Clearly, he who has attained mastery over his passions. To teach astronomy and kindred sciences we have teachers who have gone through a course of training in them and are masters of their art. Even so must we have as teachers of sexual science, *i.e.*, the science of sex control, those who have studied it and have acquired mastery over self. Even a lofty utterance, that has not the backing of sincerity and experience, will be inert and lifeless, and will utterly fail to penetrate and quicken the hearts of men, while the speech that springs from self-realization and genuine experience is always fruitful.

Today our entire environment—our reading, our thinking, our social behaviour—is generally calculated to subserve and cater for the sex urge. To break through its coils is no easy task. But it is a task worthy of our highest endeavour. Even if there are a handful of teachers endowed with practical experience, who accept the ideal of attaining self-control as the highest duty of man, and are fired by a genuine and undying faith in their mission, and are sleeplessly vigilant and active, their labour will light the path of the children of Gujarat, save the unwary from falling into the mire of sexuality and rescue those who might be already engulfed in it. *(Harijan, 22 November 1936 (CW 64, pp. 59-62))*

An Ideal Hostel

Since a Hostels' Conference is to be held this month in this city, I was asked to express my views as to what would be an ideal hostel. I have been running students' hostels since 1904 according to my lights. I am therefore inclined to claim that I have some knowledge and experience of how hostels should be run and managed. Here, we would do well to take a wider sense of the term "hostel". Every person who is learning anything is a student; and the place where more than one such student live I consider a students' hostel. The first and the most important condition for the success of such hostels is that the superintendents must be men of good character.

A hostel should never be allowed to degenerate into a mere boarding house, that is, a place where students live together for the sake of obtaining their meals. Students should cultivate a family feeling towards one another, and the superintendent should take the place of a father. He should take an interest in them, take part in their social life and also have his meals with them.

An ideal hostel would be almost more important to the student than school. In fact, the hostel is the real school. In schools or colleges the students get only verbal knowledge while in the hostels they get all kinds of knowledge. An ideal hostel should not be a separate institution from the school; hence, both should be under the same management, and teachers and students should live together. Thus, we should make the hostels like home, and create in them ideal conditions for growth and development such as do not obtain even in real homes. Therefore, the thing to do would be to turn the hostels into *gurukulas*.

There are many defects in our hostels. The reason lies in the fact that students lack a sense of belonging to a family group, and those who run them do not enter fully into the life of the students.

Then, these hostels should be outside the city limits, and all the reforms which are considered necessary for the villages or cities should be carried out in them, that is, there must be the necessary arrangements for hygienic and sanitary living and the rules of such living should be strictly followed. An ideal hostel cannot be set up in a rented building. There should be good bathrooms and latrines. The building should be well-ventilated and have a garden attached to it.

An ideal hostel should be *Swadeshi* in all respects—in the way the building is constructed, furnished and decorated. There should be too a reflection of village arts and crafts and way of life. The building itself should be in keeping with our need and our means, considering the poverty of India. Thus, hostels—as built in properous and affluent Western countries cannot serve as models for ours. Climate conditions abroad and here differ. Hence, the type of building put up must be in accordance with prevailing conditions. There must be nothing in the ideal hostel which might encourage indolence and delicacy, or lead to waywardness. Therefore, the food served there should be simple—as becomes the life of seekers of knowledge. There should be regular prayers, and rules governing work, rest and sleep.

An ideal hostel will be a *brahmacharyashram*, *i.e.*, a colony of students living the life of *brahmacharis*. The word student is of recent origin—a modern word. The old word for a student—*Brahmachari*—is richer in meaning and connotes the ideal of student life more truly.

Brahmacharya or spiritual discipline—control of the senses, purity of body and mind, and devotion to studies with a view to attaining the Ultimate Reality—is absolutely necessary during the period of study. In the rather topsy-turvy conditions obtaining today, I would like married students also, if admitted into the hostel, to observe *Brahmacharya* until the completion of their studies. This means, among other things, that during this period they should live away from their wives.

The readers should remember that I have described what would be an ideal hostel. It is understandable that all hostels may not be able to realize this goal. But, if the ideal described above is accepted as the standard, then every hostel should strive to reach it, and assess their achievement by comparison with it. *(Navajivan, 3 March 1929 (CW 40, pp. 72–73))*

True Prayer

As feed food is necessary for the body, prayer is necessary for the soul. A man may be able to do without food for a number of days,—as Mac Swiney did for over 70 days—but believing in God, man cannot, should not, live a moment without prayer. You will say that we see lots of people living without prayer. I dare say they do, but it is the existence of the brute which, for man, is worse than death. I have not the shadow of a doubt that the strife and quarrels with which our atmosphere is so full today are due to the absence of the spirit of true prayer. You will demur to the statement, I know, and contend that millions of Hindus, Musalmans and Christians do offer their prayers.

It is because I had thought you would raise this objection that I sued the words 'true prayers'. The fact is we have been offering our prayers with the lips but hardly ever with our hearts, and it is to escape, if possible, the hypocrisy of the lip-prayer, that we in the Ashram repeat every evening the last verses of the second chapter of the Bhagavad Gita. The condition of the 'Equable in Spirit' that is described in those verses, if we contemplate them daily, is bound slowly to turn our hearts towards God. If you students would base your education on the true foundation of a pure character and pure heart there is nothing so helpful as to offer your prayers every day truly and religiously. *(Speech at Students' Meeting, Berhampur .Young India, 15 December 1927 (CW 35, p. 361))*

Prayer Meetings

Here is a letter written by a student to the Principal of a national institution asking to be excused from attending its prayer meetings:

> *I beg to state that I have no belief in prayer, as I do not believe in anything known as God to whom I should pray. I never feel any necessity of supposing a god for myself. What do I lose if do not care for Him and calmly and sincerely work my own schemes?*

So far as congregational prayer is concerned, it is of no use. Can such a huge mass of men enter into any mental concentration upon a thing, however trifling it may be? Are the little and ignorant children expected to fix their fickle attention on the subtlest ideas of our great scriptures, God and soul and equality of all men and many other high-sounding phrases? This great performance is required to be done at a particular time at the command of a particular man. Can love for the so-called Lord take its root in the hearts of boys by any such mechanical function? Nothing can be more repugnant to reason than to expect the same behaviour from men of every temperament. Therefore, prayer should not be a compulsion. Let those pray who have a taste for it and those avoid who dislike it. Anything done without conviction is an immoral and degrading action.

Let us first examine the worth of the last idea. Is it an immoral and degrading act to submit to discipline before one beings to have conviction about its necessity? Is it immoral and degrading to study subjects according to the school syllabus if one has no conviction about its utility? May a boy be excused from studying his vernacular if he has persuaded himself that it is useless?

Is it not truer to say that a school boy has no conviction about the things he has to learn or the discipline he has to go through? His choice is exhausted if he had it, when he elected to belong to an institution. His joining one means that he will willingly submit to its rules and regulations. It is open to him to leave it, but he may not choose what or how he will learn.

It is for teachers to make attractive and intelligible what to the pupils may at first appear repulsive or uninteresting.

It is easy enough to say, 'I do not believe in God.' For God permits all things to be said of Him with impunity. He looks at our acts. And any breach of His law carried with it, not its vindictive, but its purifying, compelling, punishment. God's existence cannot be, does cannot be, does not need to be, proved. God is. If He is not felt, so much the worse for us. The absence of feeling is a disease which we shall some day throw off nolens volens.

But a boy may not argue. He must, out of a sense of discipline, attend prayer meetings if the institution to which he belongs requires such attendance. He may respectfully put his doubts before his teachers. He need not believe what does not appeal to him. But if he has respect for his teachers, he will do without believing what he is asked to do, not out of fear, not out of churlishness, but with the knowledge that it is right for him so to do and with the hope that what is dark to him today will some day be made clear to him.

Prayer is not an asking. It is a longing of the soul. It is a daily admission of one's weakness. The tallest among us has a perpetual reminder of his nothingness before death, disease, old age, accidents, etc. We are living in the midst of death. What is the value of "working for our own schemes" when they might be reduced to naught in the twinkling of an eye, or when we may be equally swiftly and unawares be taken away from them? But we may feel strong as a rock, if we could truthfully say: "We work for God and his schemes." Then all is as clear as day-light. Then nothing perishes. All perishing is then only what seems. Death and destruction have then, but only then, no reality about them. For death or destruction is then but a change. An artist destroys his picture for creating a better one. A watchmaker throws away a bad spring to put in a new and useful one.

A congregational prayer is a mighty thing. What we do not often do alone, we do together. Boys do not need conviction. If they merely attend in obedience to the call to prayer without inward resistance, they feel the exaltation. But many do not. They are even mischievous. All the same the unconscious effect cannot be resisted. Are there not boys who at the commencement of their career were scoffers but who subsequently became mighty believers in the efficacy of congregational prayer? It is a common experience for men who have no robust faith to seek the comfort for congregational prayer. All who flock to churches, temples, or mosques are not scoffers or humbugs. They are honest men and women. For them congregational prayer is like a daily bath, a necessity, of their existence. These places of worship are not a mere idle superstition to be swept away at the first opportunity. They have survived all attacks up to now and are likely to persist to the end of time. *(Young India, 23 September 1926 (CW 31, pp. 439–41))*

Essence of Prayer

I am glad that you all want me to speak to you on the meaning of and the necessity for prayer. I believe that prayer is the very soul and essence of religion, and therefore prayer must be the very core of the life of man, for no man can live without religion. There are some who in the egotism of their reason declare that they have nothing to do with religion. But it is like a man saying that he breathes but that he has no nose. Whether by reason, or by instinct, or by superstition, man acknowledges some sort of relationship with the divine.

The rankest agnostic or atheist does acknowledge the need of a moral principle, and associates something good with its observance and something bad with its non-observance. Bradlaugh, whose atheism is well known, always insisted on proclaiming his innermost conviction. He had to suffer a lot for thus speaking the truth, but he delighted in it and said that truth is its own reward. Not that he was quite insensible to the joy resulting from the observance of truth. This joy however is not at all worldly, but springs out of communion with the divine. That is why I have said that even a man who disowns religion cannot and does not live without religion.

Now I come to the next thing, *viz.*, that prayer is the very core of man's life, as it is the most vital part of religion. Prayer is either petitional or in its wider sense is inward communion. In either case the ultimate result is the same. Even when it is petitional, the petition should be for the cleansing and purification of the soul, for freeing it from the layers of ignorance and darkness that envelop it. He therefore who hungers for the awakening of the divine in him must fall back on prayer.

But prayer is no mere exercise of words or of the ears, it is no mere repetition of empty formula. Any amount of repetition of Ramanama is futile if it fails to stir the soul. It is better in prayer to have a heart without word than words without a heart. It must be in clear response to the spirit which hungers for it. And even as a hungry man relishes a hearty meal, a hungry soul will relish a heartfelt prayer. And I am giving you a bit of my experience and that of my companions when I say that he who has experienced the magic of prayer may do without food for days together but not a single moment without prayer. For without prayer there is no inward peace.

If that is the case, someone will say, we should be offering our prayers every minute of our lives. There is no doubt about it, but we erring mortals, who find it difficult to retire within ourselves for inward communion even for a single moment will find it impossible to remain perpetually in communion with the divine. We therefore fix some hours when we make a serious effort to throw off the attachments of the world for a while, we make a serious endeavour to remain, so to say, out of the flesh. You have heard Surdas's hymn. It is the passionate cry of a soul hungry for union with the divine. According to our standards he was a saint, but according to his own he was a proclaimed sinner. Spiritually he was miles ahead of us, but he felt the separation from the divine so keenly that he has uttered that anguished cry in loathing and despair.

I have talked of the necessity for prayer, and therethrough I have dealt with the essence of prayer. We are born to serve our fellowmen, and we cannot properly do so unless we are wide awake. There is an eternal struggle raging in man's breast between the powers of darkness and of light, and he who has not the sheet-anchor of prayer to rely upon will be a victim to the powers of darkness.

The man of prayer will be at peace with himself and with the whole world, the man who goes about the affairs of the world without a prayerful heart will be miserable and will make the world also miserable. Apart therefore from its bearing on man's condition after death, prayer has incalculable value for man in this world of the living. Prayer is the only means of bringing about orderliness and peace and repose in our daily acts. We inmates of the Ashram who came here in search of truth and for insistence on truth professed to believe in the efficacy of prayer, but had never up to now made it a matter of vital concern. We did not bestow on it the care that we did on other matters. I awoke from my slumbers one day and realized that I had been woefully negligent of my duty in the matter. I have therefore suggested measures of stern discipline and far from being any the worse, I hope we are the better for it. For it is so obvious. Take care of the vital thing and other things will take care of themselves. Rectify one angle of a square, and then other angles will be automatically right.

Begin therefore your day with prayer, and make it so soulful that it may remain with you until the evening. Close the day with prayer so that you may have a peaceful night free from dreams and nightmares. Do not worry about the form of prayer. Let it be any form, it should be such as can put us into communion with the divine. Only, whatever be the form, let not the spirit wander while the words of prayer run on out of your mouth.

If what I have said has gone home to you, you will not be at peace until you have compelled your hostel superintendents to interest themselves in your prayer and to make it obligatory. Restraint self-imposed is no compulsion. A man, who chooses the path of freedom from restraint, *i.e.*, of self-indulgence, will be a bondslave of passions, whilst the man who binds himself to rules and restraints releases himself. All things in the universe, including the sun and the moon and the stars, obey certain laws. Without the restraining influence of these laws the world would not go on for a single moment. You, whose mission in life is service of your fellowmen, will go to pieces if you do not impose on yourselves some sort of discipline, and prayer is a necessary spiritual discipline. It is discipline and restraint that separates us from the brute. If we will be men walking with our heads erect and not walking on all fours, let us understand and put ourselves under voluntary discipline and restraint. *(Speech at Prayer Meeting, Sabarmati Ashram, 17 January 1930 (CW 42, pp. 411–13))*

Sound Mind in a Sound Body

Exercise is just as essential to mankind as are air, water and food, though it is true that man cannot get on for a long time without air, water and food as he can without exercise. It is a fact of common experience, however, that one cannot enjoy really good health without exercise. We have to interpret exercise in the same way that we did "food". Exercise does not necessarily mean *moidanda* football, cricket or going out for a walk. Exercise means physical and mental activity. Just as food is necessary for the mind as much as for bones and flesh, so also is exercise necessary both for body and mind. If the body has no exercise, it is sickly and, if the mind has none, it is dull. Stupidity should also be regarded only as a kind of illness. It betrays sheer ignorance to describe as healthy a wrestler who, though adept at wrestling, is mentally a boor. There is a saying in English that he alone is healthy who has a sound mind in a sound body.

What is this exercise? Nature has so arranged things for us that we can be continuously taking exercise in one way or another. If we but think calmly enough, we shall see that a majority of people in the world live on agriculture. All members in a farmer's family have some form of exercise. It is only if they work eight, ten or even more hours every day in the fields or elsewhere that they can get their daily bread. They need no separate exercise for the mind. A farmer cannot work without applying his mind. He must be able to test the nature of his soil, must watch changes of weather, must know how to manipulate his plough skilfully and be generally familiar with the movements of the stars, the sun and the moon. However clever a city-dweller may be, every time he goes to a farmer's house, he feels altogether out of his element.

The farmer can say how seed should be sown; he is familiar with all the by-ways in the vicinity and knows all the men in the neighbourhood. By looking at the stars he can judge the direction even at night. He can make certain deductions from the voice and speed of birds; for instance, when certain birds cluster or sing together, he sees in it a sign of the approach of the monsoon or some other similar phenomenon. Thus, the farmer knows enough of astronomy, geography and geology to serve his needs. He has to feed his children and has, therefore, some idea of the duties of man, and, residing as he does in the vast open spaces of this earth, he naturally becomes aware of the greatness of God. Physically, it goes without saying, he is always sturdy. He is his own physician, when ill. Thus, we can see, he does have an educated mind.

But all men are not going to be farmers. Moreover, these chapters are not being written for the benefit of farmers. The question is, what should those who have gone into business or some similar profession do in this regard? The farmer's life has been described at some length in order that we may find a rational answer to this problem, that we who are not farmers can arrange our way of life somewhat on the pattern of his and that we may realize that, in so far as our manner of living differs from the farmer's, we would enjoy poorer health. We can conclude from a farmer's way of living that a man should do physical work for eight hours a day and that of a kind that would stimulate our mental powers in the very process of doing it.

Now, merchants and others certainly obtain mental exercise in the course of their work, but this is one-sided. A businessman does not know astronomy or geography or history, as the farmer does. He may be able to judge about movements of prices and may be proficient in the art of salesmanship, but this is not enough to exercise fully his mental faculties. In this type of work, the body does perform some movements now and then, but they are too slight to be of any account.

In the West, they have invented games like cricket for such people. Another way is to observe some days in the year as holidays, when more games are played, and to do some light reading by way of mental exercise. This is one method which we may consider. To be sure, spending time in sports does give some exercise to the body, but exercise of this kind does nothing to improve the mind. We can see the truth of this from numerous instances. What proportion of men of high intellectual calibre shall we find among those who regularly play cricket or from among the large number who play football? In India, what do we observe as regards the mental development of the princes who give their time to sports? Again, how many of those with well-developed intellectual powers are sportsmen? Experience shows that highly intellectual men are seldom sportsmen as well.

The British nowadays are very much given to sports. Their own poet, Kipling has described these sportsmen as enemies of the mind, and adds that they will also prove themselves enemies to their country. In India, our intellectuals seem to have found a different way. They provide exercise for their minds but relatively very little or none for their bodies. These people are lost to us. Their bodies are enfeebled by excessive intellectual work. They are continually pursued by some ailment or other and just when they have gained enough experience to be of real use to the country, they pass away. From this we may conclude that neither exercising the brain alone nor the body alone is enough and also that exercise which serves no useful purpose, namely, that derived from sports, has little meaning. Real exercise is that which trains, continuously, both mind and body alike. He alone who takes such exercise can preserve good health. The farmer is the only such person.

Then, what are those to do who are not farmers? The exercise obtained from sports such as cricket leaves much to be desired. We must, therefore, think of a form of exercise something like what the farmer gets. Businessmen and others similarly placed can make a garden round their house and regularly spend two to four hours a day digging there. Hawkers get exercise from their own work itself. If we are living in a rented room, we should not raise any difficulty about working in another's land, for that would indicate a small mind. We would derive nothing but benefit from working on land, whosoever's it might be. The appearance of our house would be improved and we would have the satisfaction of having looked after another's land.

It is necessary to say a few words for those who cannot find an opportunity to work on land or who do not favour such work in any circumstances. Apart from working on land, the best form of exercise is walking. It has been truly described as the king of physical exercises. Our *fakirs* and *sadhus* are very healthy. One reason for this is that they do not use horses, carriages or other vehicles. Their journeys are always performed on foot. There has been a famous American writer named Thoreau who has written a highly thought-provoking book on the subject of walking. According to him, the writings of one who refuses to leave his house on the excuse of lack of time and who undertakes no physical activity, are bound to be anaemic like himself. Speaking of his own experience, he says that when he wrote his best books he was doing his longest walking. He thought nothing of walking four or five hours at a stretch. Just as we cannot work when we are hungry, so it should be with exercise. We do not know how to measure mental work, therefore, we are not able to realize that mental work done unaccompanied by physical exercise will inevitably be dull and ineffectual.

Walking results in rapid circulation of blood in all the parts of the body, promotes movements in every organ and strengthens it. One should remember that the arms move during walking. We obtain fresh air by going for a walk and behold the beauties of Nature. One should not take walks always in the same place or in narrow lanes but go out into fields and groves. We will then be able to appreciate in some measure the beauty of Nature. A walk of a mile or two can scarcely be called walking. A walk, to be worth the name, should cover ten or twelve miles. Those who cannot do this regularly can take long walks on Sundays. A certain patient, who used to suffer from indigestion, went one day to an experienced *vaidya* for some pills.

The *vaidya* advised him to take short but regular walks. The patient protested that he was too weak. The *vaidya* realized that he was, in fact, a timid man. He thereupon took the patient with him in his carriage. On the way he purposely dropped his whip. The patient, out of politeness, had to get out to pick it up. The *vaidya* immediately drove off. The poor patient had to follow, panting hard for breath. The *vaidya* having made sure that the former had covered a fairly long distance, turned the carriage back, picked him up and told him that, since walking was the only medicine for him, he—the *vaidya*—had forced him to walk even at the risk of appearing cruel. By this time, however, the patient was ravenously hungry and had forgotten all about the whip episode. He thanked the doctor, went home and ate his fill. Those who are not in the habit of walking and suffer from indigestion and its accompanying ills should try the experiment. *(Indian Opinion, 12 April 1913 (Translated from Gujarati) (CW 12, pp. 22–27))*

Walking is the Best Exercise

We are as careless about exercise as about diet. To stroll one or two miles at a leisurely pace is no exercise. To hit a billiard ball one or two hundred times with a cue is also no exercise. When exercise is taken in this manner in a room with foul-smelling air, the effect is bound to harmful. In our predicament, when no other form of exercise is convenient, walking is the best exercise. But exercise is worth the name only if one can walk six miles at a stretch in the morning and again in the evening. The walking should be done briskly, at a speed of four miles an hour. Thoreau used to walk for eight hours daily when he wrote his best book. Tolstoy testifies to the fact that while writing his best books he never used to sit at his desk before he had plenty of exercise. He always used to work on a farm. [Some people say]: "I cannot spare a minute from the client's work or from public work, and take exercise." Such talk is sheer vanity. It would seem to proceed from a belief that but for us public work would go to the dogs. The Grand Old Man of India, Dadabhai has been observing all the general rules of hygiene and has never departed from his routine of exercise, etc. Hence, we see him alive to this day, and it would in no way be surprising if this rishi were to live a hundred years like those of old times. *(Prajabandhu, 23 April 1916 (CW 13, p. 270) (Translated from Gujarati))*

Indigenous Games

They have included various games, etc. in physical training. But, in this sphere too, nobody seems to have realized their true meaning and purpose, and our indigenous games have been left out. Tennis, cricket and football have gained in popularity. Admittedly, these three games are enjoyable. But if we had not been carried away by enthusiasm for these Western forms of sport, we would not have given up our inexpensive but equally interesting indigenous games like *gend-balla, gilli-danda, kho-kho, sat-tali, kabaddi,* etc. The old *akhadas,* which provided training in wrestling and various Indian forms of bodily exercise, have nearly gone out of existence for want of use. I think that the only western item in this field we may well copy is 'drill'. A friend once remarked that we do not know how to walk—particularly when there are more than one, and we have to walk in step. We totally lack the ability to walk quietly and regularly, to the accompaniment of *tal,* in formation of twos and fours, when there are hundreds or thousands of us.

It is not that such drilling is useful only in actual battle. It may prove quite useful in many acts of service also. For example, in extinguishing fire, in rescuing people from drowning, in carrying the sick and disabled in *doli,* etc. previous practice in drill is a valuable aid. Thus, it is necessary to introduce in our schools indigenous games, exercise and the Western type of drill. Speech at Second Gujarat Educational Conference, Broach, 20 October 1917. *(CW 14, pp. 30–31)*

Inexpensive Exercises

Many students feel that it is not necessary to make any special effort for health. However, regular exercise is absolutely necessary for the body. What can be expected of a student who is not well-equipped in health? Just as milk cannot be held in a paper container, so also education is not likely to remain for long in the paper-like bodies of our students. The body is the abode of the spirit and, therefore, holy like a place of pilgrimage. We must see that it is well protected.

Walking regularly and energetically for an hour and a half in the morning and for the same period in the evening in open air keeps it healthy and the mind fresh. The time thus spent is not wasted. Such exercise, coupled with rest, will invigorate both the body and the intellect, enabling one to learn things more quickly. I think games like cricket have no place in a poor country like India. We have a number of inexpensive games of our own which afford innocent joy. *(CW 14, pp. 135–36)*

Ancient Indian Asanas

In my opinion the physical training for our students should follow the old Indian system—that of *pranayam, asanas,* etc. I believe that the system of physical education developed by Muller and others in the West, who have written on this subject and also demonstrated the efficacy of their system through practical results, has its roots in the old Indian system. What these writers have done is to set it out in modern scientific language and perhaps to improve it in places. I am conscious that we have done very little work in this direction. Having gone through a course of training according to this old system, those who further want to learn the present day wrestling, etc.

may be given the facilities to do so. But training *lathi* and sword, etc. should not be considered necessary. I do not think that it is necessary to give lathi-training, etc. to the boys. Lathi does not seem to have much to do with the toning up of the body or with the development of its different parts. It is not therefore a part of the physical training but a part of the training useful in one's defence or similar purposes.

Compulsory Physical Training

I was glad to hear that physical training and games have been made compulsory. Let us make compulsory for ourselves all that is good. Gujarati and Sanskrit, etc. we consider good and necessary and therefore prescribe them as compulsory subjects. We did not consider physical training and games equally necessary and had left them to the choice of the students. Now that we have made them compulsory it means that we consider them as necessary as Gujarati. Restraints imposed upon us against our will tend to make slaves of us, but restraints willingly accepted augment our true independence.

Brahmacharya and Ahimsa

'You know,' said he, 'that I am a man conscious of my limitations and it is not in my nature to have more things than I can attend to. But I could not resist Dr. Patwardhan's request. I was glad to be told that this gymnasium was open to Hindus and Musalmans alike, and that not only Musalman but 'untouchable' youths are members of it. I rejoice to see that the institution is thus free from communalism.

'Our Shastras say that a boy who would keep his body fit and strong and make the best use of it should observe *Brahmacharya.* I have travelled all over the country and one of the most deplorable things I have noticed is the rickety bodies of young men. So long as we labour under the curse of child marriage, and so long as many members of our society are children of such marriages, so long much bodily exercise is an impossibility. Who will recommend physical exercise to consumptives? We should therefore lay the axe at the root of this curse, if we would see our young men and women strong and healthy and India on the path of vigorous and healthy growth. Manu has laid down that a student should observe *Brahmacharya* up to his 25th year at least. All physical exercise will be futile so long as these conditions are not satisfied.

'But there is another thing to which I should like to draw your attention. You know that I am pledged to have nothing to do with things even remotely connected with violence. Whatever others may say, I am convinced that the way of nonviolence is the only way and the highest and permanent religion for me. How is it then, some one might ask, that an avowed votary of nonviolence like me has at all associated himself with an institution like this? The reason is clear. *Ahimsa* or nonviolence means the renunciation of the capacity to use violence. He who has not that capacity is therefore incapable of exercising nonviolence.

Nonviolence is a mighty spiritual force, but its votary should have the power to use physical force and should consciously and deliberately refuse to exercise that force. Not that physical training is a *sine qua non* for acquiring capacity for violence, but we may not encourage our youths to have feeble physiques in order to be capable of *ahimsa.* You cannot make a man nonviolent by depriving him of arms. One of the many crimes of the British rule in India is that we have been forcibly deprived of our arms—not indeed with a view to making us nonviolent even if such a thing was possible but to emasculating us. I want India to be strong and free to exercise its strength and yet to renounce it.

'Thus I like institutions like these for physical training. But let me utter a word of warning. No institution that has as its object the subjection of a community, whether Hindu, Musalman, Parsi or Christian, can have my blessings. Only that institution can have my blessings which aims at the growth of the physical culture of all communities, of all the youths of the nation, to whatever creed or community they belong. I should not have come here, did I not know that the gymnasium I have opened belonged to the latter type. Congratulating you once more I wish and pray that you may all be true and pure, and your lives may be consecrated to the service of our nation and of our religions.' *(Speech at Vyayam Mandir, Amaraoti, Young India, 30 December 1926 True Education, pp. 108-109))*

Physical versus Spiritual Strength

I install this image of Maruti here, not merely because Maruti had the strength of a giant. Even Ravana had that strength. But Maruti had the strength of soul, and his physical strength was only a manifestation of his spiritual strength which in its turn was the direct fruit of his exclusive devotion to Rama and his *Brahmacharya.* May you therefore be like Maruti of matchless valour born out of your *Brahmacharya* and may that valour be dedicated to the service of the Motherland. *(Speech at Vaisya Vidyashram Gymnasium, Young India, 17 March 1927 (CW 33, p. 143))*

Time for Exercise

'But you do not even go out for walks,' said I. 'Is it surprising that you should be always ailing? Should public work leave no time for physical exercise?'

'When do you ever find me free to go out for a walk?' He replied.

I had such a great regard for Gokhale that I never strove with him. Though this reply was far from satisfying me, I remained silent. I believed then and I believe even now, that no matter what amount of work one has, one should always find some time for exercise, just as one does for one's meals. It is my humble opinion that, far from taking away from one's capacity for work, it adds to it. *(An Autobiography, Vol. I, p. 348 (CW 39, pp. 188–9))*

Mass Drill

The object of mass drill is to enable large bodies of people to perform any movement rhythmically and swiftly and with absolute precision. What a saving in national time and energy it would mean if we could do that in our public meetings and functions! There is a silent music in disciplined movement of masses of men and women. Just now I asked you to move a little towards me so that my low voice may reach you. Had you advanced far enough in your drill, you would have been able to perform that movement with ease without any noise or confusion.

There is a rhythm and music in drill that makes action effortless and eliminates fatigue. If the whole nation of 300 millions could be drilled so as to move together and act together and if necessary to die together as one man, we should attain independence without striking a blow and set an example of a peaceful revolution for the whole world to emulate. *(Speech at Scouts Rally Segaon, 22 December 1938 (CW 68, pp. 232-3))*

Right to Punish

> *"I believe that corporal punishment does not improve anyone If, in spite of my belief, I still punish the students of my class, would it be regarded as violence on my part on not? Again, if I do not punish them myself and send a boy who is mischievous or dull to the Headmaster knowing that he will award him physical punishment, would I be deemed to be guilty of violence or not?"*

There is certainly violence in punishing the students—whether one punishes them oneself, or sends them to the Headmaster to be punished by him. The question whether a teacher may at all punish any student has not been explicitly asked, but it is implied in the original question. I can imagine a situation when it may be one's duty to punish even a young boy if he has committed a wrong and is conscious of it. Every teacher must decide for himself what course of action to take. But, as a general rule, a teacher should never inflict corporal punishment on students.

The right to punish them belongs to the parents, if at all. A punishment is just only if it is accepted by the student himself. Such occasions, however, do not often arise. Even when they arise, punishment should never be inflicted if there is any doubt about its justness. Lastly, no punishment should be inflicted in anger. *(Navajivan, 27 September 1925 (CW 28, p. 242))*

Teaching sans Punishment

A teacher in a *Vinaya Mandir* (national high school) asks:

1. Is there any justification for corporal punishment being meted out to boys in schools, especially in national schools?

2. Some teachers opine: "We may not punish boys who fail to fulfil the assignments given them; but there would be nothing wrong in punishing them if they commit mischief or moral offence?" Is this opinion correct?
3. Some friends say that they punish boys at times in order to improve them, but they are also sorry for having done so afterwards and no blame, therefore, attaches to them. Could we excuse the teacher who punishes his pupils and makes this plea afterwards?
4. What other forms of punishment, besides the corporal, should be prohibited in national schools?
5. What forms of punishment will imply a breach of the pledge of nonviolence on the part of the teacher in a national school?

The above questions have not been put to you through idle curiosity. The teachers of this school have been discussing them for some time past, and the arguments which I have quoted were actually used by some of them.

Because they are of practical importance, your considered opinion on them will provide guidance to a large number of teachers. You may answer them in the columns of the *Harijan*—if you will be so kind.

I hold the view that it is wrong to inflict punishment on the boys in any form whatsoever. It diminishes the love for, and pride in, their students which teachers should have. The old system of punishing students in order to teach them is fast disappearing in modern educational methods. I know that occasions crop up when even the best teachers cannot help punishing the offender among students. But, fortunately, such occasions are few, and, in any case, it would not be right to justify them. If a teacher feels compelled to resort to punishment it should be taken as implying a deficiency, to that extent, in his profession. Educationists like Spencer have held as improper every form of punishment, though he could not always stick by his precept.

After giving the above answer, it does not seem necessary to reply the other questions in detail. As a general rule, nonviolence and punishment cannot go together. I can certainly imagine cases in which punishment would not be punishment. But such examples would not be useful to teachers. For instance, if a father is very sad over his son's misconduct and, unable to bear the grief, beats him, his beating the boy might well be regarded as the punishment of love. The boy would also not consider it violence. Those who nurse a patient in delirium have, at times, to slap him in order to control him. This would also be not violence, but nonviolence. But such examples are worthless to teachers. They must acquire the art of disciplining students and of teaching them without punishing them. There are examples of teachers who have never used punishment. Other forms of punishment, besides corporal punishment, are: to make the students get down from their seat, to make them do the stand-and-sit exercise, to abuse them, etc. According to me, the teacher should not punish students at all.

To punish the boys first for improving them and then be sorry for it is no true penitence. Besides, if the teachers adopt this practice and act on it, it will ultimately become a behaviour pattern of people in our society. Punishment has led us to believe in the illusion that improvement can be brought about through the use of violence. I hold the view that a teacher, who deliberately uses punishment, commits a breach of his pledge in regard to non violence. *(Navajivan, 21 October 1928 (CW 37, pp. 399–400))*

Spare the Rod

I am a teacher. I try to follow the principle of nonviolence in dealing with my schoolboys and my own children. I am successful to a great extent in case of the school children, excepting a bully whom I would send to the Head Master. But in case of my own children I often feel like beating, though I successfully restrain myself. I find that these are readily obedient to my uncle who, unlike me, believes in the old saying 'Spare the rod, spoil the child.' What should I do with my own children? How should a nonviolent Head Master deal with a bully?

I am quite clear that you must not inflict corporal or other punishment on your children or pupils. You can punish yourself, if you like and are qualified, in order to melt your children's or pupils' hearts. Many mothers are known to have corrected their children in this manner. I have on many occasions. I had to deal with wild boys in South Africa—Muslims, Christians, Hindus and Parsis. With one exception; I do not remember ever having punished a single boy. The nonviolent method invariably succeeded. When a bond is established between a teacher and his pupils, the latter will generally yield before their teachers' suffering for their sake. In the case of your 'bully' if he has no respect for you, you can non-co-operate with him by sending him away from your school. Nonviolence does not compel you to keep in your school a student who does not carry out disciplinary rules. *(Harijan, 13 July 1940 (CW 72, p. 226))*

Library

I have some ideas about libraries—about what they should be and what they should do. I will place them before you. First, you must so plan the building of the library that it can be enlarged as the library expands without marring its symmetry. The later additions should not appear as extraneous accretions to the original building. It should provide facilities for arranging occasional lectures, and for students and scholars engaged in research work to come and make use of the books there in an atmosphere of peace. We should aim at making this library the biggest and the best in the world. If we have the will, God will give us the strength to do it. Kakasaheb has suggested that the collection of books with the Vidyapith may be kept here. There is no dearth of art in Gujarat. The famous lattice-work in stone in the mosque at Bhadra has no match in the whole world. Similarly, the needle-work of Ahmedabad is perhaps unrivalled. The delicacy of stone-work of the masons of Ahmedabad has surprised me. I have seen them living in dark and dingy hovels. Artists do not wait for encouragement. If we could find another donor ready to offer fifty thousand rupees, for a museum, we could set up one in this very building. We have to work in such a way that the library may grow and develop from day to day.

It would be better if we could get one or two men who would devote most of their time to it. Don't choose a money-minded businessman, who would merely keep the books safe and in good condition, for the post of librarian. Choose someone who could be depended upon to appreciate the relative worth of different books and select them. In case no one volunteers his services for it free, you should be ready to offer a good salary and appoint a really qualified man. Harijans should be allowed to use the library without any fee, and if books are spoiled or damaged or even stolen, the loss should be borne by the library itself. The Harijans are the poorest of the poor and are entitled to special consideration. In fact, you may extend this concession to all poor people. That will enhance the glory of the institution.

I also repeat the request made by Bhai Rasiklal, namely, the managing body for the library should be carefully chosen from a body of scholars so as to keep the institution alive and growing. Do not think that this body should be composed only of men of practical wisdom, for scholars understand what a library should be like and how it can be made to shine. Carnagie gave large donations to many libraries. The conditions he attached to his donations were accepted by most scholars, except those of Scotland. They frankly told Carnagie that if he insisted on his conditions they would not accept the donation. How could he know, they asked, what books would be useful to the library? The artists do not sell their art. There are in Gujarat large collections of precious books.

But they are in the possession of *banias*. The Jains have fine collections of old books of great historical value, but they are lying useless tied up in silken sheaths. I have wept over the sight of these books which serve no purpose by being in the hands of the *banias* who know nothing except how to make money. I would go as far as to say that in their hands the Jaina religion itself is dying of starvation by being in the stranglehold of money. Is it possible to count dharma against money? In fact, money should be only the means of dharma. I, therefore, ask you to include able scholars in the managing body of the library. Find out how to do this, and see that you do it. *(Extract from speech delivered at foundation-laying ceremony of the Ahmedabad Sangrahalaya, Satyagraha Ashram—Harijanbandhu, 1 October 1933, (True Education, pp. 169–70))*

Textbooks

I have written a book called *Balpothi,* not much worth talking about. If I sit down to read it, I can finish it in five minutes. If I read it a little carefully, I would finish it in ten minutes. I have not read the comments on it which have been received. I know that many of these are not likely to please me much. There is no measure in the praise or censure generally showered on me and, therefore, either has little effect on me. However that be, the idea behind that book is great.

It is that a teacher should impart education only by word of mouth; that he cannot do so with the help of books and textbooks. Who knows what stuff gets into the brains of children in countries where there are heaps of textbooks! The devil takes possession of them, the children's thinking power is reduced to nil.

This conclusion of mine is based on my experience of countless children and on discussions with many teachers. I used to move about with wide-open eyes in South Africa. There was a conflagration in the country, and moving even in the midst of that I observed this thing. Let us compare two schools: one in which teachers are supplied with textbooks and another in which they have to teach without the use of a single textbook.

The teachers in both are equally gifted. The one, then, which has no textbooks to use will be able to give more to the pupils than the one which has them. I do not want children to have any text books. The teachers may, if they wish, read them. We may write as much for them as we choose. If you write for children, you will make the teachers mechanical and destroy their originality and initiative.

I do not, of course, wish to arrest the progress of teachers. I merely want that you should also know this point of view of mine. The authors of textbooks are experienced writers. Where the people need their books, by all means let them buy them, but please understand what lies behind my attitude.

You may ask me if I have worked as a teacher. My view is based on considerable experience and I have thought a great deal about education. Kindly think about the matter from the point of view indicated by me and go a little slow. The point of what I am saying is that, if you wish to bring out books for lakhs of children, well, Gujarat does not have the money for that and it will lose interest in this business; secondly, we should not burden the children's brains with these books. *(Navajivan 3 August 1924 (CW 24, pp. 488–90))*

Choking Load of Books

Pupils should know to discriminate between what should be received and what rejected. It is the duty of the teacher to teach his pupils discrimination. If we go on taking in indiscriminately we would be no better than machines. We are thinking, knowing beings and we must in this period distinguish truth from untruth, sweet from bitter language, clean from unclean things and so on.

But the student's path today is strewn with more difficulties than the one of distinguishing good from bad things. The *rishis* taught their pupils without books. They only gave them a few *mantras* which the pupils treasured in their memories and translated in practical life. The present day student has to live in the midst of heaps of books, sufficient to choke him. *(Young India, 29 January 1925 (Towards New Education pp. 39-37))*

Textbooks for Teachers

For India a multiplicity of textbooks means deprivation of the vast majority of village children of the means of instruction. Textbooks, therefore, in India must mean, principally and for the lower standards, textbooks for teachers, not pupils. Indeed, I am not sure that it is not better for the children to have much of the preliminary instruction imparted to them vocally. To impose on children of tender age a knowledge of the alphabet and the ability to read before they can gain general knowledge is to deprive them, whilst they are fresh, of the power of assimilating instruction by word of mouth. Should, for instance, a lad of seven wait for learning the Ramayana till he can read it? The results that we arrive at when we think of the few lakhs living in the cities of India are wholly different from those we obtain, we think, in terms of the millions of rural India. *(Young India, 16 September 1926 (CW 31, p. 410))*

Books versus Need-based Learning

There seems to me to be no doubt that in the public schools the books used, especially for children, are for the most part useless when they are not harmful. That many of them are cleverly written cannot be denied. They might even be the best for the people and the environment for which they are written. But they are not written for Indian boys and girls, not for the Indian environment. When they are so written, they are generally undigested imitations hardly answering the wants of the scholars. In this country, wants vary according to the provinces and the classes of children. For instance, want of Harijan children are, in the beginning stages at least, different from those of the others.

I have, therefore, come to the conclusion that books are required more for the teachers than for the taught. And every teacher, if he is to do full justice to his pupils, will have to prepare the daily lesson from the material available to him. This too, he will have to suit to the special requirements of his class.

Real education has to draw out the best from the boys and girls to be educated. This can never be done by packing ill, assorted and unwanted information into the heads of the pupils. It becomes a dead weight crushing all originality in them and turning them into mere automata. If we were not ourselves victims of the system, we would long ago have realized the mischief wrought by the modern method of giving mass education, especially in a case like India's.

Attempts have undoubtedly been made by many institutions to produce their own textbooks with more or less success. But in my opinion they do not answer the vital needs of the country. I lay no claim to originality for the views I have endeavoured to set forth here. They are repeated here for the benefit of the managers and teachers of Harijan schools, who have a tremendous task before them. They dare not be satisfied with mere mechanical work resulting in simply making the children under their charge indifferently and in a parrotlike manner learn the books chosen anyhow. They have undertaken a great trust which they must discharge courageously, intelligently and honestly.

The task is difficult enough but not so difficult as one would imagine, provided the teacher or the manager puts his whole heart into the work. If he becomes a parent to his pupils, he will instinctively know what they need and set about giving it to them. If he has it not to give, he will proceed to qualify himself. And seeing that we have started with the idea that the boys and girls have to have instruction in accordance with their wants, no extraordinary cleverness or possession of external knowledge is required in a teacher of Harijan and, for that matter, any other children.

And when it is remembered that the primary aim of all education is, or should be, the moulding of the character of pupils, a teacher who has a character to keep need not lose heart. *(Harijan, 1 December 1933 (CW 56, pp. 295-6))*

Craze for Changing Textbooks

The craze for ever-changing textbooks is hardly a healthy sign from the educational standpoint. If textbooks are treated as a vehicle for education, the living word of the teacher has very little value. A teacher who teaches from textbooks does not impart originality to his pupils. He himself becomes a slave of textbooks and has no opportunity or occasion to be original. It therefore seems that the less textbooks there are the better it is for the teacher and his pupils. Textbooks seem to have become an article of commerce. Authors and publishers who make writing and publishing a means of making money are interested in a frequent change of textbooks. In many cases teachers and examiners are themselves authors of textbooks.

It is naturally to their interest to have their books sold. The selection board is again naturally composed of such people. And so the vicious circle becomes complete. And it becomes very difficult for parents to find money for new books every year. It is a pathetic sight to see boys and girls going to school loaded with books which they are ill able to carry. The whole system requires to be thoroughly examined. The commercial spirit needs to be entirely eliminated and the question approached solely in the interest of the scholars. It will then probably be found that 75 per cent of the textbooks will have to be consigned to the scrap-heap. If I had my way, I would have books largely as aids to teachers rather than for the scholars. Such textbooks as are found to be absolutely necessary for the scholars should be circulated among them for a number of years so that the cost can be easily borne by middle class families. The first step in this direction is perhaps for the State to own and organize the printing and publishing of textbooks. This will act as an automatic check on their unnecessary multiplication. *(Harijan, 9 September 1939 (CW 70, p. 153))*

Unhealthy Textbooks

There is in Wardha a girls' school. Several girls are preparing there for the Sammelan examination. Both teachers and girls complain that not all the prescribed textbooks are fit to be read. It has been complained that they are too full of erotic matter. There is erotic literature in Hindi. Shri Benarsidas Chaturvedi had drawn my attention to this a few years ago. The literature of the language which we wish to make our national language should be pure, radiant and lofty. Nowadays there is a good deal of obscene literature in Hindi. Editors of periodicals are either not careful or they deliberately encourage obscenity in the writings. In my opinion the Sammelan should not remain indifferent in this matter. Good writers should get encouragement from the Sammelan. People should also get some help from the Sammelan in choosing the right books. The task no doubt is difficult but we cannot run away from difficulties. *(Speech at Hindi Sahitya Sammelan, Indore, 20 April 1935 (CW 60, pp. 449–50))*

Teacher and Textbooks

Nowadays the teacher's task has in fact been reduced to that of a postman or a foreman. It consists only of placing books written by educationists in the hands of pupils and of supervising whether they make use of these or not. In addition to this, what other skill do you expect the teachers to possess?

The science of education has been developed to the extent where the term 'teacher' may be defined as one who can clarify the meaning of difficult passages and prepare abstracts of long chapters. Why should we not now accept this ideal?

I keep on feeling that teachers in the true sense of the word are essential, no matter how good the textbooks are. A good teacher would never content himself with summarizing or explaining the meaning of difficult passages. Time and again, he would go beyond the textbooks and present his subject to the pupil in a vivid manner in the same way as an artist does. The best textbook may be compared to the best photograph. However, just as a painting by an artist although second rate is invariably superior to a photograph, similar is the case with a real teacher. A true teacher introduces the pupil to his subject, creates in him interest for the subject and enables him to understand it independently. In my opinion, one who explains difficult passages and prepares abstracts can never be regarded a good teacher. Our endeavours should be to turn out true teachers who could be infused with a spirit of service. It is not that stray instances of such teachers are not to be found even today. *(Navajivan, 16 June 1928 (CW 36, pp. 352–3) (Translated from Gujarati))*

Language and Spellings

The anarchy prevailing in Gujarati spelling is perhaps unparalleled in any other language. It is not found in Marathi, Bengali, Tamil or Urdu. I have not heard of it in any other Indian language. It is to be found in no European language. What epithet except barbarous can one apply to a people who speak a language with unorganized spelling? Man's language develops as he progresses. A man can be judged in several matters by the language he speaks.

The Government of Bombay took quite some time to come to a decision, but they deserve to be congratulated on having at last arrived at one. I hope all journalists and authors will be guided by the dictionary prepared by the Vidyapith. The Vidyapith should provide the necessary means to facilitate this. Every lover of language must have in his pocket or on his desk a Gujarati dictionary as he would have an English dictionary if he were writing English. Gujarati writers must be as proud of the purity of their language as the English are of theirs. An Englishman who cannot spell correctly is considered uncivilized. But let us leave aside English. Why should we not devote as much attention to our mother tongue as the students studying in our English schools give or are required to give to English spelling? The Vidyapith should immediately provide facilities for this purpose. The Vidyapith dictionary is of course there. But a simpler and cheaper pocket edition should be prepared. An attempt has been made in the said dictionary to include as many words as possible along with their meanings in brief. It is enough if the pocket edition gives only the spelling and not all words need be included. Only words whose spelling is doubtful should be included. *(Harijanbandhu, 4 February 1940 (Translated from Gujarati) (CW 71, pp. 176-7))*

Music

Nowhere do I find a place given to music. It exercises a powerful influence over us. We do not realize this vividly enough, otherwise we would have done everything possible to teach music to our boys and girls. The Vedic hymns seem to follow musical tunes in their composition. Harmonious music has the power to soothe the anguish of the soul. At times, we find restlessness in a large gathering. This can be arrested and calmed if a national song is sung by all. That hundreds of boys may sing a poem full of courage and the spirit of adventure and bravery and be inspired with the spirit of heroism is no commonplace fact. We have an example of the power of music in the fact that boatmen and other labourers raise, in unison, the cry of Harahar and Allabeli and this helps them in their work. I have seen English friends trying to fight cold by singing songs.

Our boys learn to sing songs from popular plays in all manner of tunes and without regard to time and place, and try their hands, on noisy harmoniums and other instruments, and this does them harm. If, instead, they were to be correctly trained in music, they would not waste their time singing, or attempting to sing, music-hall songs. Just as a trained singer never sings out of tune or at the wrong time, even so one who has learnt classical music will not go in for street music. Music must get a place in our efforts at popular awakening. *(CW 14, p. 30)*

Mass Music

Music means rhythm, order. Its effect is electrical. It immediately soothes. Unfortunately like our *shastras*, music has been the prerogative of the few. It has never become nationalized in the modern sense. If I had any influence with volunteer boy scouts and Seva Samiti organizations, I would make compulsory a proper singing in company of national songs. And to that end I should have great musicians attending every Congress or Conference and teaching mass music. *(Young India, 8 September 1920 (CW 18, p. 241))*

Music and Other Arts

Our conversation having that morning centred round music, Mahatmaji told me in passing how fond he really was of music even though he could not boast of the power of any expert or analytic appreciation. He had said:

> *I am so fond of music that once, while I was in a South African Hospital and ailing from a bruise on my upper lip, I felt greatly soothed as the daughter of a friend of mine sang the song 'Lead, Kindly Light' at my request.*

On my asking him if he knew any of the beautiful songs of Mirabai, he said:

> *Yes, I have heard a good many of them. They are so beautiful. It's because they come from the heart and not from any desire to compose or to please a public.*

I called the same evening at his request. After the music, I saw that it had affected him visibly. For I thought I saw his eyes glisten even in that none-too-bright light of the hospital.

"I feel," said I after a short pause, "that our beautiful music has been sadly neglected in the schools and colleges." Mahatmaji replied:

Yes, it has, I have always said so.

Srijut Mahadeo Desai who was present throughout our conversation corroborated this. "I am glad to hear you say so. Because I have been all along under the impression that you would be against all arts such as music."

I! Against music! Well, I know, I know.......There are so many superstitions rife about me that it has become now almost impossible for me to overtake those who have set them afloat. As a result, my friends only smile at me when I try to lay any claim to being an artist myself.

"I am glad to hear this; because I have been given to understand that in your philosophy of life, which is one of unqualified asceticism, arts like music can hardly aspire to any place." Mahatmaji emphatically said:

But I maintain that asceticism is the greatest art in life.

"What I however meant by art just now is a somewhat different activity such as music or painting or sculpture for the matter of that. And I had thought that you would be rather opposed to them than otherwise." Mahatmaji said:

I, opposed to arts like music! Why, I cannot even conceive of an evolution of the religious life of India without music. I do say I am a lover of music as well as the other arts. Only, my values may be different from the accepted ones, that's all. I am doubtless against much that passes for art in these days. I do not for instance call that art which demands an intimate knowledge of its technique for its appreciation. If you go to the Satyagraha Ashram, you will find the walls bare. And my friends object to this. I admit I don't have paintings on the walls of my Ashram. But that is because I think that the walls are meant for sheltering us, and not because I am opposed to art as such. For have I not gazed and gazed at the wonderful vault of the starry sky—hardly ever tiring of the same? And I do say that I can never conceive of any painting superior to the star-studded sky in its satisfying effect on the mind. It has bewildered me, mystified me—sent me into the most wonderful ecstatic thrills imaginable. Side by side with this wondrous mystery of God's artistic handi-work, does not that of man appear to be the merest tinsel?

I said: "I agree with you when you say that Nature is a great artist, as also when you inveigh against the regrettable prostitution of art, which unhappily so often passes for art. I differ also from those artists who have acquired the habit of saying that art is even greater than life."

Exactly. Life is and must always be greater than all the arts put together. I go still further. For I say that he is the greatest artist who leads the best life. For what is art without the background and setting of a worthy life? An art is to be valued only when it ennobles life. I object emphatically only when people say that art is everything, that it does not matter even if life has to be held subservient to its (*i.e.*, art's) fulfilment. I have then to say that my values are different, that is all. But fancy people saying that I am opposed to all arts on that account!

An interview with Dilip Kumar Roy, an exponent of Indian music and inmate of the Aurobindo Ashram, Pondicherry. *(The Bombay Chronicle, 5 February 1924 (CW 23, pp. 192–4))*

Music—A Divine Art

Why do you always attach so much importance to music?

It is sad that the study of music is generally neglected in our country today. Without it, the entire educational system seems to me to be incomplete. Music brings sweetness to the individual and to the social life of the people. Even as *pranayama is* necessary for the regulation of breath, so is music for disciplining the voice. Dissemination of the knowledge of music among the people will greatly help in controlling and stopping the music which is a usual feature of public meetings in this country. Music pacified anger and its judicious use is highly helpful in leading a man to the vision of God.

It does not mean shouting and shrieking a tune anyhow like a rigmarole, nor does it mean the singing of stage songs. I have already referred to its ordinary meaning above, but its deeper meaning is that our whole life should be sweet and musical like a song. It goes without saying that life cannot be made like that without the practice of virtues such as truth, honesty, etc. To make life musical means to make it one with God, to merge it in Him. He who has not rid himself of raga and dwesha, *i.e.*, likes and dislikes, who has not tasted of the joy of service, cannot have any understanding of celestial music. A study of music, which does not take account of this deeper aspect of this divine art, has little or no value for me. *(Navjivan, 1 July 1928 (CW 37, pp. 2–3) (Translated from Gujarati))*

Music and Harmony

There is a famous classical saying which has now become a proverb that the man 'that hath no music in himself' is either an ascetic or a beast. We are far from being ascetics, and to the extent that we are devoid of music we are near allied to beasts. To know music is to transfer it to life. The prevalent discord of today is an indication of our sad plight. There can be no Swaraj where there is no harmony, no music.

Where there is discord and every one striking his own tune, there is bad government or anarchy. Work for Swaraj fails to appeal to us because we have no music in us. When we have millions of people singing together in harmony or taking God's name in unison, making one music, we shall have taken the first step to Swaraj. If we cannot achieve this simple thing, how can we win Swaraj.

Where there is filth and squalor and misery there can be no music. It implies an atmosphere quite the contrary. If we put a broad interpretation on music, *i.e.*, if we mean by it union, concord, mutual help, it may be said that in no department of life can we dispense with it.

Music today has been degraded to mean the vocal effort of a singing girl. We fight shy of sending our sisters and daughters to music schools. There seems to be a superstition that their voice is best when it is devoid of sweetness. That explains why Dr. Hariprasad has had to express satisfaction with an attendance of ten students.

Music, truly speaking, is an ancient and sacred art. The hymns of Samaveda are a mine of music, and no ayat of the Koran can be recited unmusically. David's Psalms transport you to raptures and remind you of the hymns from Samaveda. Let us revive this art and patronize the school of music.

We see Hindu and Musalman musicians sitting cheek by jowl and partaking in musical concerts. When shall we see the same fraternal union in other affairs of our life? We shall then have the name of Rama and Rahman simultaneously on our lips.

I am glad some of you here are patronizing music. If many more send their children to the music class it will be part of their contribution to national uplift.

But to go a step further. If we would see music in millions of our homes, we should all wear Khadi and spin. The music we have had today was sweet indeed but it is a privilege of the favoured few. The music of the spinning wheel can be a free gift to all and is therefore sweeter. It is the hope and solace and mainstay of the millions, and for me therefore truly good music. *(Young India, 15 April 1926 (CW 30, pp. 159–60))*

Music Fills the Soul

A student of the Gujarat Vidyapith asks:

"What has been the influence of music on your life?"

Music has given me peace. I can remember occasions when music instantly tranquillized my mind when I was greatly agitated over something. Music has helped me to overcome anger. I can recall occasions when a hymn sank deep into me though the same thing expressed in prose had failed to touch me. I also found that the meaning of hymns discordantly sung has failed to come home to me and that it burns itself on my mind when they have been properly sung. When I hear Gita verses melodiously recited I never grow weary of hearing and the more 1 hear the deeper sinks the meaning into my heart. Melodious recitations of the Ramayana which I heard in my childhood left on me an impression which years have not obliterated or weakened.

I distinctly remember how when once the hymn 'The path of the Lord is meant for the brave, not the coward' was sung to me in an extraordinarily sweet tune, it moved me as it had never before. In 1907 while in the Transvaal I was almost fatally assaulted, the pain of the wounds was relieved when at my instance Olive Doke gently sang to me 'Lead kindly light'.

Let no one infer from this that I know music. On the contrary it would be more correct to say that my knowledge of music is very elementary. I cannot critically judge music. All I can claim is that I have a natural ear for good homely music.

I do not mean to suggest either that because the influence of music has been uniformly good on me it must act similarly on others. On the contrary I know that many people employ music to feed their carnal passions. To sum up, therefore, we may say that the influence of music will differ according to temperaments. As Tulsidas has sung:

The Lord of Creation created everything in this world as an admixture of good and evil. But a good man selects the good and rejects the evil even as the fabled swan is said to help himself to cream leaving the water in the milk. (Young India, 10 January 1929 (CW 38, p. 90))

Music in Schools

Pandit Khare of Gandharva Mahavidyalaya, who has dedicated his life to the spread of pure music among boys and girls, reports the great progress being made in Ahmedabad in particular and Gujarat in general, and he deplores the fact that the education authorities do not seem to countenance the introduction of music in the curricula of education. In the Pandit's opinion, based upon wide experience, it should form part of the syllabus of primary education. I heartily endorse the proposition. The modulation of the voice is as necessary as the training of the hand. Physical drill, handicrafts, drawing and music should go hand in hand in order to draw the best out of the boys and girls and create in them a real interest in their tuition. *(Harijan, 11 September 1937 (CW 66, p. 121))*

True Art is Expression of the Soul

How is it that many intelligent and eminent men, who love and admire you, hold that you consciously or unconsciously have ruled out of the scheme of national regeneration all considerations of Art? I am sorry that in this matter I have been generally misunderstood. There are two aspects of things—the outward and the inward. It is purely matter of emphasis with me. The outward has no meaning except in so far as it helps the inward. All true Art is thus the expression of the soul. The outward forms have value only in so far as they are the expression of the inner spirit of man.

Hesitatingly: The great artists themselves have declared, that Art is the translation of the urge and unrest in the soul of the artist into words, colours, shapes, etc.

Yes, Art of that nature has the greatest possible appeal for me. But I know that many call themselves as artists, and are recognized as such, and yet in their works there is absolutely no trace of the soul's upward urge and unrest.

Have you any instance in mind?

Yes, take Oscar Wilde. I can speak of him, as I was in England at the time that he was being much discussed and talked about. I have been told that Oscar Wilde was one of the greatest literary artists of modern times.

Yes, that is just my trouble. Wilde saw the highest Art simply in outward forms and therefore succeeded in beautifying immorality. All true Art must help the soul to realize its inner self. In my own case, I find that I can do entirely without external forms in my soul's realization. I can claim, therefore, that there is truly sufficient Art in my life, though you might not see what you call works of Art about me. My room may have blank walls; and I may even dispense with the roof, so that I may gaze out upon the starry heavens overhead that stretch in an unending expanse of beauty.

What conscious Art of man can give me the panoramic scenes that open out before me, when I look up to the sky above with all its shining stars? This, however, does not mean that I refuse to accept the value of productions of Art, generally accepted as such, but only that I personally feel how inadequate these are compared with the eternal symbols of beauty in Nature. These productions of man's Art have their value only so far as they help the soul onward towards self-realization.

But the artists claim to see and to find Truth through outward beauty. Is it possible to see and find Truth in that way?

I would reverse the order. I see and find Beauty in Truth or through Truth. All Truths, not merely true ideas, but truthful faces, truthful pictures, or songs, are highly beautiful. People generally fail to see Beauty in Truth, the ordinary man runs away from it and becomes blind to the beauty in it. Whenever men begin to see Beauty in Truth, then true Art will arise.

But cannot Beauty be separated from Truth, and Truth from Beauty?

I should want to know exactly what is Beauty. If it is what people generally understand by that word, then they are wide apart. Is a woman with fair features necessarily beautiful?

Yes.

Even if she may be of an ugly character?

But her face in that case cannot be beautiful. It will always be the index of the soul within. The true artist with the genius of perception will produce the right expression.

But here you are begging the whole question. You now admit that mere outward form may not make a thing beautiful. To a true artist only that face is beautiful which, quite apart from exterior, shines with the Truth within the soul. There is then, as I have said, no Beauty apart from Truth. On the other hand, Truth may manifest itself in forms which may not be outwardly beautiful at all. Socrates, we are told, was the most truthful man of his time and yet his features are said to have been the ugliest in Greece. To my mind he was beautiful, because all his life was a striving after Truth, and you may remember that his outward form did not prevent Phidias from appreciating the beauty of Truth in him, though as an artist he was accustomed to see Beauty in outward forms also!

But, Bapuji, the most beautiful things have often been created by men whose own lives were not beautiful.

That only means that Truth and untruth often coexist; good and evil are often found together. In an artist also not seldom the right perception of things and the wrong coexist. Truly beautiful creations come when right perception is at work. If these moments are rare in life they are also rare in Art.

If only truthful or good things can be beautiful, how can things without a moral quality be beautiful?....... Is there truth, Bapuji, in things that are neither moral nor immoral in themselves? For instance, is there truth in a sunset or a crescent moon that shines amid the stars at night?

Indeed these beauties are truthful, inasmuch as they make me think of the Creator at the back of them. How else could these be beautiful, but for the Truth that is in the centre of creation? When I admire the wonder of a sunset or the beauty of the moon my soul expands in worship of the Creator. I try to see Him and His mercies in all these creations. But even the sunsets and sunrises would be mere hindrances, if they did not help me to think of Him. Anything which is a hindrance to the flight of the soul, is a delusion and a snare; even, like the body, which often does hinder you in the path of salvation.

I am grateful to hear your views on Art, and I understand and accept them. Would it not be well for you to set them down for the benefit of the younger generation in order to guide them aright? That I could never dream of doing, for the simple reason that it would be an impertinence on my part to hold forth on Art. I am not an art student, though these are my fundamental convictions. I do not speak or write about it, because I am conscious of my own limitations. That consciousness is my only strength. Whatever I might have been able to do in my life has proceeded more than anything else out of the realization of my own limitations. My functions are different from the artist's and I should not go out of my way to assume his position. In conversation with Ramachandran, a young student from Shantiniketan. *(Young India, 13 November 1924 and 20 November 1924 (CW 25, pp. 248–50))*

Music and Painting

The art of painting means expression of the emotions of the artist through line and colour. If this definition of painting were to be accepted, would you include painting as an essential part of the scheme of national education which should be universally taught to all? I have never disparaged drawing and painting, though I have certainly deprecated the blots of ink and colour passing under its name. I doubt if painting as defined by the artist could be made universal. There is this difference between music and painting: While painting can be learnt only by a few who have a natural aptitude for it, music must be and can be learnt by all. In painting too, drawing of straight lines and the figures of animate and inanimate objects can be taught to all. It is certainly useful and necessary and I want it to be taught to every child before it is taught the alphabet. *(Navajivan, 1 July 1928 (CW 37, p. 3))*

The Speaking Painting

Though I was happy and proud to see what I saw in the Exhibition this morning, and felt that I had not seen anything of the kind before in Gujarat, let me tell you that I missed what I would call a speaking painting. Why should I need an artist to explain a work of art to me? Why should it not speak out to me itself? I tell you what I mean. I saw in the Vatican art collection a statue of Christ on the Cross which simply captured me and kept me spell-bound. I saw it five years ago, but it is still before me. There was no one there to explain its charm to me. Here in Belur in Mysore I saw in the ancient temple a bracket in stone made of a little statuette which spoke out to me without anyone to help me to understand it. It was just a woman, half-naked, struggling with the folds of her cloths to extricate herself from the shafts of Cupid who is after all lying defeated at her feet in the shape of a scorpion. I could see the agony on the form—the agony of the stings of scorpion. That at any rate was my interpretation of it. *(Harijan. 14 November 1936 (True Education, p. 176))*

Literature in Quest for Truth

I ask writers: "Will you, through your creations, bring me sooner to God?" If their reply is in the affirmative, I will be a slave to their works. If the work of any writer bores me, it is not my dullness that is to blame but his art itself. A gifted writer should so perfect his art that the reader would be simply absorbed in his work. I am sorry that our literature has little of this kind of thing. There is nothing the masses can learn from the literature of today. There is not one idea in this literature by virtue of which it may endure for a week, or a year or a whole age.

Let us, then, see what literature we possess in the holy books we have had with us from ancient times. The satisfaction they give we don't derive from our modern literature. Even a barely passable translation of any of those works is more interesting to read than anything of the latter. There is much indeed, some will say, in contemporary literature. That may be, but it is an exhausting task to search for that "much". Whoever gives us today anything like what Tulsidas and Kabir gave?

Live as you may,

Realize God anyhow, anyway.

We never see these days anything of this kind. Where do we find now what we received in the age of Akha?

I returned to India after twenty years in South Africa and, looking around, I discovered that we lived in a state of fear. A people in such a state cannot express itself fearlessly. If we have to write under the weight of suppression, the springs of poetry in us will not flow nor will truth come floating on the wave. The same is true about newspapers. With the Press Act hanging over him, the editor cannot write uninhibitedly. With the same Act hanging over the writers, not a single line is written in freedom and hence it is that truth is not presented as it ought to be.

This is a period of transition in India. Crores of people feel that great changes are about to take place, that our poverty will give place to glory, that now the Age of Truth will dawn upon us. I hear these hopes expressed wherever I go. Large numbers of people think that India is about to turn a new leaf. If it does, what sort of writing shall we find on that new leaf? The Reforms which will have been granted will only prove to be a collar and we shall continue to be driven like bullocks, as we are driven today. At such a time, I ask the servants of literature nothing less than that they help us to a vision of God and Truth. They must demonstrate that India is not given to sinful ways, that she will not betray one's faith [in her].

No Indian in Madras has served South India so well as did Pope —not the Pope of the *Iliad* fame. I am ever in love with human beings and would, therefore, always want to steal people's hearts. In order that I might steal the hearts of my brothers of the South, I had to learn their language. I cannot just now quote anything from the writings of the Rev. Pope, but this I will tell you that the poems, or rather the poetry, in Tamil, which even the peasant can enjoy as he waters his field, is just superb.

The watering of the field begins even before the sun has risen. *Bajri* and wheat, everything is covered with pearly dew. The liquid drops on the tree leaves shine like pearls. This is what the men, these peasants, as they water the fields sing about. When I lived at Kochrab, I used to watch the peasants and listen to their songs. Found obscene words in their mouth.

Why should this be so? I should like to have an answer to this from Shri Narasinharao here and from the Chairman.

I say to the Sahitya Parishad that, unless you help remove the filthy language from the mouths of our peasants, the sin of our degradation will be on your heads. I want to know from the servants of literature what the condition of the majority of our people is and what they will write for this majority. I will say only this to the Sahitya Parishad and repeat it over and over again: rid yourselves of all your shortcomings.

Lewis thought of writing a book and wrote one for his children. They read it to their profit; men, women and children today may also read it and profit by it. I ask for such literature from our men of letters. I want, not Banabhatta's *Kadambari* but Tulsidas's *Ramayana.* I have my doubts whether *Kadambari* will be with us for ever, but Tulsidas's work will certainly endure. Let us at present get just *roti,* ghee and milk from our literature. Later on we shall add almonds, pistachio nuts, etc. and produce something like *Kadambari.*

If the meek people of Gujarat—a people filled with sweetness, whose goodness is without bounds, a people so very simple-minded and having unswerving faith in God—if these people are to go forward, their men of letters should sing and write for labourers and peasants in the fields.

It is my heartfelt prayer that our people may learn to write the truth, speak the truth and live the truth. *(Speech at Gujarat Sahitya Parishad, Ahmedabad. Navajivan, 4 April 1920 (CW 17, pp. 301–03) (Translated from Gujarati))*

Literature for the Deprived

I want art and literature that can speak to the millions. I have given you an outline of the picture; you will fill in the details. I have had my say. My heart is weeping at the present moment, but time has made it hard enough not to break even when there are occasion for it. As I think of Segaon and its skeletons, (at this stage he did, however, break down! After a little pause he continued) as I think of Segaon and its folk, I can't help saying that our literature is a miserable affair. Principal Anandshankar Dhruva sent me a list of a hundred books, but none of them would do for them. What am I to place before them? And their women! Is there any relation, I wonder, between them and the Ahmedabad ladies I see in front of me?

The Segaon women know no literature. They cannot even repeat the *ramadhun* with me. They simply know how to drudge and slave away. Reckless of sun or rain, of snakes or scorpions, they fetch water, they cut grass and hew wood, and look upon me as their benefactor if I give them work and a few coppers. What am I to take to these dumb sisters? Those dumb millions do not live in Ahmedabad but in the Indian villages. I know what to take to them. But I cannot tell you. I am no speaker, neither is the pen my profession. I have written what I have, because I could not help it, and at one time I was dumb, so much so that my friends used to call me a dunce, until I went to the courts where too it was with difficulty that I opened my lips. It is not my business to speak or to write. My business is to live amongst them and show them how to live. The key to Swaraj is not in the cities but in the villages, and so I have settled in a village—a village too, not of my seeking, but which came to me." *(Harijan, 14 November 1936 (True Education, p. 177))*

Wrong Apotheosis of Women

He next dwelt on a topic on which he had spoken in the Subjects Committee, but could not have any resolution thereon as he did not find the proper atmosphere. The occasion was a letter addressed to him by the ladies in charge of a women's movement called *Jyoti Sangh.* The letter enclosed copy of a resolution they had passed condemning the present-day tendencies in literature regarding the presentation of women. There was, Gandhiji felt, considerable force in the complaint, and he said: "The gravest of their charge is that the present-day writers give an entirely false picture of women. They are exasperated at the sickly sentimentality with which you delineate them, at the vulgar way in which you dwell on their physical form. Does all their beauty and their strength lie in their physical form, in their capacity to please the lustful eye of men? Why, the writers of the letter justly ask, should we be eternally represented as meek submissive women for whom all the menial jobs of the household are reserved, and whose only deities are their husbands?

Why are they not delineated as they really are? We are, they say, neither etherial damsels, nor dolls, nor bundles of passions and nerves. We are as much human beings as men are, and we are filled with the same urge for freedom. I claim to know them and their minds sufficiently well. There was a time in South Africa when I was surrounded by numerous women, all their menfolk having gone to jails. There were some sixty inmates and I had become the brother and father of all the girls and women. Let me tell you that they grew in strength and spirit under me, so much so that they ultimately marched to jails themselves.

"I am told that our literature is full of even an exaggerated apotheosis of women. Let me say that it is an altogether wrong apotheosis. Let me place one simple test before you. In what light do you think of them when you proceed to write about them? I suggest that before you put your pens to paper, think of women as your own mother, and I assure you the chastest literature will flow from your pens even like the beautiful rain from heaven which waters the thirsty earth below. Remember that a woman was your mother before a woman became your wife.

Far from quenching their spiritual thirst some writers stimulate their passions, so much so that poor ignorant women waste their time wondering how they might answer to the description our fiction gives of them. Are detailed descriptions of their physical form an essential part of literature, I wonder? Do you find anything of the kind in the Upanishads, the Quran or the Bible? And yet do you know that the English language would be empty without the Bible? Three parts Bible and one part Shakespeare is the description of it. Arabic would be forgotten without the Quran. And think of Hindi without Tulsidas! Do you find in it anything like what you find in present day literature about women? *(Harijan, 21 November 1936 (True Education, pp. 179–180))*

Folk Literature

We must not only seek to know the picturesque language of the village folk, but also to spread a knowledge of modern useful literature among the villagers. It is a shame that

Chaitanya's lyrics are a sealed book to people outside Bengal and Orissa. Few of us here may know the name of Tiruvalluvar. People in the North are innocent even of the great saint's name. Few saints have given us treasures of knowledge contained in pithy epigrams as he has done.

In this context, I can at this moment recall the name only of Tukaram.

But for that purpose not only the existing literary treasures had to be made available in a language which could be easily learnt by the masses in all the provinces, but even new literature had to be created—new literature of a healthy and health-giving type. *Harijan,* 2 May 1936 (*CW* 62, p. 346)

Global Culture versus Mother Tongue

I do not want my house to be walled in on all sides and my windows to be stuffed. I want the cultures of all lands to be blown about my house as freely as possible. But I refuse to be blown off my feet by any. I would have our young men and women with literary tastes to learn as much of English and other world languages as they like, and then expect them to give the benefits of their learning to India and to the world like a Bose, a Roy or the Poet himself. But I would not have a single Indian to forget, neglect or be ashamed of his mother tongue, or to feel that he or she cannot think or express the best thoughts in his or her own vernacular. Mine is not a religion of the prison-house. *(Young India, 1 June 1921)*

Cultural Diversity

Nothing can be farther from my thought than that we should become exclusive or erect barriers. But I do respectfully contend that an appreciation of other cultures can fitly follow, never precede, an appreciation and assimilation of our own.

It is my firm opinion that no culture has treasures so rich as ours has. We have not known it, we have been made even to deprecate its study and depreciate its value. We have almost ceased to live it. An academic grasp without practice behind it is like an embalmed corpse, perhaps lovely to look at, but nothing to inspire or ennoble.

My religion forbids me to belittle or disregard other cultures, as it insists under pain of civil suicide upon imbibing and living my own.

It stands for synthesis of the different cultures that have come to stay in India, that have influenced Indian life, and that, in their turn, have themselves been influenced by the spirit of the soil. This synthesis will naturally be of the Swadeshi type, where each culture is assured its legitimate place....

It [Indian civilization] is a mingling of the cultures represented by the different faiths and influenced by the geographic and other environments in which the cultures have met. Thus Islamic culture is not the same in Arabia, Turkey, Egypt and India, but it is itself influenced by the conditions of respective countries. Indian culture is, therefore, Indian. It is neither Hindu, Islamic nor any other, wholly. It is a fusion of all and essentially Eastern. And everyone who calls himself or herself an Indian is bound to treasure that culture, be its trustee and resist any attack upon it.

The Indian culture of our times is in the making. Many of us are striving to produce a blend of all the cultures which seem today to be in clash with one another. No culture can live if it attempts to be exclusive.

There is no such thing as pure Aryan culture in existence today in India. Whether the Aryans were indigenous to India or were unwelcome intruders does not interest me much. What does interest me is the fact that my remote ancestors blended with one another with the utmost freedom and we of the present generation are a result of that blend. Whether we are doing any good to the country of our birth and the tiny globe which sustains us or whether we are a burden, the future alone will show.

Either people of different faiths having lived together in friendship have produced a beautiful blend of cultures, which we shall strive to perpetuate and increasingly strengthen the shape [of], or we shall cast about for the day when there was only one religion represented in Hindustan and retrace our steps to that exclusive culture.

It is just possible that we might not be able to find any such historical date and if we do and we retrace our steps, we shall throw our culture back to that ugly period and deservedly earn the execration of the universe.

Western vs Eastern Culture

Of myself, whilst I have freely acknowledged my debt to Western culture, I can say that whatever service I have been able to render to the nation has been due *entirely* to the retention by me of Eastern culture to the extent it has been possible. I should have been thoroughly useless to the masses as an anglicized, denationalized being, knowing little of, caring less for and perhaps even despising their ways, habits, thoughts and aspirations. European civilization is no doubt suited for the Europeans, but it will mean ruin for India if we endeavour to copy it. This is not to say that we may not adopt and assimilate whatever may be good and capable of assimilation by us, as it does not also mean that even the European will not have to part with whatever evil might have crept into it.

The incessant search for material comforts and their multiplication is such an evil; and I make bold to say that the Europeans themselves will have to remodel their outlook if they are not to perish under the weight of the comforts to which they are becoming slaves. It may be that my reading is wrong, but I know that for India to run after the Golden Fleece is to court certain death.

Medium of Instruction: Mother Tongue

I am hoping that this University will see to it that the youths who come to it will receive their instruction through the medium of their vernaculars. Our language is the reflection of ourselves, and if you tell me that our languages are too poor to express the best thought, then I say that the sooner we are wiped out of existence the better for us. Is there a man who dreams that English can ever become the national language of India? (Cries of 'Never') Why this handicap on the nation? Just consider for one moment what an unequal race our lads have to run with every English lad. I had the privilege of a close conversation with some Poona professors.

They assured me that every Indian youth, because he reached his knowledge through the English language, lost at least six precious years of life. Multiply that by the number of students turned out by our schools and colleges and find out for yourselves how many thousand years have been lost to the nation. The charge against us is, that we have no initiative. How can we have any if we are to devote the precious years of our life to the mastery of a foreign tongue? We fail in this attempt also.... I have heard it said that after all it is English-educated India which is leading and which is doing everything for the nation.

It would be monstrous if it were otherwise. The only education we receive is English education. Surely we must show something for it. But suppose that we had been receiving during the past fifty years education through our vernaculars, what should we have today? We should have today a free India, we should have our educated men, not as if they were foreigners in their own land, but speaking to the heart of the nation; they would be working amongst the poorest of the poor, and whatever they would have gained during the past fifty years would be a heritage for the nation (Applause). Today even our wives are not sharers in our best thought. Look at Professor Bose and Professor Ray and their brilliant researches. Is it not a shame that their researches are not the common property of the masses? *(Speech at Banaras Hindu University, 6 February 1916—Speeches and Writings of Mahatma Gandhi, pp.318–20 (CW 13, pp. 211–12))*

Foreign Medium

The foreign medium has caused brain fag, put an undue strain upon the nerves of our children, made them crammers and imitators, unfitted them for original work and thought, and disabled them for filtrating their learning to the family or the masses. The foreign medium has made our children practically foreigners in their own land. It is the greatest tragedy of the existing system. The foreign medium has prevented the growth of our vernaculars. If I had the powers of a despot, I would today stop the tuition of our boys and girls through a foreign medium, and require all the teachers and professors on pain of dismissal to introduce the change forthwith. I would not wait for the preparation of textbooks. They will follow the change. It is an evil that needs a summary remedy. *(Young India, 1 September 1921 (CW 21, p. 40))*

Vernacular versus Foreign Medium

But for the fact that the only higher education, the only education worth the name has been received by us through the English medium, there would be no need to prove such a self-evident proposition that the youth of a nation to remain a nation must receive all instruction including the highest in its own vernacular or vernaculars. Surely, it is a self-demonstrated proposition that the youth of a nation cannot keep or establish a living contact with the masses unless their knowledge is received and assimilated through a medium understood by the people.

Who can calculate the immeasurable loss sustained by the nation owing to thousands of its young men having been obliged to waste years in mastering a foreign language and its idiom of which in their daily life they have the least use and in learning which they had to neglect their own mother tongue and their own literature? There never was a greater superstition than that a particular language can be incapable of expansion or expressing abstruse or scientific ideas. A language is an exact reflection of the character and growth of its speakers.

Among the many evils of foreign rule this blighting imposition of a foreign medium upon the youth of the country will be counted by history as one of the greatest. It has sapped the energy of the nation, it has shortened the lives of the pupils, it has estranged them from the masses, it has made education unnecessarily expensive. If this process is still persisted in, it bids fair to rob the nation of its soul. The sooner therefore educated India shakes itself free from the hypnotic spell of the foreign medium, the better it would be for them and the people. *(Young India, 5 July 1928 (CW 37, p. 22))*

De-Indianizing Education

I find daily proof of the increasing and continuing wrong being done to the millions by our false de-Indianizing education.

These graduates who are my valued associates themselves flounder when they have to give expression to their innermost thoughts. They are strangers in their own homes. Their vocabulary in the mother tongue is so limited that they cannot always finish their speech without having recourse to English words and even sentences. Nor can they exist without English books. They often write to one another in English. I cite the case of my companions to show how deep the evil has gone. For we have made a conscious effort to mend ourselves.

It has been argued that the wastage that occurs in our colleges need not worry us if, out of the collegians, one Jagadish Bose can be produced by them. I should freely subscribe to the argument, if the wastage was unavoidable. I hope I have shown that it was and is even now avoidable. Moreover the creation of a Bose does not help the argument. For Bose was not a product of the present education. He rose in spite of the terrible handicaps under which he had to labour. And his knowledge became almost intrans-missible to the masses. We seem to have come to think that no one can hope to be like a Bose unless he knows English. I cannot conceive a grosser superstition than this. No Japanese feels so helpless as we seem to do.

The medium of instruction should be altered at once and at any cost, the provincial languages being given their rightful place. I would prefer temporary chaos in higher education to the criminal waste that is daily accumulating.

In order to enhance the status and the market-value of the provincial languages, I would have the language of the law courts to be the language of the province where the court is situated. The proceedings of the provincial legislatures must be in the language, or even the languages of the province where a province has more than one language within its borders. I suggest to the legislators that they could, by enough application, inside of a month understand the languages of their provinces. There is nothing to prevent a Tamilian from easily learning the simple grammar and a few hundred words of Telugu, Malayalam, and Kanarese all allied to Tamil. At the centre Hindustani must rule supreme.

In my opinion this is not a question to be decided by academicians. They cannot decide through what language the boys and girls of a place are to be educated. That question is already decided for them in every free country. Nor can they decide the subjects to be taught. That depends upon the wants of the country to which they belong. Theirs is a privilege of enforcing the nation's will in the best manner possible. When this country becomes really free the question of medium will be settled only one way. The academicians will frame the syllabus and prepare textbooks accordingly. And the products of the education of a free India will answer the requirements of the country as today they answer those of the foreign ruler. So long as we the educated classes play with this question, I very much fear we shall not produce the free and healthy India of our dream. We have to grow by strenuous effort out of our bondage, whether it is Educational, Economical, Social or Political. The effort itself is three-fourths of the battle. *(Harijan, 9 July 1938 (CW 67, pp. 162–63))*

State Languages

If the medium is changed at once and not gradually, in an incredibly short time we shall find textbooks and teachers coming into being to supply the want. And if we mean business, in a year's time we shall find that we need never have been party to the tragic waste of the nation's time and energy in trying to learn the essentials of culture through a foreign medium. The condition of success is undoubtedly that provincial languages are introduced at once in Government offices and courts, if the Provincial Governments have the power or the influence over the courts. If we believe in the necessity of the reform, we can achieve it in no time. *(Harijan, 30 July 1938 (CW 67, p. 212))*

Richness of Dialects

Gandhiji deprecated the suggestion that it would need a lot of research and preparation to enable them to impart technical education through the medium of the mother tongue. Those who argued like that, were unaware of the rich treasure of expressions and idioms that were buried in the dialects of our villages. In Gandhiji's opinion there was no need to go to Sanskrit or Persian in search for many expressions. He had been in Champaran and he had found that the village folk there, could fully express themselves with ease and without the help of a single foreign expression or idiom. As an illustration of their resourcefulness, he mentioned the word *hava gadi* which they had coined to denote a motor car. *(Harijan, 18 August 1946 (CW 85, p. 144))*

National Language

It behoves us to devote attention to a consideration of a national language, as we have done to that of the medium of instruction. If English is to become a national language, it ought to be treated as a compulsory subject. Can English become the national language? Some learned patriots contend that even to raise the question betrays ignorance. In their opinion, English already occupies that place. His Excellency the Viceroy in his recent utterance has merely expressed a hope that English will occupy that place. His enthusiasm does not take him as far as that of the former. His Excellency believes that English will day after day command a larger place, will permeate the family circle, and at last rise to the status of a national language. A superficial consideration will support the viceregal contention. The condition of our educated classes gives one the impression that all our activities would come to a standstill if we stop the use of English. And yet deeper thought will show that English can never and ought not to become the national language of India. What is the test of national language?

1. For the official class it should be easy to learn.
2. The religious, commercial and political activity throughout India should be possible in that language.
3. It should be the speech of the majority of the inhabitants of India.
4. For the whole of the country it should be easy to learn.
5. In considering the question, weight ought not to be put upon momentary of shortlived conditions.

The English language does not fulfil any of the conditions above-named. The first ought to have been the last, but I have purposely given it the first place, because that condition alone gives it the appearance of being applicable to the English language. But upon further consideration we should find that for the officials even at the present moment it is not an easy language to learn. In our scheme of administration, it is assumed that the number of English officials will progressively decrease, so that in the end only the Viceroy and others whom one may count on one's finger-tips will be English. The majority are of Indian nationality today, and their number must increase.

And every one will admit that for them, English is more difficult to be learnt than any Indian language. Upon an examination of the second condition, we find that until the public at large can speak English, religious activity through that tongue is an impossibility. And a spread of English to that extent among the masses seems also impossible. English cannot satisfy the third condition, because the majority in India do not speak it. The fourth, too, cannot be satisfied by English, because it is not an easy language to learn for the whole of India.

Considering the last condition we observe that the position that English occupies today is momentary. The permanent condition is that there will be little necessity for English in national affairs. It will certainly be required for imperial affairs. That, therefore, it will be an imperial language, the language of diplomacy, is a different question. For that purpose its knowledge is a necessity. We are not jealous of English. All that is contended for is, that it ought not to be allowed to go beyond its proper sphere. And as it will be the imperial language, we shall compel our Malaviyajis, our Shastriars and our Banerjees to learn it. And we shall feel assured that they will advertise the greatness of India in other parts of the world. But English cannot become the national language of India. To give it that place is like an attempt to introduce Esperanto. In my opinion, it is unmanly even to think that English can become our national language. The attempt to introduce Esperanto merely betrays ignorance. Then which is the language that satisfies all the five conditions? We shall be obliged to admit that Hindi satisfies all those conditions.

I call that language Hindi which Hindus and Mohammedans in the North speak and write, either in the Devanagari or the Urdu character. Exception has been taken to this definition. It seems to be argued that Hindi and Urdu are different languages. This is not a valid argument. In the Northern parts of India, Musalmans and Hindus speak the same language. The literate classes have created a division. The learned Hindus have Sanskritized Hindi. The Musalmans, therefore, cannot understand it. The Moslems of Lucknow have Persianized their speech and made it unintelligible to the Hindus. These represent two excesses of the same language. They find no common place in the speech of the masses. I have lived in the North. I have freely mixed with Hindus and Mohammedans and although I have but a poor knowledge of Hindi, I have never found any difficulty in holding communion with them. Call the language of the North what you will, Urdu or Hindi, it is the same. If you write it in the Urdu character, you may know it as Urdu. Write the same thing in the Nagari character and it is Hindi.

There, therefore, remains a difference about the script. For the time being Mohammedan children will certainly write in the Urdu character, and Hindus will mostly write in the Devanagari. I say mostly, because thousands of Hindus use the Urdu character, and some do not even know the Nagari character. But when Hindus and Mohammedans come to regard one another without suspicion, when the causes begetting suspicion are removed, that script which has greater vitality will be more universally used, and therefore, become the national script. Meanwhile those Hindus and Mohammedans who desire to write their petitions in the Urdu character, should be free to do so and should have the right of having them accepted at the seat of the National Government.

There is not another language capable of competing with Hindi in satisfying the five conditions. Bengali comes next to Hindi. But the Bengalis themselves make use of Hindi outside Bengal. No one wonders to see a Hindi-speaking man making use of Hindi, no matter where he goes. Hindu preachers and Mohammedan Moulvis deliver their religious discourses throughout India in Hindi and Urdu and even the illiterate masses follow them. Even the unlettered Gujarati going to the North, attempts to use a few Hindi words whereas a gatekeeper from the North declines to speak in Gujarati even to his employer, who has on that account to speak to him in broken Hindi. I have heard Hindi spoken even in the Dravid country.

It is not true to say that in Madras one can go on with English. Even there I have employed Hindi with effect. In the trains I have heard Madras passengers undoubtedly use Hindi. It is worthy of note that Mohammedans throughout India speak Urdu and they are to be found in large numbers in every Province. Thus Hindi is destined to be the national language. We have made use of it as such in times gone by. The rise of Urdu itself is due to that fact. The Mohammedan kings were unable to make Persian or Arabic the national language. They accepted the Hindi grammar but employed the Urdu character and Persian words in their speeches. They could not, however, carry on their intercourse with the masses through a foreign tongue. All this is not unknown to the English. Those who know anything of the sepoys, know that for them military terms have had to be prepared in Hindi or Urdu.

Thus we see that Hindi alone can become the national language. It presents some difficulty in the case of the learned classes in Madras. For men from the Deccan, Gujarat, Sind and Bengal it is easy enough. In a few months they can acquire sufficient command over Hindi to enable them to carry on national intercourse in that tongue. It is not so for the Tamils. The Dravidian languages are distinct from their Sanskrit sister in structure and grammar. The only thing common to the two groups is their Sanskrit vocabulary to an extent. But the difficulty is confined to the learned class alone. We have a right to appeal to their patriotic spirit and expect them to put forth sufficient effort in order to learn Hindi. For in future when Hindi has received State recognition, it will be introduced as a compulsory language in Madras as in other Provinces, and intercourse between Madras and them will then increase. English has not permeated the Dravidian masses. Hindi, however, will take no time. *(Speeches and Writings of Mahatma Gandhi, pp. 395-99)*

Hindustani

Do not consider for one moment that you can possibly make English a common medium of expression between the masses. Twenty-two crores of Indians know Hindustani—they do not know any other language. And if you want to steal into their hearts Hindustani is the only language open to you. *(Young India, 2 February 1921 (CW 19, p. 314))*

Richness of the Hindi Language

You talk of the poverty of Hindi literature—you talk of the poverty of today's Hindi, but if you dive deep into the pages of Tulsidas, probably you will share my opinion that there is no other book that stands equal to it in the literature of the world in modern languages. That one book has given me faith and hope which no other book has given. I think that it is a book which can stand any criticism and any scrutiny, alike in literary grace, in metaphor and in religious fervour. *(Young India, 9 February 1921 (CW 19, p. 322))*

National Languages versus State Languages

A fear had been expressed, observed Gandhiji, that the propagation of Rashtrabhasha or the national tongue would prove inimical to the provincial languages. That fear was rooted in ignorance. Provincial tongues provided the sure foundation on which the edifice of the national tongue should rest. The two were intended to complement, not supplant each other. *(Harijan, 18 August 1946 (Towards New Education, p. 74))*

Place of English

I do not dislike English; its riches are infinite. It is the language of administration and is rich with the wealth of knowledge. All this notwithstanding, I hold that it is not necessary for every Indian to learn it. But of this, I do not wish to speak more here. Students have been learning English and they have no option but to do so till some other system is devised and the present schools undergo a revolution. I shall, therefore, end this all-important subject of the mother tongue here, merely saying in conclusion that in their dealings with one another, and whenever possible, people should use only their mother tongue and that others, besides students, who are present here should strive their utmost to make the mother tongue the medium of education. *(Speech at Bihar Students Conference, Bhagalpur—17 July 1917 (CW 14, p. 133))*

English versus Mother Tongue

English is a language of international commerce, it is the language of diplomacy, and it contains many a rich literary treasure, it gives us an introduction to Western thought and culture. For a few of us, therefore, a knowledge of English is necessary. They can carry on the departments of national commerce and international diplomacy, and for giving to the nation the best of Western literature, thought, and science. That would be the legitimate use of English, whereas today English has usurped the dearest place in our hearts and dethroned our mother tongues. It is an unnatural place due to our unequal relations with Englishmen. The highest development of the Indian mind must be possible without a knowledge of English. It is doing violence to the manhood and specially the womanhood of India to encourage our boys and girls to think that an entry into the best society is impossible without a knowledge of English. It is too humiliating a thought to be bearable. To get rid of the infatuation for English is one of the essentials of Swaraj. *(Young India, 2 February 1921 (CW 19, pp. 314–15))*

English: Language and Culture

My uncompromising opposition to the foreign medium has resulted in an unwarranted charge being levelled against me of being hostile to foreign culture or the learning of the English language. No reader of *Young India* could have missed the statement often made by me in these pages, that I regard English as the language of international commerce and diplomacy and therefore consider its knowledge on the part of some of us as essential. As it contains some of the richest treasures of thought and literature, I would certainly encourage its careful study among them who have linguistic talents and expect them to translate those treasures for the nation in its vernaculars. *(Young India, 1 September 1921 (CW 21, p. 40))*

English versus Hindi

I know this tussle between English and Hindi is almost an eternal tussle. Whenever I have addressed student audiences, I have been surprised by the demand for English. You know, or ought to know, that I am a lover of the English language. But I do believe that the students of India, who are expected to throw in their lot with the teeming millions and to serve them, will be better qualified if they pay more attention to

Hindi than to English. I do not say that you should not learn English; learn it by all means. But, so far as I can see, it cannot be the language of the millions of Indian homes. It will be confined to thousands or tens of thousands, but it will not reach the millions. *(Harijan, 17 November 1933 (Towards New Education, p. 80))*

Literary Treasure in English

I must not be understood to decry English or its noble literature. The columns of the *Harijan* are sufficient evidence of my love of English. But the nobility of its literature cannot avail the Indian nation any more than the temperate climate or the scenery of England can avail her. India has to flourish in her own climate, and scenery, and her own literature, even though all the three may be inferior to the English climate, scenery and literature. We and our children must build on our own heritage. If we borrow another, we impoverish our own. We can never grow on foreign victuals. I want the nation to have the treasures contained in that language and, for that matter, in other languages of the world, through its own vernaculars. I do not need to learn Bengali in order to know the beauties of Rabindranath's matchless productions. I get them through good translations. Gujarati boys and girls do not need to learn Russian to appreciate Tolstoy's short stories. They learn them through good translations. It is the boast of Englishmen that the best of the world's literary output is in the hands of that nation in simple English inside of a week of its publication. Why need I learn English to get at the best of what Shakespeare and Milton thought and wrote? *(Harijan, 9 July 1938 (CW 67, p. 161))*

English as an Optional Language

English is today admittedly the world language. I would therefore accord it a place as a second, optional language, not in the school but in the university course. That can only be for the select few—not for the millions. Today when we have not the means to introduce even free compulsory primary education, how can we make provision for teaching English? Russia has achieved all her scientific progress without English. It is our mental slavery that makes us feel that we cannot do without

English. I can never subscribe to that defeatist creed. *(Harijan, 25 August 1946)*

Sanskrit and Education

For the purpose of marriage ceremonies, *sandhya, yajna* rituals and prayers, Sanskrit verses are used in our age. The verses are recited by the person officiating on these occasions and those who have engaged him join him in reciting the verses without understanding their meaning. Sanskrit is no longer our mother tongue. Many institutions ask the people to use that language for prayers, *sandhya, yajna* rituals, etc. But the people do not understand the language. How, then, can they concentrate attention on what is being recited? Sanskrit, moreover, is a difficult language. Learning the verses by heart and remembering their meanings seems to me, therefore, a double burden. When Sanskrit was people's mother tongue, all their work was done in it and that was but right. That is no longer the position now. It helps people to use their mother tongue for all their work, but our present practice is different. The religious ceremonies mentioned above are performed in Sanskrit among the general public.

My view is that Sanskrit should be used in all Hindu religious ceremonies. However good a translation, it cannot give us the meaning which lies in the sounds of certain words in the original. Moreover, by translating into regional languages, and remaining content with such translations, verses which belong to a language which has acquired a certain refinement over thousands of years and in which those verses have always been recited, we diminish the air of solemnity which attaches to them. But I have no doubt at all in my mind that the meaning of every verse and every step in the ceremony should be explained in their own language to the people for whose benefit they are being recited or performed. It is also my view that the education of every Hindu is incomplete without an elementary knowledge of Sanskrit. I simply cannot conceive the continued existence of Hinduism without a widespread knowledge of Sanskrit. The language has been made difficult by the type of curriculum we follow in teaching it, in itself it is not difficult at all. Even if it is, the practice of dharma is still more difficult and, therefore, to those who wish to follow it in life the means of doing so should seem easy, however difficult they may actually be. *(Navajivan, 28 March 1926 (CW 30, p. 195) (Translated from Gujarati))*

Sanskrit and Other Languages

"It is the duty of every Indian student to learn Sanskrit—the duty not only of the Hindus but also of the Muslims, because, after all, Rama and Krishna were as much their ancestors as of the Hindus, and to understand them they must learn Sanskrit. But it is equally the duty of the Hindus to learn the language of the Muslims in order to keep in touch and communicate with them. Today we run away from each other's language because we have turned mad. Be sure that an institution which preaches hate and fear is not, cannot be, national." *(Speech at National Educational Conference, Hardwar—20 March 1927 (CW 33, p. 170))*

Sanskrit Scriptures

And remember that since you are in a vast majority, the responsibility rests on your shoulders to make Jaffna, and through Jaffna Ceylon also perfectly dry. Hinduism does not permit you to drink. And if the board of education will do its duty, you will encourage Sanskrit study in your schools. I regard the education of any Hindu child as incomplete unless he has some knowledge of Sanskrit. And so far as I have been able to see we have in Hinduism no book so compact and so acceptable all round as the *Bhagavad Gita*. If you will, therefore, saturate your children and yourselves with the spirit of Hinduism, you will endeavour to understand the spirit of the teachings of the *Gita*. You should also cultivate a common knowledge of the *Mahabharata* and the *Ramayana*. *(Speech to Ceylon Hindus, Jaffna, 27 November 1927 (CW 35, p. 337))*

Sanskrit versus State Languages

Do you know that the Patna University has practically tabooed the study of Sanskrit? Do you approve of the step? If you do not, will you express your opinion in *Harijan*?

I do not know what the Patna University has done. But I quite agree with you that the study of Sanskrit is being sadly neglected. I belong to a generation which believed in the study of the ancient languages. I do not believe that such a study is a waste of time and effort. I believe it is an aid to the study of modern languages. This is truer of Sanskrit than of any other ancient language so far as India is concerned, and every nationalist should study it because it makes a study of the provincial languages easier than otherwise. It is the language in which our forefathers thought and wrote. No Hindu boy or girl should be without a knowledge of the rudiments of Sanskrit, if he will imbibe the spirit of his religion. Thus the Gayatri is untranslatable. No translation can give the music of the original which I hold has a meaning all its own. The Gayatri is but one example of what I have said. *(Harijan, 23 March 1940 (CW 71, p. 346))*

Pronunciation

By all means study Sanskrit. The effort made for learning correct pronunciation will not be wasted. Chaste pronunciation is a requisite for [learning] any language. But perhaps for Sanskrit accuracy of pronunciation is imperative. It is not at all necessary for you to study English. Assimilate the knowledge you already have and add to it. *(Letter to Balvant Sinha, 21 October 1944 (CW 78, p. 217))*

Languages versus Composite Culture

Every cultured Indian should know in addition to his own provincial language, if a Hindu, Sanskrit; if a Mohammedan, Arabic; if a Parsee, Persian; and all, Hindi. Some Hindus should know Arabic and Persian; some Mohammedans and Parsees, Sanskrit. Several Northerners and Westerners should learn Tamil. A universal language for India should be Hindi, with the option of writing it in Persian or Nagari characters. In order that the Hindus and Mohammedans may have closer relations, it is necessary to know both the characters. *(Hind Swaraj, p. 107)*

Language Chasm

Our love of the English language in preference to our own mother tongue has caused a deep chasm between the educated and politically-minded classes and the masses. The languages of India have suffered impoverishment. We flounder when we make the vain attempt to express abstruse thought in the mother tongue. There are no equivalents for scientific terms. The result has been disastrous. The masses remain cut off from the modern mind. We are too near our own times correctly to measure the disservice caused to India by this neglect of its great languages. It is easy enough to understand that unless we undo the mischief the mass mind must remain imprisoned. The masses can make no solid contribution to the construction of swaraj. It is inherent in swaraj based on nonviolence that every individual makes his own direct contribution to the Independence movement. The masses cannot do this fully unless they understand every step with all its implications. This is impossible unless every step is explained in their own languages. *((CW 75, p. 156-57))*

Place for Languages in Curriculum

It is now my opinion that in all Indian curricula of higher education there should be a place for Hindi, Sanskrit, Persian, Arabic and English, besides of course the vernacular. This big list need not frighten anyone. If our education were more systematic, and the boys free from the burden of having to learn their subjects through a foreign medium, I am sure learning all these languages would not be an irksome task, but a perfect pleasure. A scientific knowledge of one language makes a knowledge of other languages comparatively easy. *(Autobiography, p. 30)*

Multiplicity of Scripts

If we are to make good our claim as one nation, we must have several things common. We have a common culture running through a variety of creeds and sub-creeds. We have common disabilities. I am endeavouring to show that a common material for our dress is not only desirable but necessary. We need also a common language not in suppression of the vernaculars, but in addition to them. It is generally agreed that medium should be Hindustani—a resultant of Hindi and Urdu, neither highly Sanskritized, nor highly Persianized or Arabianized. The greatest obstacle in the way are the numerous scripts we have for the vernaculars. If it is possible to adopt a common script, we should remove a great hindrance in the way of realizing the dream, which at present it is, of having a common language.

A variety of scripts is an obstacle in more ways than one. It constitutes an effectual barrier against the acquisition of knowledge. The Aryan languages have so much in common that, if a great deal of time had not to be wasted in mastering the different scripts, we should all know several languages without much difficulty; for instance, most people who have a little knowledge of Sanskrit would have no difficulty in understanding the matchless creation of Rabindranath Tagore, if it was all printed in Devanagari script. But the Bengali script is a notice to the non-Bengalis—"hands off". Conversely, if the Bengalis knew the Devanagari script, they would at once be able to enjoy the marvellous beauty and spirituality of Tulsidas and a host of other Hindustani writers. When I returned to India in 1905, I had a communication from a society whose headquarters were, I believe, in Calcutta, and whose object was to advocate a common script for all India. I do not know the activities of that society, but its object is worthy, and a great deal of substantial work can be done by a few earnest workers in this direction.

There are obvious limitations. A common script for all India is a distant ideal. A common script for all those who speak the Indo-Sanskrit languages, including the Southern stock, is a practical ideal, if we can but shed our provincialisms. There is little virtue, for instance, in a Gujarati clinging to the Gujarati script. A provincial patriotism is good where it feeds the larger stream of all-India patriotism, as the latter is good to the extent that it serves the still larger end of the universe.

But a provincial patriotism that says "India is nothing, Gujarat is all", is wickedness. I have selected Gujarat because it is the halfway house, and because I am myself a Gujarati. In Gujarat, somewhat fortunately those who settled the principles of primary education, decided to make Devanagari script compulsory. Every Gujarati boy or girl, who has passed through a school, therefore knows both the Gujarati and the Devanagari scripts. If the committee had decided upon purely Devanagari script, it would have been better still. No doubt, the research scholars would still have learnt the Gujarati script for deciphering old manuscripts, but the Gujarati boy's energy would have been spared for more useful labour, if he had to learn only one instead of two scripts. The committee that settled the education scheme for Maharashtra, was more enlightened, and it simply required the Devanagari script.

The result is that a Mahratta reads, so far as mere reading is concerned, Tulsidas with as much facility as he reads Tukaram, and Gujaratis and Hindustanis read Tukaram with equal facility. The committee in Bengal, on the other hand, ruled otherwise, with the result we all know and many of us deplore. The treasures of the richest Indian vernacular have been rendered most difficult of access as if by design. That Devanagari should be the common script, I suppose, does not need any demonstration—the deciding factor being that it is the script known to the largest part of India.

These reflections arise, because, I was called upon to solve, during my visit to Cuttack, a practical question. There is a tribe wedged between the Hindi-speaking people in Bihar and Uriya-speaking people of Orissa. What was to be done for the education of its children? Were they to be taught through Uriya or through Hindi? Or were they to be taught their own dialect, and if they were, was the script to be Devanagari or a new invention? The first thought of the Utkal Friends was to absorb the tribe amongst the Uriyas.

The Biharis would think of absorbing them in Bihar, and if the elders of the tribe were consulted, they would most probably and naturally say that their dialect was just as good as the Uriya or the Bihari, and that it should be reduced to writing. And for them it would be a toss whether the script to be adopted should be Devanagari or Uriya, if not even a newly invented script, as has happened in modern times in at least two instances I know. Endeavouring to think in terms of all-India I suggested to my friends that, whilst it was proper for them to strengthen the Uriya language among the Uriya-speaking people, the children of this tribe should be taught Hindi and naturally the script should be Devanagari. A spirit that is so exclusive and narrow as to want every form of speech to be perpetuated and developed, is anti-national and anti-universal.

All undeveloped and unwritten dialects should, in my humble opinion, be sacrificed and merged in the great Hindustani stream. It would be a sacrifice only to be nobler, not a suicide. If we are to have a common language for cultured India, we must arrest the growth of any process of disintegration or multiplication of languages and scripts. We must promote a common language.

The beginning must naturally be made with the script, and until the Hindu–Muslim question is solved, confined perhaps to Hindu India. If I could have my way, I would make the learning of Devanagari script and Urdu script, in addition to the established provincial script, compulsory in all the provinces and I would print in Devanagari chief books in the different vernaculars with a literal translation in Hindustani. *(Young India, 27 August 1925 (CW 26, pp. 119–22))*

One Script, Many Languages

Although it is my firm conviction that there should be one script for all the Indian languages, and that script can only be Devanagari, I could not follow the correspondent's advice for the reasons stated in my note in *Navajivan,* and which I need not reiterate here. But there is no doubt that we ought to seize the opportunity that the great national awakening gives us, of not merely popularizing the idea but of doing something concrete in that direction. The Hindu–Muslim madness no doubt stands in the way of a thorough reform. But before the acceptance of Devanagari script becomes a universal fact in India, Hindu India has got to be converted to the idea of one script for all the languages derived from Sanskrit and the Dravidian stock.

At the present moment we have Bengali script in Bengal, Gurmukhi in the Punjab, Sindhi in Sind, Oriya in Utkal, Gujarati in Gujarat, Telugu in Andhradesha, Tamil in Tamil Nadu, Malayalam in Kerala, Kanarese in Karnataka, not to speak of Kaithi in Bihar and Modi in the Deccan. If all these scripts could be replaced by Devanagari for all practical and national purposes, it would mean a tremendous step forward. It will help to solidify Hindu India and bring the different provinces in closer touch. Anyone who has any knowledge of the different Indian languages and scripts knows to his cost what time it takes to master a new script. For the love of his country, no doubt, nothing is difficult, and time spent in mastering the different scripts, some of which are very beautiful, is in no way idly spent.

But this spirit of abandon is not to be expected of millions. National leaders have to make things easy for them. Therefore, we must have an easily adaptable universal script for all India, and there is nothing so adaptable and readymade as Devanagari script. There is, or there used to be, an all-India organization for this very purpose. I do not know what its activities are at present. But if the work has to be done, either the original association should be strengthened, or a new one formed for this purpose. The movement should in no way be confused with the spread of Hindi or Hindustani as the lingua franca. The latter work is going on very slowly, but steadily. Use of one script will facilitate the spread of one language.

But the functions of the two run parallel only up to a point. Hindi or Hindustani is not designed to replace the provincial languages, but is intended to supplement them, and to be used for interprovincial contact. And till the Hindu–Muslim tension lasts it takes the form either of Urdu written in the Persian script, and containing preponderance of Persian or Arabic words, or Hindi written in Devanagari and containing a preponderance of Sanskrit words.

When the hearts of the two meet, the two forms of the same language will be fused together, and we shall have a resultant of the two, containing as many Sanskrit, Persians, Arabic or other words as may be necessary for its full growth and full expression. But one script is undoubtedly designed to displace all the different scripts so as to render it easy for people belonging to different provinces to learn provincial languages. The best way of achieving the purpose is first to make the learning of Devanagari script compulsory at least for Hindus in all the schools, as it is in Gujarat, and secondly to print the important literature in different Indian languages in Devanagari script.

Such effort has already been made to a certain extent. I have seen *Gitanjali* printed in Devanagari script. But the effort requires to be made on a large scale, and there should be propaganda carried on for the spread of such books. *(Young India, 14 July 1927 (CW 34, pp. 168–69))*

Devanagari and National Unity

The object of this conference is to collect gems from all provincial literatures and to make them available through Hindi. For this purpose I would make an appeal to you. Of course everyone must know his own language thoroughly well, and he should also know the great literature of other Indian languages through Hindi. But it is also the object of this conference to stimulate in our people the desire to know languages of other provinces, *e.g.*, Gujaratis should know Tamil, Bengalis should know Gujarati and so on. And I tell you from experience that it is not at all difficult to pick up another Indian language. But to this end a common script is quite essential.

It is not difficult to achieve in Tamil Nadu. For look at this simple fact: over 90 per cent our people are illiterate. We have to start with a clean slate with them. Why should we not start making them literate by means of a common script? In Europe they have tried the experiment of a common script quite successfully. Some people even go the length of saying that we might adopt the Roman script from Europe. After a good deal of controversy there is a consensus of opinion that the common script can be Devanagari and none else. Urdu is claimed as a rival, but I think neither Urdu nor Roman has the perfection and phonetic capacity of Devanagari. Please remember that I say nothing against your languages. Tamil, Telugu, Malayalam, Kannada must be there and will be there. But why not teach the illiterate in these parts these languages through the Devanagari script. In the interest of the national unity we desire to achieve, the adoption of Devanagari as a common script is so essential. Here it is a question of just shedding our provincialism and narrowness, there are no difficulties at all. *(The Hindu, 27 March 1937 (CW 65, p. 27))*

Universalising Devanagari

I understand that some of the tribes in Assam are being taught to read and write through the Roman script instead of Devanagari. I have already expressed my opinion that the only script that is ever likely to be universal in India is Devanagari, either reformed or as it is. Urdu or Persian will go hand in hand unless Muslims, of their own free will, acknowledge the superiority of Devanagari from a purely scientific and national standpoint. But this is irrelevant to the present problem. The Roman cannot go hand in hand with the other two scripts. Protagonists of the Roman script would displace both. But sentiment and science alike are against the Roman script. Its sole merit is its convenience for printing and typing purpose. But that is nothing compared to the strain its learning would put upon millions.

It can be of no help to the millions who have to read their own literature either in their own provincial scripts or in Devanagari. Devanagari is easier for the millions of Hindus and even Muslims to learn, because the provincial scripts are mostly derived from Devanagari. I have included Muslims advisedly. The mother tongue of Bengali Muslims, for instance, is Bengali as is Tamil of Tamil Muslims. The present movement for the propagation of Urdu will, as it should, result in Muslims all over India learning Urdu in addition to their mother tongue. They must, in any case, know Arabic for the purpose of learning the Holy Koran. But the millions whether Hindus or Muslims will never need the Roman script except when they wish to learn English. Similarly, Hindus who want to read their scriptures in the original have to and do learn the Devanagari script. The movement for universalizing the Devanagari script has thus a sound basis. The introduction of the Roman script is a superimposition which can never become popular. And all superimpositions will be swept out of existence when the true mass awakening comes, as it is coming, much sooner than anyone of us can expect from known causes. Yet the awakening of millions does take time. It cannot be manufactured. It comes or seems to come mysteriously. National workers can merely hasten the process by anticipating the mass mind. *(Harijan, 11February 1939 (CW 68, pp. 380–81))*

One Script for Sister Languages

The question of having one script for the Indian languages which are daughters of Sanskrit by birth or adoption has been before the public for a number of years. Yet in these days of aggressive provincialism, perhaps, any plea for one script will be regarded as an impertinence. But the literacy campaigns raging all over the country should compel a hearing for the advocates of one script. I have been one such for years. I remember having even adopted in South Africa Devanagari script for my Indian correspondence with Gujaratis in select cases. Interprovincial intercourse will be much facilitated by such adoption, and the learning of the various provincial languages will be made infinitely easier than it is today.

If the educated people of the land were to put their heads together and decide upon one script, its universal adoption should be an easy thing. To the millions who are illiterate it is a matter of indifference what script is prescribed to them. If the happy consummation comes to pass, there will be only two scripts in India—Devanagari and Urdu, and every nationalist will deem it his duty to master the two scripts. I am a lover of all Indian languages. I have tried to learn as many scripts as possible.

And if only I had the time, even at the age of seventy I have energy enough to learn more Indian languages. That would be a recreation for me. But in spite of all my love for the languages I must confess that I have not learnt all the scripts. But if the sister languages were written in one script, I should pick up a workable knowledge of the principal languages of the provinces in very little time. And Devanagari has nothing to be ashamed of in point of symmetry or beauty. I hope that those who are engaged in the literacy campaigns will give a passing thought to my suggestion. If they will adopt Devanagari script, they will save for the future generations tons of labour and time and earn their blessings. *(Harijan, 5 August 1939 (CW 70, pp. 46–47))*

National versus International Language

Where is the need for a national language? Will not the mother tongue and an international language suffice? And then why not the Roman script for both? Your question surprises me. English no doubt is the international language. But can it ever be our national language? The latter must be the common property of millions of our people. How can they sustain the burden of learning the English tongue? Hindustani is the natural national language, for it is already understood by 21 crores. The remainder of the population can also easily understand it. But English may be said to be the mother tongue of a mere handful—say, a lac at the most. If India is a nation, it must have a national language. English will appropriately remain the international language with the Roman script. But the latter can never be the script of the national language. *(Harijan, 26 April 1942 (CW 76, p. 49))*

Religious Education

The question of religious education is very difficult. Yet we cannot do without it. India will never be godless. Rank atheism cannot flourish in this land. The task is indeed difficult. My head begins to turn as I think of religious education. Our religious teachers are hypocritical and selfish; they will have to be approached. The Mullas, the Dasturs and the Brahmins hold the key in their hands, but if they will not have the good sense, the energy that we have derived from English education will have to be devoted to religious education. This is not very difficult. Only the fringe of the ocean has been polluted, and it is those who are within the fringe who alone need cleaning. We who come under this category can even cleanse ourselves, because my remarks do not apply to the millions. In order to restore India to its pristine condition, we have to return to it. *(Hind Swaraj, p.107)*

Dharma and Scriptures

This brings me to the subject of dharma. Where there is no dharma, there can be neither knowledge nor wealth, nor health, nor anything else. Where there is no dharma, life is devoid of all joy, is mere emptiness. We have had to go without instruction in dharma; we are in much the same position as the bridegroom's party at a wedding without the bridegroom. Students cannot have innocent joy without a knowledge of dharma. That they may have such joy, it is necessary for them to study the Shastras, to reflect over their teaching and bring their conduct in comformity with their ideals. Smoking a cigarette the first thing in the morning or idle gossip does good to nobody. Nazir has said that, even the sparrows as they twitter, sing the name of the Lord morning and evening, when we are still lying in our beds full-length.

It is the duty of every student to acquire the knowledge of dharma in any manner he can. Whether or not dharma is taught in schools, it is my prayer to students who have assembled here that they introduce its essential principles in their life. What exactly is dharma?

In what manner can instruction in religion be imparted? This is not the place for a discussion of this subject. But I shall give you this practical advice, based on my own experience, that you should take to the *Ramacharitamanasa* [of Tulsidas] and the *Bhagavad Gita* in love and reverence. You have a real jewel in the latter; seize it. But see that you study these two books in order to learn the secret of dharma.

The seers who wrote these works did not set out to write history but only to teach dharma and morals. Millions of people read these books and lead pure lives. They read them with a guileless heart and live in this world full of innocent joy. It never occurs to them even in a dream to ask whether or not Ravana was a historical figure or whether they might not kill their enemies as Rama killed Ravana. Even when face to face with enemies, they pray for Ramachandra's protection and ramain unafraid. Tulsidas, the author of the *Ramayana*, had nothing but compassion by way of a weapon. He desired to kill none. He who creates, destroys.

Rama was God; He had created Ravana and so had the right to kill him. When any of us becomes God; he may consider whether he is fit to have the power to destroy. I have ventured to say this by way of introduction to these great books. I was, myself, a sceptic once and lived in fear of being destroyed.

I have grown out of that stage and become a believer. I have thought it fit here to describe the influence which these books have had on me. For Muslim students, the *Koran* is the best book in this respect. I would counsel them as well that they study this book in a spirit of devotion. They should understand its true message. I feel, too, that both Hindus and Muslims should study each other's religious scriptures with due respect and try to understand them. *(CW 14, pp. 136–37)*

State versus Religious Instruction

If India is not to declare spiritual bankruptcy, religious instruction of its youth must be held to be at least as necessary as secular instruction. It is true that knowledge of religious books is no equivalent of that of religion. But if we cannot have religion, we must be satisfied with providing out boys and girls with what is next best. And whether there is such instruction given in the schools or not, grown-up students must cultivate the art of self-help about matters religious as about others. They may start their own class just as they have their debating, and now, spinners' clubs.

I do not believe that the State can concern itself or cope with religious education. I believe that religious education must be the sole concern of religious associations. Do not mix up religion and ethics. I believe that fundamental ethics is common to all religions. Teaching of fundamental ethics is undoubtedly a function of the State.

By religion I have not in mind fundamental ethics but what goes by the name of denominationalism. We have suffered enough from State-aided religion and a State Church. A society or a group, which depends partly or wholly on State aid for the existence of its religion, does not deserve, or, better still, does not have any religion worth the name.

Religious Education and the Teacher

You have rightly found place for religious instruction. I have experimented with quite a number of boys in order to understand how best to impart religious instruction and whilst I found that book instruction was somewhat of an aid, by itself it was useless. Religious instruction, I discovered, was imparted by teachers living the religion themselves.

I have found that boys imbibe more from the teachers' own lives than they do from the books that they read to them, or the lectures that they deliver to them with their lips. I have discovered to my great joy that boys and girls have unconsciously a faculty of penetration whereby they read the thoughts of their teachers. Woe to the teacher who teaches one thing with his lips, and carries another in his breast. *(24 November 1927 (CW 35, p. 306))*

Liberal Education

I shall say to the 75 per cent Hindus receiving instruction in this College that your lives will be incomplete unless you reverently study the teaching of Jesus. I have come to the conclusion, in my own experience, that those who, no matter to what faith they belong, reverently study the teaching of other faiths broaden their own, instead of slackening their hearts.

Personally, I do not regard any of the great religions of the world as false. All have served in embellishing mankind and are even now serving their purpose. A liberal education to all should include, as I have put it, a reverent study of other faiths, but I do not want to labour this point, nor have I the time to do so.